A Language for Psychosis
Psychoanalysis of Psychotic States

A Language for Psychosis

Psychoanalysis of psychotic states

Edited by
PAUL WILLIAMS PhD

Anglia Polytechnic University

W
WHURR PUBLISHERS
LONDON AND PHILADELPHIA

© 2001 Whurr Publishers Ltd

First published 2001 by Whurr Publishers Ltd
19b Compton Terrace, London N1 2UN, England

British Library Cataloguing in Publication Data
A catalogue record for this book is available from the
British Library.

ISBN 1 86156 166 0

Cover
Fool's Cap World Map. 1590
Reproduced with kind permission of Peter Whitfield,
Wychwood Editions.

Printed and bound in the UK by Athenaeum Press Ltd,
Gateshead, Tyne & Wear

Contents

Series foreword

After the first hundred years of its history, psychoanalysis has matured into a serious, independent intellectual tradition, which has notably retained its capacity to challenge established truths in most areas of our culture. The biological psychiatrist of today is called to task by psychoanalysis, as much as was the specialist in nervous diseases of Freud's time, in turn of the century Vienna. Today's cultural commentators, whether for or against psychoanalytic ideas, are forced to pay attention to considerations of unconscious motivation, defences, early childhood experience and the myriad other discoveries which psychoanalysts brought to 20th century culture. Above all, psychoanalytic ideas have spawned an approach to the treatment of mental disorders, psychodynamic psychotherapy, which has become the dominant tradition in most countries, at least in the Western world.

Little wonder that psychoanalytic thinking continues to face detractors, individuals who dispute its epistemology and its conceptual and clinical claims. While disappointing in one way, this is a sign that psychoanalysis may be unique in its capacity to challenge and provoke. Why should this be? Psychoanalysis is unrivalled in the depth of its questioning of human motivation, and whether its answers are right or wrong, the epistemology of psychoanalysis allows it to confront the most difficult problems of human experience. Paradoxically, our new understanding concerning the physical basis of our existence – our genes, nervous systems and endocrine functioning – rather than finally displacing psychoanalysis, has created a pressing need for a complementary discipline which considers the memories, desires and meanings which are beginning to be recognised as influencing human adaptation even at the biological level. How else, other than through the study of subjective experience, will we understand the expression of the individual's biological destiny, within the social environment?

It is not surprising, then, that psychoanalysis continues to attract some of the liveliest intellects in our culture. These individuals are by no means all psychoanalytic clinicians, or psychotherapists. They are distinguished scholars in an almost bewildering range of disciplines, from the study of mental disorders with their biological determinants to the disciplines of literature, art, philosophy and history. There will always be a need to explicate the meaning of experience. Psychoanalysis, with its commitment to understanding subjectivity, is in a premier position to fulfil this intellectual and human task. We are not surprised at the upsurge of interest in psychoanalytic studies in universities in many countries. The books in this series are aimed at addressing the same intellectual curiosity that has made these educational projects so successful.

We are proud that the Whurr Series in Psychoanalysis has been able to attract some of the most interesting and creative minds in the field. Our commitment is to no specific orientation, to no particular professional group, but to the intellectual challenge to explore the questions of meaning and interpretation systematically, and in a scholarly way. Nevertheless, we would be glad if this series particularly spoke to the psychotherapeutic community, to those individuals who use their own minds and humanity to help others in distress.

Our focus in this series is to communicate the intellectual excitement which we feel about the past, present and future of psychoanalytic ideas. We hope that our work with the authors and editors in the series will help to make these ideas accessible to an ever-increasing and worldwide group of students, scholars and practitioners.

Peter Fonagy
Mary Target
University College London
October 2000

Acknowledgements

Thanks are due in particular to the authors of the contributing papers, all of whom responded enthusiastically to the idea of a psychoanalytic book on contemporary conceptual and clinical perspectives on psychosis. Mary Target and Peter Fonagy suggested that the book become part of a new psychoanalytic series envisaged by them. Peter Fonagy, Kathy Leach and Mary Target provided valuable comments on the manuscript. David Tuckett, editor-in-chief of the *International Journal of Psychoanalysis,* kindly gave permission for reproduction of the paper by Franco De Masi. I am grateful to my colleagues Drs Tom Freeman and Murray Jackson for their intellectual and moral support. No discussion of psychosis can take place without the patients who agree to share their stories with us: to them we owe a particular debt of gratitude.

Chapter 10 is reproduced by kind permission of the Analytic Press and Psychoanalytic Dialogues.

Paul Williams

For Cindy and Oscar

Introduction

Psychoanalysts, not to mention psychiatrists and psychologists, have written extensively on the subject of psychosis. This book does not attempt to review these contributions: rather, it has been prompted by the extent to which psychotic states and psychotic mental mechanisms continue to pose significant theoretical and clinical problems for mental health workers of all kinds. Each paper in the book sets out to explore a psychoanalytic language for the understanding and treatment of psychosis. The papers demonstrate the value of contemporary concepts and techniques, and they also point to how psychoanalytic insights and formulations can provide a treatment focus for multi-disciplinary approaches. Despite the efforts of researchers and clinicians from a range of disciplines there remains no comprehensive solution to the impact of the schizophrenias, manic-depressive conditions or other formally diagnosed psychotic states. This is not to devalue advances made in the understanding of the biological, pharmacological, social and psychological dimensions of psychotic conditions. In particular, recent developments in the understanding of brain function, in cognitive functioning, in evolutionary psychology and in pharmacology offer renewed hope that a cure for these conditions may eventually prove to be a reality. This book, however, recognizes how much still remains to be grasped and how important it is to draw attention to the creative uses of existing knowledge being made by experienced psychoanalytic clinicians who are conversant with multi-disciplinary thinking.

Despite the limits to our knowledge of what psychosis actually is, psychoanalysis provides a fundamental theoretical and technical contribution that touches the core of the patient's crisis – the destruction of meaning – which is the hallmark of psychosis. The papers in this book address how and why the destruction of meaning occurs and the ways in which clinicians from different psychoanalytic orientations approach the task of restoring meaning. The constructive and moving results evident in

1

the papers are a powerful reminder to governments, funding agencies and health service providers of the necessity of persisting with the painful and urgent task of improving methods of addressing the unimaginable sufferings of individuals afflicted with psychosis. Were the same havoc to be wreaked upon patients and their families by better recognized physical illnesses, there is no doubt that greater funding and improved conditions would be forthcoming. Yet provision for some of the most seriously ill members of society – those with first-rank symptoms of psychosis – remains woefully inadequate. In the UK many clinicians have reported that conditions are a national disgrace, with mental health workers operating in inadequately resourced settings whilst being asked to meet unrealistic goals (Jackson and Williams, 1994).

A further obstacle hindering improvements in the treatment of psychosis lies less in scientific ignorance (despite the constraints on our knowledge, we have today more of it than at any time in the history of psychosis studies) and more in a failure by those associated with the mental health services to co-ordinate knowledge. Too often clinical disciplines (psychiatry, psychoanalysis, clinical psychology, neuro-psychology, nursing and so forth) work separately rather than together, employing languages that are seen as mutually incomprehensible. As a result patients are unlikely to have their needs met in an integrated manner or, if they do, good treatment is likely to be patchy. The most important and repeatedly conveyed requests by individuals with psychosis are that they want to have their symptoms relieved and their plight understood by a professional, caring clinician. Physiological and mental distress reduction, and the acquisition of understanding and insight within a secure relationship – these are what patients seek.

One of the messages of this book is to stress the benefits of disciplines working together. Collaboration rather than competition is not easy to achieve: conceptual and technical bridges are difficult, sometimes impossible, to create. Professional rivalries and ivory-tower attitudes can promote mistrust where little or none is warranted, so that attitudes of mutual incomprehension between disciplines are maintained unnecessarily. One of the most recurrent interdisciplinary misunderstandings in clinical work derives from the different ways in which psychoanalysts and general psychiatrists talk about psychosis. Many general psychiatrists find analysts hard to understand because the latter often use the term 'psychosis' to describe a state of acute psychotic anxiety or else a mental process characterized by psychotic thinking. This differs from the formal, structural and diagnostic categories employed by psychiatry, which, to some analysts, omit crucial unconscious and subjective dimensions of experience. Neither orientation is exclusive or comprehensive.

Clarification of and respect for inter-disciplinary terminology is needed if we are to avoid elementary misunderstandings.

Within psychoanalysis there are many theoretical and technical problems facing clinicians who work with psychosis. For example, the problem of modification of analytic technique for the treatment of psychosis creates conflict between those who see this as a deviation from 'pure' psychoanalytic principles and those who find that 'pure' psycho-analysis does not adequately account for or ameliorate psychotic states. At the level of metapsychology, some consider the psychotic personality to be the product of a separate developmental line. Michael Robbins, a psych-iatrist and psychoanalyst working in the US, has articulated this position, suggesting that Freud's theoretical abstractions with regard to psychosis arose not only from sources once-removed from the clinical situation, unlike his work on neurosis, but also in apparent disregard of his assertion that psychosis was not amenable to psychoanalysis (Robbins, 2000). Others continue to find Freud's theory of the roles of fantasy, delusion and hallucination in psychosis germane and the basis of successful attempts to achieve a *psychoanalytic* understanding of the meaning of psychotic states. Linked to problems of definition is the important question of what constitutes a patient with psychosis. It has often been noted how few psychoanalysts actually work with patients who are formally diagnosed as suffering from a psychosis, and how many analysts and papers in the analytic literature discuss cases of psychosis, which, when measured against DSM or ICD diagnostic criteria, are more likely to resemble cases of serious personality disorder falling within the borderline/narcissistic/paranoid-schizoid spectrum. Those who are criticized argue that such patients nevertheless suffer genuine psychotic illnesses and that they are amenable to psychoanalytic treatment.

At the time of writing, one debate in particular, amongst many, is taking place in the UK and elsewhere on the nature of the superego in its more extreme and murderous forms and its impact on the patient's sense of self. At its most violent a pathological superego is not only capable of driving the individual mad but also of ending life altogether. Where does this fatal, anti-life power come from? Is its highly destructive form an attenuation of a neurotic structure or something inherently psychotic, and if the latter what is its relation to neurosis? What part does the death instinct play? Or is something else occurring of a nature and bizarreness that escapes our current psychoanalytic theorizing? A longstanding debate exists around the question of whether patients with psychosis lack mental structure in comparison to neurotic patients. In other words, is psychosis a different type of mental structure operating according to principles that are distinct from neurosis? None of these questions has yet been answered satisfactorily. However, it would be wrong to conclude that psychoanalytic inquiry into psychosis is in any way static: the opposite is the case. An indication of progress in recent years is given in the papers in this volume, where we see individual analytic work of a high order taking place with highly disturbed adults and children. Also described are multi-disciplinary, analytically based approaches within the public health services and there are several examples of original psychoanalytic theorizing. One reference, which crops up here and elsewhere regularly with regard to multi-disciplinary thinking, is the well-known work on psychosis carried out in Scandinavia in recent years. The best known example of this is the innovatory 'need-adapted' model of treatment which originated in Finland under Yrjo Alanen and which has demonstrated how life-changing opportunities and cost-effective treatment can be achieved if careful attention is paid to co-ordination of the pharmacological, psychoanalytic, family and social needs of patients (Alanen, 1997). The increasing importance of multi-disciplinary thinking derives from research into the varying needs of patients with psychosis, all of which need to be met at different times if durable improvements are to be achieved. Pharmacological treatments alone, like psychoanalytic therapy alone, do not offer the best prognosis for cases of psychosis. A judicious, flexible combination of minimal pharmacotherapy and psychoanalytic therapy (in the context of a multi-disciplinary regime) is far more likely to succeed in the long term. At the heart of a multi-disciplinary approach lies the therapeutic relationship between the patient and his or her psychoanalyst, psychodynamically oriented psychiatrist or psychotherapist. This relationship informs the other main aim of this book: to demonstrate the centrality of an analytic or analytically informed perspective as a prerequisite for the therapy of psychosis. Psychoanalytic ideas and techniques can act as a beacon to illuminate the patient's state of mind, areas of vulnerability to psychosis, developmental crises and the nature of intra-psychic and interpersonal processes, which at their most malignant can destroy the sense of life's meaning. Without a grasp of the meaning of the patient's unconscious and conscious preoccupations, it is likely that the patient with psychosis will not feel sufficiently contained or understood to permit the integration of psychotic and non-psychotic experiences in a way that will shift the balance of psychic investment from psychosis to neurosis. A number of papers (Prado de Oliveira, Rosenfeld, Williams) stress the dynamic features of this developmental shift within the analytic relationship, its phases and the therapeutic outcome. Others (for example, Freeman, Cullberg, Jackson, Martindale) illustrate how the analytic relationship can be properly situated within a multi-disciplinary context and how this creates a conceptual and clinical framework within which treatment can proceed.

The papers in the book divide, broadly, into two types – those that delineate, from a psychoanalytic perspective, the necessary components of treatment and those that illustrate the use of psychoanalytic knowledge within the clinical setting.

The first contributor, James Grotstein, is a clinical Professor of Psychiatry at the University of California, Los Angeles, and training and supervising analyst at the Psychoanalytic Center of California. He is a prolific author on the subject of severe disturbance and he discusses the clinical substrate in schizophrenic illnesses in relation to overt psychotic states and their consequences for the personality. He offers a practical way of integrating contemporary neuro-biological knowledge into clinical theory and practice, but one in which the objectives of psychoanalytic treatment of psychosis need to be modified to incorporate the notion of rehabilitation.

Brian Martindale is a psychiatrist in the British National Health Service, a psychoanalyst and a member of the Executive Board of the International Society for the Psychological Treatments of Schizophrenia and other Psychoses. His chapter stresses how and why organizations – particularly hospitals – find dealing with psychosis so dreadfully painful. This can lead to defensive relations with patients and to confusion and conflict amongst staff. Martindale reminds us that we have long known why this is so yet we persist in setting aside available, useful knowledge as part of a wider wish to repudiate the impact of madness on individuals and institutions.

Murray Jackson is Emeritus Consultant Psychiatrist at the Maudsley Hospital, London and a well-known psychoanalyst with long experience of the treatment of patients with psychosis. He was recently awarded honorary life membership of the ISPS. In his chapter he enumerates the core treatment conditions needed for the therapy of psychotic states. He specifies a 'patients' charter of rights' and conveys how psychoanalytic knowledge of the meaning of psychotic thinking may be integrated within general psychiatric and nursing practice.

Thomas Freeman is a widely respected psychiatrist and psychoanalyst whose career has been spent studying, treating and teaching on the subject of psychosis. He has been highly influential in the maintenance of a psychoanalytic presence in general psychiatry in Northern Ireland, and has written extensively on the schizophrenias and other psychoses. Here he reflects on aspects of his life's work with schizophrenic patients, especially his efforts to integrate the phenomenology of these conditions with psychoanalytic thinking.

Franco De Masi is a medical doctor and psychiatrist, a training analyst of the Italian Psychoanalytical Society and author of papers in the *International Journal of Psychoanalysis* and the *Rivista Italiana di Psicoanalisi*. In 1999 he published a book on sadomasochistic perversions (*La perversione sadomasochistica*. Torino: Boringhieri). In a highly original chapter he draws attention to how psychoanalysts employ differing definitions of the unconscious, and proposes his own distinction between an 'emotional' and a 'dynamic' unconscious in order to clarify the nature of the impact of psychosis on the capacity to think and to symbolize.

Johan Cullberg is Professor of Psychiatry at the Karolinska Institute in Stockholm. He is a member of the Swedish Psychoanalytic Society and a past chairman of the ISPS. He has worked clinically and as a researcher on several large-scale social psychiatric projects in Sweden. His chapter describes 'The Parachute Project', a government-funded programme that tackles first episode psychosis in a 'need-adapted' way and that has achieved impressive results.

Andrzej Werbart is an associate member of the Swedish Psychoanalytical Society and Research Director at the Institute of Psychotherapy, Stockholm County Council. He is editor of *Freud's Case Studies* in the Swedish edition of *Collected Papers of Sigmund Freud*.

Marika Lindbom-Jakobson is a psychologist who works in private practice and is a consultant to a variety of groups and organizations and a former member of staff at the Red Cross Centre for Tortured Refugees in Stockholm. She has published articles on torture and trauma. Together, Werbart and Lindbom-Jakobson consider some of the clinical consequences of torture in relation to the experience of psychotic illness, and how these consequences may be addressed in the treatment setting.

Luiz Eduardo Prado de Oliveira is a Brazilian psychoanalyst who has spent most of his professional life in Paris (he is a Guest Member of the Société Psychoanalytique de Paris). He is the co-ordinator of a team of psychoanalysts and psychotherapists at the Centre Hospitalier Sainte-Anne and has written a number of books on psychosis; amongst his interests are the psychological *sequelae* of autism and he provides a sensitive chapter on the analysis of a boy diagnosed as autistic. The paper is striking for the manner in which it addresses the needs of the parents of the patient, something analysts rarely feel confident in undertaking.

David Rosenfeld, a member of the Argentinian Psychoanalytic Society and a psychiatrist, has wide experience of the psychoanalytic treatment of psychosis and has published extensively. His clinical paper elucidates the nature and meaning of a psychotic addictive state to a contemporary problem – computers and video games.

Paul Williams is a Member of the British Psychoanalytical Society and Visiting Professor in the School of Community Health and Social Studies at Anglia Polytechnic University, UK. He is co-author, with Murray Jackson, of *Unimaginable Storms* (Jackson and Williams, 1994) and editor of the book *Psychosis* (*Madness*) published by the Institute of Psychoanalysis, London. His chapter explores theoretical and technical obstacles in the interpretation of psychotic transference states in a borderline patient.

Paul Williams
London
June 2001

References

Alanen Y (1997) Schizophrenia. Its Origins and Need Adapted Treatment. London: Karnac.

Jackson M, Williams P (1994) Unimaginable Storms: a Search for Meaning in Psychosis. London: Karnac.

Robbins M (2000) Bulletin No. 290 of the Internet Discussion of the International Journal of Psychoanalysis, www.ijpa.org

A rationale for the psycho-analytically informed psychotherapy of schizophrenia and other psychoses

Towards the concept of 'rehabilitative psychoanalysis'

JAMES S GROTSTEIN

Introduction

As we enter into a new millennium a summing up seems appropriate to reassess the progress and changes that have taken place and continue to take place in our conceptions of treatment for those who suffer from psychoses and related conditions. Psychoanalysis and psychoanalytically informed ('dynamic') psychotherapy entered the scene early on, in part because of the enthusiasm of some of Freud's adherents who were eager to apply his 'depth psychology' to psychotic patients. This enthusiasm approached its acme in Great Britain after the Second World War, especially with some of the followers of Melanie Klein. Simultaneously, great interest in the application of psychoanalytic understanding developed in the USA, particularly in psychiatric hospitals on the eastern seaboard, such as Austen Riggs, the Institute of Living, Chestnut Lodge, and Sheppard and Enoch Pratt, as well as some inland hospitals such as Menninger's Hospital, Michael Reese Hospital and others. One psychoanalyst, John Rosen, who founded his own hospital for schizophrenics in Doylestown, Pennsylvania, propounded the application of 'direct psychoanalysis' on these patients under the premise that psychosis and dreams were virtually identical phenomena. Such stalwart psychoanalytic pioneers in Britain as Hanna Segal, Herbert Rosenfeld, and Wilfred Bion devoted their careers to the psychoanalytic treatment of psychotics. In the US, such names as Harold Searles, Frieda Fromm-Reichmann, L Bryce Boyer, and Peter Giovacchini stand out.

Close upon the heels of this psychoanalytic enthusiasm the new discipline of psychopharmacology pounded at the gates. As newer and significantly effective anti-psychotic medications came to market, the psychoanalytic/psychotherapeutic hegemony became increasingly challenged. The challenge was significant in a number of ways, particularly in the USA. For a generation after the Second World War a significant number of the chairmen of departments of psychiatry in the USA were psychoanalysts, and a significant number of medical students were so influenced by them that an unusually high percentage of psychiatrists emerged who became interested in psychoanalysis. All this changed as psychopharmacology and neurobiology secured their toehold on the psychiatric scene. A turf war ensued as to what was or was not the proper treatment of the psychoses.

The emergence of diagnostic specificity: 'state' versus 'trait'

An important part of the question of 'ownership' devolved into issues of diagnosis. One aspect of this was a useful diagnostic clue that emerged from DSM I and its descendants, namely the distinction between what are termed 'Axis I' and 'Axis II' disorders. This translates into 'states' and 'traits' respectively. In other words, a patient may be psychotic in regard to being 'possessed', as it were, by an abnormal, unrealistic state of mind, but what about this patient's ongoing, relatively more stable personality? At the Conference on the Treatment of Schizophrenia in London in 1997 many contributors to the conference spoke of their successes in curing or ameliorating their patients' 'psychoses', suggesting that their treatments constituted a cure for their patients. In my own address to that conference I emphasized that a psychosis may be a transitory, sub-acute, or even chronic aberrant state (Axis I) that becomes superimposed upon an underlying permanent personality or temperament (Axis II) and emerges ultimately from defects, deficits, and/or deficiencies, both primarily neurobiological and psycho-social, ultimately developing into a psychical conflict of 'to be or not to be'. Consequently, the issue of the difference between state and trait is of enormous conceptual and clinical importance. It may be much easier to terminate a psychotic state therapeutically than it is to treat the underlying personality disorder (Trait) that periodically or permanently subtends the psychosis. Further, whereas anti-psychotic medications, like all psychotropic agents, affect state disorders like psychosis, no medication affects trait disorders. The role of psychotherapy is appropriate and indicated, consequently, in approaching the underlying trait disorders – and may even be effective for state disorders. More co-operative interdisciplinary research is necessary to settle this issue, however, as was indicated in the introduction to this volume.

The shrinking of the schizophrenic cohort

The gradual refinement of diagnostic criteria for psychoses had other facets. A significant number of what were formerly called 'manic-depressive' psychotics, and which were later called 'unipolar' and 'bipolar disorders', became located within many of those patients who had formerly been called schizophrenics. One of the problems of diagnosis was the apparent isomorphism of psychotic characteristics in the psychotic state – as compared with the pre-psychotic or non-psychotic trait. By far the biggest subtraction from the schizophrenic cohort was the emergence of the borderline condition and, along with it, a new collection of diagnostic entities, roughly designated as 'primitive mental disorders', which included lower-level narcissistic personality disorders, addictions, eating disorders, and perversions.

Diagnostic matters had already been made complicated in the UK, for instance, by Klein's exploration of the earliest mental and emotional states of the infant. While she held on to the formulation of the orthodox/classical concept of the infantile neurosis, which she had retro-extended to the oral stage of development, she often spoke of 'infantile psychosis', and suggested that the origins of schizophrenic and manic-depressive psychoses lay in these phases. One of her staunchest followers, Edward Glover, was to part company with her because of what he believed was her unfounded presumptions about medical issues. As it has turned out, he seems to have been correct. One still finds some British analysts who, when describing the presence of omnipotence in his or her patient, as for instance in the manic defence, will frequently attribute 'psychosis' (State, Axis I) to this patient, whereas Americans would attribute 'narcissism' (Trait, Axis II).

The change in the concept of the psychopathology of the psychoses

For many years there existed a major debate in psychoanalysis between the conflict school and the ego defect school in terms of the psychopathology of psychoses, which I have detailed elsewhere (Grotstein, 1975, 1976, 1977a, 1977b, 1986, 1989, 1990, 1997). The conflict school, whether Kleinian or classical, depended for its provenance on the orthodox canon of unconscious psychic determinism. The ego defect school emphasized Freud's (1958) concept of decathexis, which, though nondescript as to origin, implied a constitutional inability in the patient to be able to 'cathect' objects – to 'invest' love in them and to attach to them. Thomas Freeman (1969) and Milton Wexler (1971) were among the more prominent members of this group. Mauritz Katan (1954) and Wilfred Bion (1957) virtually simultaneously and independently came up with the conceptualization of a distinction between the psychotic as distinguished from the neurotic portions of these otherwise psychotic patients. What this dual track accomplished was a reconciliation in part between the two schools. The concept of ego defect (decathexis) later became supplanted by another defect or deficiency school, that of self psychology and later of intersubjectivity, each of which owes its origins in some measure to the contributions of Fairbairn and Winnicott in the UK and to Harry Stack Sullivan in the US. In the former of these the idea of self–object deficiencies is postulated, whereas in the latter, failures of ongoing intersubjective affect attunement of the infant/child is cited.

In the meanwhile, however, findings from neurobiological research were burgeoning. Their studies ultimately concluded that schizophrenia was due to a constitutional genotype with an as-yet-undetermined genetic pattern plus a psychosocial phenotype that predisposes the emergence of the genotype. What this means is that psychical conflict and psychosocial traumata are incapable per se of creating schizophrenia. What is needed for the expression of this illness is a constitutional predisposition. It has been shown that one type of schizophrenia evolves ultimately from a viral illness due to influenza in the future schizophrenic's mother during the second trimester of pregnancy. The rationale is as follows: in the second trimester neuroblasts in the neural plate of the foetus begin to migrate to their final destination in the cerebral cortex. Certain neuroblasts that are located on this neural plate and that are genetically consigned to the hippocampus begin their migration upward to their destination. On the way they must climb stem cells, somewhat analogous to microscopic palm trees. Their ability to climb these stem cells is contingent upon secretion by the stem cells of a cellular adhesive molecule (CAM) factor. If the mother falls ill with influenza during the stage of this neuroblastic trek (second trimester), the stem cell fails to secrete the CAM factor. The consequences of this failure are that the neuroblasts fail to reach their ultimate destination in the hippocampal cortex and fall by the wayside alongside the stem cells. These ill-fated neuroblasts form a graveyard-pattern known as 'palisading' and they are now observable to researchers.

A newer conception of the neurological defects in schizophrenia – one that, like the preceding one, is also neuro-developmental – is the possibility of developmental synaptic death because of an 'apoptotic cascade' (cell death). Hoffman and McGlashan (1997, p. 1683) state:

> After peaking during childhood, synaptic density in the human frontal cortex declines by 30%–40% during adolescence because of progressive elimination of synaptic connections. The characteristic age of onset of schizophrenia–late adolescence and early adulthood–suggests that the disorder should arise from irregularities involving this neuro-developmental process.

Using computer model techniques, they concluded that the model demonstrates perceptual advantage of selective synaptic elimination as well as selective neuronal loss, suggesting a functional explanation for these aspects of neuro-development. The model predicts that psychosis arises from a pathological extension of one of these neuro-developmental trends, namely synaptic elimination (p. 1683). The apoptotic cascade is a normal developmental phenomenon in which an overabundance of synapses are initially produced in utero, many of which gradually undergo cell death (apoptosis) in order to shape and prune the central nervous system. Without this 'pruning' we should have web fingers, for instance. It is hypothesized by Hoffman and McGlashan and others that the onset of schizophrenia may be due in part to an idiopathic hyper-functioning of the apoptotic propensity.

Garver (1997) states that there are two kinds of schizophrenia, with different causes and treatments: one, the neuro-degenerative, involves progressive brain atrophy and cell membrane degeneration during adulthood, and the other, the neuro-developmental type, becomes more stabilized. I assume that the latter type is one that lends itself more to psychoanalytically informed psychotherapy.

Two further studies emphasize the difficulties schizophrenics have with memory. Fletcher (1998, p. 266) states: 'Schizophrenics perform poorly on memory tasks. A new study [Heckers et al., 1998] suggests that this may be due to abnormal interactions between the hippocampus and prefrontal cortex.' Heckers et al.'s (1998) findings are that poor attention and impaired memory are enduring and core features of schizophrenia. These impairments have been attributed either to global cortical dysfunction or to perturbations of specific components associated with the dorsolateral prefrontal cortex (DLFC), hippocampus and cerebellum. Here, we used positron emission tomography (PET) to dissociate activations in DLFC and hippocampus during verbal episodic memory retrieval. We found reduced hippocampal activation during conscious recollection of studied words, but robust activation of the DLFC during the effort to retrieve poorly encoded material in schizophrenic patients. This finding provides the first evidence of hippocampal dysfunction during episodic memory retrieval in schizophrenia (p. 318).

The significance of these findings is far reaching. Compromised memory retrieval capacity may predispose these patients to a difficulty in forming mature object relationships based on mourning and separation – tasks that these patients characteristically find difficult. Moreover, the hypofrontality syndrome that these findings confirm suggests one of the principal reasons why schizophrenics are emotionally labile. The pathological involvement of the hippocampus indicates that they also have difficulty in the personal, subjective encoding of emotions in relationship to their experiences.

Conclusion

The long and the short of the above is as follows:

- Schizophrenia constitutes both a trait and a state disorder. The former may be considered as the 'non-psychotic schizophrenic personality', which may be a variant of the 'schizotypal personality disorder'. The latter is the intervening psychotic state itself.
- Schizophrenia is a dementia, that is, a constitutionally predisposed illness that prevents the formation of several areas of neocortex, finally emanating in a syndrome characterized by defective mental processing, particularly in visual as well as auditory processing.
- The schizophrenic brain is generally characterized by progressive deterioration of cortical mass and compensatory enlargement of the cerebral ventricles. There is 'word-of-mouth' suggestion that there are some schizophrenics who do not deteriorate and who become 'psycho-analytic schizophrenics'. Little is known about the degree of pervasiveness of the cerebral deterioration.
- They also suffer from over-inclusion or 'perceptual enslavement', by which is meant that they have considerable difficulty in sorting out, prioritizing, and hierarchizing the importance of incoming stimuli. It is as if they have no effective sensory filter. They pay equal attention to all stimuli and thereby become prisoners of the perception.
- They consequently have problems in being able to achieve the capacity to symbolize (make internal maps of) objects. As a result they have trouble in achieving object permanence, constancy and of self-reflection (the depressive position).

Unipolar and bipolar illnesses

Thus far, I have been discussing schizophrenic illness as an interlocking relationship between state and trait (Axis I and Axis II). Similar considerations exist with regard to unipolar and bipolar illnesses, formerly referred to as 'depressive' and 'manic-depressive' illnesses. We now realize that an individual may become melancholic and/or hypomanic without actually becoming psychotic, whereas others in these categories may actually plummet into a depressive or a manic psychosis, or a mixture of both. The psychobiological predisposition to unipolar and/or bipolar illness is due fundamentally to disregulation of energy, depressives suffering from having too little and hypomanics from too much. The decisive factor in whether psychosis intervenes in the illnesses depends on the presence or absence of reality testing and the intactness or non-intactness of the capacity for self-reflection (Fonagy, 1991).

I have seen many melancholic and hypomanic patients who were aware or who became aware of their energy transformations and who were able to employ a corrective, mental form of 'manual override' to correct it. Whereas the key biological defect in the schizophrenic seems to be cognitive and perceptual, the principal defect of the unipolar and bipolar patient is one in which they fail to some degree or another to be able to regulate their affective dispositions. Research is being done on the pre-morbid or inter-episode personality types of these patients. Although antidepressant and/or mood-regulating medication seem to be very helpful with a large number of these patients, psychotherapy and psycho-analysis have been gainfully administered to them with success – along with, and often without, medication.

Psychoses other than schizophrenic or unipolar/bipolar

Over and above these diagnostic considerations, a cluster of patients exists in which psychotic episodes may become manifest or may be so subtly insinuated into the non-psychotic aspects of the personality that the clinician must be all the more alert to its presence (Katan, 1954; Bion, 1957). This phenomenon frequently occurs in borderlines and lower-level or lower-functioning narcissistic disorders. In most of the cases in this category psychoanalysis, often without the use of medication, is indicated.

What kinds of therapies are warranted?

Unipolar and bipolar states

In light of the above consideration that schizophrenia and unipolar/bipolar illness are both trait and state disorders and that the former is a neuro-biologically founded dementia, somewhat akin to autism, and the latter a neuro-biologically founded affect regulation disorder, what are the appro-priate treatment modalities that are warranted for them? The answer to the case of the unipolar/bipolar disorder illnesses is easier to come by. Since these patients do not, as a rule, seem to suffer from significant dementia or mental deterioration, i.e., since their axis II status does not always corres-pond directly to or may be unrelated to their axis I disorder, they can and probably should be treated by psychoanalysis or psychoanalytically informed psychotherapy – with the proviso that psychopharmacological intervention should be seriously considered as well. Further, psychoana-lytically based therapies can now parallel or even replace cognitive and/or behaviour-modification therapies in these disorders by helping the patient to focus on and to anticipate the arrival of axis I phenomena with a view to holding them in check. These adjusted techniques seem to work, but corroboration so far is only by way of hearsay, not by any formal clinical research.

Schizophrenic conditions

The problem about the application of psychoanalysis and/or psychoanalytically informed psychotherapy to schizophrenics is a more complicated one. First, one must ask, as stated above, whether one is dealing with axis I schizophrenia or axis II schizotypal personality disorder ('non-psychotic schizophrenia'). Second, one must ask what kind of schizophrenia it is: a progressively deteriorating one or one that is stabilized over time. Yet another question is what kind of psychoanalysis or therapy is appropriate. Kernberg (1984) has written extensively on the issue of the types of psychotherapies that are indicated for borderlines and other primitive mental disorders – expressive and supportive. Furthermore, what schools of psychoanalytic thought deserve to be considered – orthodox Freudian, classical Freudian (ego psychology), Kleinian, Bionian, object relations (Winnicott, Fairbairn), Lacanian, intersubjective, relational, self psychological? Although no significant clinical research has been done on this issue, word of mouth and individual case reports in the literature suggest that psychoanalytic psychotherapy has been of great benefit for most schizophrenic patients, the therapeutic goals and outcomes for whom, however, must be constrained by their residual condition.

The rationale for using psychoanalysis and/or psychoanalytically informed psychotherapy with schizophrenics

One way to look at the problem is as follows: virtually anyone who suffers from a mental disorder, irrespective of diagnosis or prognosis, needs to be listened to, to be 'debriefed', as it were, of their tensions and to be effectively attuned, and so forth. Winnicott's (1960) concept of a holding environment and Bion's (1962) concept of the 'container' and 'contained' come to mind as apposite depictions of this need. I should also like to use the simile of renal dialysis, in which toxins are removed from the blood stream. The idea of cure is irrelevant to the dialysis patient. All (s)he knows is that without it there is no hope. Thus, even though the patient may be undergoing a deteriorative process, (s)he still needs to be listened to – all the more so because his/her self-healing, self-soothing, self-attuning, and self-reflecting capacities are compromised and consequently require the intervention of a professional therapist. Furthermore, and this is the heart of the matter, schizophrenic patients, because of their very condition, whether axis I or axis II, need all the more to have someone help them make sense of their 'topsy-turvy' mental processes, to help attune and settle their sense of mental and emotional lostness, disillusionment and helplessness, and continue to certify them as worthwhile human beings who can generate mental and emotional meaning in an analytic session, meaning that the therapist can grasp, reflect upon, and return to the patients with an expansion of their psyche.

Psychoanalysis, more than any other treatment modality, offers schizophrenics what they really need – assistance in and the restoration of their capacity to find meaning in their fractionated thinking. This function is all but neglected in all those proposed alternative psychotherapies that eschew insight. Psychoanalysis and psychoanalytically informed psychotherapy are well constituted to attend to these tasks – provided something else is added, and that 'something else' is the rehabilitative factor! I shall deal with that shortly, after reviewing other therapy techniques.

Other psychotherapy modalities

Munich (1997), in his survey paper on the treatment of schizophrenia, recommends, along with psychopharmacological interventions, the following psychotherapy modalities: supportive psychotherapy, psycho-education, group psychotherapy, family therapy, and rehabilitative treatment.

Kernberg's technical recommendations

Kernberg (1984), speaking from his own clinical experience and from his research in the long-term treatment project on borderlines at the Menninger Foundation, concludes that higher functioning borderlines do well when they are treated with expressive psychotherapy, whereas lower-level functioning borderlines do better with supportive psychotherapy. Expressive psychotherapy, though psychoanalytically informed, is modified in many ways; for example, reconstructions are avoided, transference is marginalized in favour of content. He also favours the 'structured interview' in severe borderline and psychotic patients, in which technique boundary issues and incongruities are dealt with.

Personal psychotherapy

Hogarty et al. (1997a, 1997b) report on a new psychotherapeutic technique – 'personal psychotherapy'. After favourably comparing their technique with psychodynamic psychotherapy, supportive psychotherapy, case management, and behaviour skills training or cognitive problem-solving approaches, they state (1997a, p. 1505):

Our interest in the development of a more disorder-relevant, individual psychological approach to schizophrenia arose not only from an awareness of these methodological constraints but from our observation that a maintenance skills training approach and a family psycho-educational intervention that we developed appeared to be of decreasing effectiveness against late relapse in the second year after discharge.

They then go on to state (p. 1505):

More central to the treatment of schizophrenia is the requirement that psychological treatment accommodate important neuropsychological impairments as well as the timing of treatment components to reflect the patients' level of clinical recovery. Negative effects of dynamic psychotherapy found in past studies might have represented the imposition of cognitive demands that exceeded the patients' capacities at different stages of recovery.

Personal therapy is defined as seeking to intercept the late (second-year) relapse of schizophrenics, a phenomenon that happens quite commonly with other approaches. It deals directly with the patient's affect disregulation, which either preceded and/or provoked a psychotic relapse. Personal therapy is applied as a systematic approach characterized by a graduated, three-stage protocol in order to adjust the schizophrenic patients' sensitivities to a new therapeutic technique. It employs a technique called 'internal coping', in which the patient is encouraged to identify the stressful affective, cognitive, and physiological experience. The attempt is to focus on their individual characteristic responses to stress. It avoids symbolic interpretation and clarification of unconscious motives and drives. Personal therapy focuses on the patient's internal sources of disregulation. This summary of personal therapy does not do justice to the intricately worked out protocol of its graduated and staged approach to the schizophrenic patient. The reader is referred to the original contributions for an in-depth picture (Hogarty et al., 1997a, 1997b).

Towards a concept of a psychoanalytically informed rehabilitative psychotherapy for schizophrenics

As I have stated elsewhere, I believe that the psychoanalytic approach to patients suffering from schizophrenic spectrum disorders remains valid. By way of the oral tradition (albeit without confirmatory empirical support for these claims) it has often been successful. Unfortunately, psychoanalysts, in the past, failed to recognize the clinical importance of the neuropsychological and neurobiological foundations of the disorder and how they subtly dominated the clinical picture of the case without the analyst or therapist becoming aware of it. Some analysts accounted for the schizophrenic illness in terms of a 'schizophrenogenic mother' or family (systems theory); others through 'decathexis', and still others in terms of the operation of the death instinct. Further complicating factors were inexactness of diagnosis, as mentioned earlier, and also a tendency, especially in UK, for analysts and therapists to speak of 'psychosis' rather than of the whole spectrum of the disorder, which certainly include the non-psychotic and/or pre-psychotic-episode personality trait disorder (axis II). I have not been able to find studies, as yet, of schizophrenic spectrum-disorder patients who have been treated by 'enlightened' psychoanalysts – 'enlightened' not only to the pharmacological intricacies of the psychotic state (axis I), but especially to the intricacies of the subtle but vast and profound neuro-psychological disarray in these patients who have a range of difficulties in maintaining their vigilance of attention (Nelson et al., 1998), their processing of objective and personal data of everyday experience, a trouble in 'gating' and prioritizing incoming stimuli, in being able to establish object constancy and permanency, in being able use their visual and auditory apparatuses for appropriate reception and memory of the perceived object, and so on. The reader is referred to Willich (1993) for a review of the literature on these neuro-developmental, neuro-psycho-logical, and neuro-biological factors.

What I am stating, in effect, is that, contrary to the verdicts of so many empirical studies on this issue – including that of Hogarty et al., psychoana-lytically informed psychotherapy is indicated in the treatment of many patients suffering from schizophrenic spectrum disorders as long as the analyst or therapist is sufficiently well-informed and sophisticated in his/her knowledge of the uniqueness of the disorders that occur in the schizo-phrenic brain/mind – their unique dementia. Thus, a psychoanalytically informed psychotherapy that is also neuro-psychologically informed may qualify as a 'rehabilitative psychoanalytically informed psychotherapy' – one that, to me, is quite suitable for many schizophrenic spectrum disorder patients: those who are able to respond to it and who do not have to be denied the dignity of unconscious insight into themselves. How can this rehabilitative therapy be adjoined to regular psychoanalysis? All the newer therapies seem to agree on the importance of specific affect attunement. That certainly would be one addition. Another would be the analyst's careful monitoring of patients' associations so as to make sure that they are manifestly coherent. When they become elliptical, the analyst should halt the patient's flow and ask for clarification for all obscurities. I have found that when I do this, the patient feels relieved. Another is to help patients sort out, organize and prioritize incoming associations by reminding them, tactfully and analytically, of their difficulty in these procedures.

Case illustration

LS is a 42-year-old high-school teacher who is married and the mother of a 12-year-old daughter. She has been in psychoanalysis with me for ten years. When I first saw her I formulated the diagnosis of a schizotypal personality (DSM IV, Axis II) with a proclivity to decompensation into psychosis (Axis I). The family history strongly suggests that her mother suffered from Asperger's disorder with a propensity toward a schizotypal disorder as well, and that her father may have suffered from a mild form of bipolar illness. One of the most important revelations from her past history was told to her by her father. Her mother attempted to breast-feed her over many weeks, but the patient lost weight without her mother becoming aware of the fact. Finally, her father intervened, consulted the family doctor, and had the patient placed on bottle feeding. She recalls that her mother rarely held her nor was she affectionate to her. There are a number of important and relevant aspects of her past and current life that would be of interest in completing the picture, but space limitations require me to focus on only a few elements that emphasize my discussion. Because, allegedly, of the emotional distance between her and her mother, the patient was predisposed to anal masturbation to soothe her self as a child. She also recalls that from her earliest years a 'bizarre object' had haunted her. This 'bizarre object' took many forms but generally began as an image of a teddy bear or some other transitional object and then became de-animated and then throbbing and menacing. During the course of the analysis she reported to me that she was pregnant. She was very frightened, she initially revealed, that her pregnancy would damage her body and her career as a teacher. She then 'visualized' her pregnancy and uttered alarm when she imaginatively perceived 'a throbbing mass of protoplasm that lacked a mouth, eyes, or nose'. I interpreted to her that her 'bizarre object' had returned. Her previously aborted foetus (of two years prior) had returned to persecute her for her having murdered it. Furthermore, she was identified, I continued, with her own mother who she felt could not bear her. I interpreted further that her earlier rejection by her mother resulted in her mother's becoming a persecutory internal demon who was now felt to be retaliating against her own foetus. The patient was silent for a moment and then uttered, 'I'm looking at my baby, and now it has a mouth, eyes, and a nose. It's human!' And she cried. The following is a clinical excerpt from an analytic session with this patient:

Adaptive context: (a) Autumn, with feelings from childhood about having to leave home and return to school; (b) daylight is beginning to diminish; (c) her teenage daughter (with whom she is very close) is going off to private school; (d) she is emotionally estranged from her husband, who still lives with her; she is in graduate school and is seeking a higher degree but experiences difficulties in concentrating on her requisite dissertation.

Patient: I had dreams over the weekend. In one I was hiking in the woods with a nondescript man and other people. The setting was like the Australian outback. It was red sandstone. There were hills in the distance and we went over to them to climb them. I went up a hill and came suddenly upon a cliff with a deep chasm marked off by chicken wire. When I got there, I saw swimming pools at the bottom of the chasm and saw people in the sky who were diving from a higher point down into these pools. Then others seemed to rise up from the bottom, climb up over the chicken wire, and dive over the side into the pools. I looked down over the edge of the precipice watching all these people diving into the pools. I was wearing hiking boots and leather socks to support my ankles. As I was waking up from the dream, I realized that I wanted to join the others in leaping into the pool, despite the apparent danger from this height. It suddenly looked less dangerous and might be fun. I figured that I could do it even though I feared the landing.

I had another dream. It was foggy. All I could see was black shapes moving mysteriously in the fog. When they came closer, they first resembled wild pigs, then they looked more like sharks. I had a compulsion to approach one of the figures and touch it. I felt its fur. I realized that it was not really dangerous but only ephemeral, like a hologram – it had shape and form but no substance. Yet I was still afraid of being eaten by these figures.

There was a third dream. A large animal, something like a dog, poked its nose into me. It reminded me of the previous dream but also of another dream where I was trapped within a smallish enclosed space which contained little creatures with fuzzy snouts. I had no clothes on, and they were crawling all over me. It was sweet and wonderful. While there, I noticed a fish bowl with a large fish in it. Suddenly the fish jumped out of the fish bowl, crawled along the floor and disappeared into a small mouse hole in the wall.

When I awakened, I thought I heard voices. Yesterday, I kept asking my daughter if the phone had just rung, and she kept reassuring me that it hadn't. I then realized that I was hallucinating. Then later I actually did hear voices, which said things to me – I forget now what they said. What was curious was that my experience of them was in the immediate past tense. In other words, I didn't actually here them at the moment they were speaking; I became aware that they had just spoken. There were many different voices, male and female. It was like seeing something out of the corner of one's eye. If you pay direct attention, they disappear.

Analyst: I think your daughter's leaving for school, the Fall season, and the weekend break, combined with the progress you've felt that we have been making are threatening to your vulnerable self. One you, a very early you, seems rooted to red sandstone hills of your early background – Mother Nature in lieu of actual mother. The nondescript man is me whom you feel may not be able sufficiently to protect you as you leap from your protective yet threatening psychotic state into the swimming pools of ordinary, sane life. Finally, you did leap, I believe, but that isn't recorded in the dreams. What we see, though, are the results of your re-entry. You were then threatened by menacing objects with fur and teeth, the former alluding to your frustrated need for your mother to touch you, and the latter alluding to your biting hunger and anger – at her then and at me now – as you feel that 'progress' is pushing you away from me, as your daughter's progress is pulling her away from you. In the third dream I believe that you were enjoying the sensuous rewards of real intercourse - with your husband on one level and a sensuous feeding contact with a mother-me on a deeper level. No sooner does that sense of sensuous union/reunion occur than the threatening voices emerge to sabotage the scene. You are then pulled back into your psychosis by these voices, as shown by the bizarre trek of the leaping and then disappearing fish. It is as if you have to pay a very heavy re-entry tax of pain and suffering in order to leave your psychotic sanctuary and return to sanity.

Patient: (tearfully). I'm scared. I'm scared to hope. Whenever I feel I'm getting better, I'm avalanched with all these terrible reminders of my being a prisoner. It's as if they let me leave only to tantalize and torment me by showing me that I'm stuck.

Analyst: The 'taxes' you seem to have to pay have developed compound interest since you first sought refuge in leaving yourself for a dissociated state of mind in order to protect yourself. When you seek to leave, you are reminded of the price you feel you had to pay in order to be safe. The price was forfeiting your own right to decision-making and turning your 'power of attorney' over to ones who are represented by the voices and who orchestrate the bizarre happenings. Yet, when you dared to touch the monsters, you found that they were phantasmal, not real. That must have been both reassuring and disappointing at the same time, disappointing because of the disillusionment and realization that psychosis is impotent and couldn't – and didn't – really save you.

Patient: Now I recall another dream. There were many little round, brown men. They were cartoon figures, two dimensional. Then they became three dimensional and then collapsed back again into cartoon figures. It was eerie.

Analyst: It's as if you had been trying to hold on to the power of your psychotic demons in order to organize yourself around them, and, now that their power seems to be subsiding because of our work, you've become even more frightened of the terror that psychosis allegedly protected you from. The little round, brown men are faeces-men, reminding you of how, ever since you were a little child, you used anal masturbation to soothe yourself, and in so doing, believed that you entered into the other world, the world of psychosis.

Patient: What am I to do? Craziness has been discredited. I'm back where I started as a child and have lost all that time. I don't feel safe.

Discussion of case

In the course of treating this patient I had to pay close attention at the beginning to a certain elliptical nature to her free associations, which at times appeared to be loose (because of overinclusion and poor gating capacity for feelings and thoughts). I found that asking her to explain and to supply connections or links between the associations was very helpful, not only in my understanding but also in hers. The patient has made considerable progress in her treatment, but every step along the way is seemingly challenged by her psychotic organization, which might be thought of in terms of endopsychic structure (Fairbairn, 1952) or as a pathological organization or psychic retreat (Steiner, 1993). It is as if she had long ago made a Faustian bargain with her anal sadistic self and its associated objects, which lured her into a psychotic world of omnipotence – one in which she did not realize the cost to herself of being unreal and also failed to take into account the retribution of omnipotence. At the height of her psychosis she felt omnipotently special, uniquely different and better than others. It has been a long journey for her to recover access to her actual uniqueness, which she could achieve only by accepting her authentic, ordinary, vulnerable, needy self. Ultimately, it is the abjectness and vulnerability of that infant self that she fears for the most. Although seen four times per week, this patient had difficulty in tolerating the intervals between sessions. I came to believe that this difficulty lay in part in her problem of holding on to her experience of me and the treatment in conjunction with a problem holding on to herself as a self. I attribute this difficulty to a deficit in her being able to utilize her visual and auditory mechanisms in apprehending the object. I emphasized this problem to her in my interventions, and it gradually seemed to subside.

Discussion

It is a tragic irony that psychoanalysts should, in the present state of the Zeitgeist, be reduced to defensiveness in pleading for the value of their approach with psychosis-disposed personalities. It is ironic insofar as they once held hegemony in the treatment of these disorders in the earlier part of the 20th century but yielded almost completely once neuropsychological, biological, and developmental research blossomed. The newer techniques lean heavily on psychopharmacology on the one hand and on supportive or cognitive modifications on the other. Medication compliance issues occupy much of the empirical literature. 'Personal therapy' has been advocated most recently. The value of the latter approach lies in specifically addressing the schizophrenic's deficiencies, including self-soothing. What is left out of this approach is the schizophrenic's quest for soothing through meaning, long the strong point of psychoanalysis. The climate of empirical opinion seems to have 'sold out' to practicality. From my experience I think that psychoanalysis and psychoanalytically informed psychotherapy can often be the treatments of choice for many psychosis-prone personalities, including the schizophrenic. However, it (they) must become not altered so much as extended to include keen focusing on the individual patient's neuro-psychological and biological labilities and defects so that intermittent psychotic episodes can be aborted through carefully planned anticipation of proneness. These patients need to be microanalysed as well as micromanaged.

I cannot leave the discussion of this issue without mentioning the example of John Nash, a frequently hospitalized schizophrenic who, late in life, won the Nobel Prize in economics for his discovery of the mathematical concept of game theory. I again refer to the works of Katan (1954) and Bion (1957), who established that there is always a non-psychotic personality that is present during psychosis. My addition is that both personalities need to be attended to psychoanalytically, non-psychotic and the psychotic. One of the reasons why many analysts deserted the field of the treatment of psychotics has to do with their having become intimidated by the growing realization of the universality and omnipresence of constitutional/biological factors in these cases. Another, one that is probably more true in the USA, is the limitations involved with the particular kind of psychoanalytic school in which American analysts were trained – specifically, ego psychology. English and South American Kleinians have been more sanguine about the applicability of their technique to psychotic personalities, as have many members of the independent school, which leans toward relationism. What is needed is further research, but research done by psychoanalysts who possess a sophisticated understanding of constitutional factors. We can no longer allow empirical researchers who have had no psychoanalytic training or experience in treating psychotics to interdict in these disorders.

References

Baher I, Cantor-Graae E, McNeil TF (1998) Neurological abnormalities in schizophrenic patients and their siblings. Journal of the American Psychiatric Association 155: 76–83.

Bion WR (1957). Differentiation of the psychotic from the non-psychotic personalities. International Journal of Psycho-Analysis 38: 266–75.

Bion WR (1962) Learning from Experience. London: Heinemann.

Fletcher P (1998) The missing link: a failure of fronto-hippocampal integration in schizophrenia. Nature Neuroscience 1: 266–7.

Fonagy P (1991) Thinking about thinking: some developmental and theoretical considerations in the psychotherapy of a borderline patient. International Journal of Psycho-Analysis 72: 639–56.

Freeman T (1969) Psychopathology of the Psychoses. New York: International Universities Press.

Freud S (1958) Psycho-analytic notes on an autobiographical account of a case of paranoia (dementia paranoides). Standard Edition. London: Hogarth Press, pp. 3–84.

Garver DL (1997) Is schizophrenia a degenerative or a developmental disorder?
Harvard Mental Health Letter 14: 8.

Grotstein JS (1975) A theoretical rationale for the psychoanalytic therapy of schizophrenia. In JG Gunderson and LR Mosher (eds). Psychotherapy of Schizophrenia.
New York: Jason Aronson, pp. 175–204.

Grotstein JS (1976) Psychoanalytic therapy of schizophrenia. In LJ West and DE Flinn
(eds) Treatment of Schizophrenia: Progress and Prospects. New York: Grune &
Stratton, pp. 131–45.

Grotstein JS (1977a). The psychoanalytic concept of schizophrenia: I. The dilemma.
International Journal of Psycho-Analysis 58: 403–25.

Grotstein JS (1977b) The psychoanalytic concept of schizophrenia: II. Reconciliation.
International Journal of Psycho-Analysis 58: 427–52.

Grotstein JS (1986) Schizophrenic personality disorder: '. . . And if I should die before
I wake.' In D Feinsilver (ed.) Towards a Comprehensive Model for Schizophrenic
Disorders. Hillsdale NJ: Analytic Press, pp. 29–74.

Grotstein JS (1989) A revised psychoanalytic conception of schizophrenia: an interdisciplinary update. Journal of Psychoanalytic Psychology 6(3): 253–75.

Grotstein JS (1990) The 'black hole' as the basic psychotic experience: some newer
psychoanalytic and neuroscience perspectives on psychosis. Journal of the
American Academy of Psychoanalysis 18(1): 29–46.

Grotstein J (1997) The impact of neurodevelopmental findings on the psychoanalytic
conception of schizophrenia: Toward the concept of rehabilitative psychoanalytic
psychotherapy. Paper presented at Building Bridges: The Psychotherapies and
Psychosis. 12th International Symposium for the psychotherapy of schizophrenia,
London, England, October 12–16.

Heckers S, Rauch SL, Goff D, Savage CR, Schacter DL, Fischman AJ, Alpert NM (1998)
Impaired recruitment of the hippocampus during conscious recollection in schizophrenia. Nature Neuroscience 1: 318–23.

Hoffman RE, McGlashan TH (1997) Synaptic elimination, neurodevelopment, and the
mechanism of hallucinated 'voices' in schizophrenia. Journal of the American
Psychiatric Association 154: 1683–9.

Hogarty GE, Kornblith SJ, Greenwald D, DiBarry AL, Cooley S, Ulrich RF, Carter M,
Flesher S (1997) Three-year trials of personal therapy among schizophrenic
patients living with or independent of family, I: Description of study and effects on
relapse rates. Journal of the American Psychiatric Association 154: 1504–13.

Hogarty GE, Greenwald D, Ulrich RF, Kornblith SJ, DiBarry AL, Cooley S, Carter M,
Flesher S (1997) Three-year trials of personal therapy among schizophrenic
patients living with or independent of family, II: Effects on adjustment of patients.
Journal of the American Psychiatric Association 154: 1514–24.

Katan M (1954) The importance of the non-psychotic part of the personality in schizophrenia. International Journal of Psycho-Analysis 35: 119–28.

Kernberg O (1984) Severe Personality Disorders: Psychotherapeutic Strategies. New
Haven and London: Yale University Press.

Matte Blanco I (1975) The Unconscious as Infinite Sets. London: Duckworth Press.

Matte Blanco I (1988) Thinking, Feeling, and Being: Clinical Reflections on the
Fundamental Antinomy of Human Beings. London/New York: Tavistock and
Routledge.

Munich RL (1997) Contemporary treatment of schizophrenia. Bulletin of the Menninger Clinic, 61:189–221.

Nasar S (1998) A Beautiful Mind. New York: Simon & Schuster.

Nelson EB, Sax KW, Strakowski, SM (1998) Attentional performance in patients with psychotic and nonpsychotic major depression and schizophrenia. Journal of the American Psychiatric Association 155: 137–9.

Wexler M (1971) Schizophrenia as conflict and deficiency. Psychoanalytic Quarterly 40: 83–100.

Willich M (1993) The deficit syndrome in schizophrenia: psychological and neurobiological perspectives. Journal of the American Psychiatric Association 41: 1135–58.

Winnicott DW (1960) The theory of the parent-infant relationship. In Winnicott DW (1965) The Maturational Processes and the Facilitating Environment: Studies in the Theory of Emotional Development. New York: International Universities Press, pp. 37–55.

CHAPTER 2

New discoveries concerning psychoses and their organizational fate

BRIAN MARTINDALE

If we are to achieve substantial long-term success with significant numbers of persons with schizophrenia in our societies, it may be of value to stand back from the tendency to focus on contemporary, promising therapeutic strategies, and instead to review what has happened in the past to many earlier, equally worthy discoveries and potential advances. What was their fate, and what can we learn from this, in psychological terms? As part of any such enquiry it would be appropriate to clarify to what extent organizational changes were made to integrate new knowledge or treatment interventions. If organizational changes were made, what sorts of changes were they? If changes were not made, it is useful to clarify why not. Pursuing such questions might help us in understanding and anticipating responses to contemporary discoveries. In this sense we should be wise to keep in mind the guiding principle embodied in Freud's compelling aphorism (made in another context): 'history not remembered will be repeated' (Freud, 1914).

Overview of some problems in implementing therapeutic strategies

In recent decades, even centuries, Western societies have had little to feel pleased about concerning their treatment and care of persons suffering psychosis. Inadequate treatment, stigmatization and marginalization have been and are commonplace. Contemporary Western patients generally have a worse prognosis than in the developing world (Jablensky et al., 1992). This is despite burgeoning 'discoveries', pharmacological 'miracles' and scientific 'advances'. The bulk of research funding in the Western world is channelled into improving medication for psychotic conditions.

This research has been successful in that it has brought important benefits in the form of symptom relief, but it is becoming increasingly likely that overall prognosis will be affected only if psycho-social factors are also taken fully into account, a perspective that is, regrettably, almost always minimal in treatment and care programmes today (Clinical Standards Advisory Group, 1995; Jones et al., 1996; Lehman, 1998; Lehman et al., 1998). It is surely appropriate that we ask if the lessons of history are being remembered, or if our errors and blind spots are merely being repeated and augmented in what appears to be the increasingly exclusive focus on and idealization of contemporary neuro-pharmacology. One is reminded of the cliché about surgical teams that claimed that their operations were successful, but (unfortunately) the patients died!

The 'infectiousness' of psychosis

Studies of interpersonal dynamics and institutional processes in relation to psychosis often describe individuals and groups of people thinking, feeling and acting very strangely (Hinshelwood, 1987). We have learned (and I would add also *not* learned from our learning) that working with the seriously emotionally disturbed is itself highly disturbing. Being in the presence of psychosis generates, sooner or later, extreme thoughts and feelings in all of us, which can be deeply unsettling. In turn, schizophrenic patients are often exquisitely sensitive to our own disturbances, whether evoked by the patient or arising independently of the patient. Harold Searles, one of many writers on this subject, has stressed the widespread need for therapists, families and hospital ward staff to at times locate and even evoke madness exclusively in the patient, in order to avoid having to recognize the experience of it within themselves (Searles, 1965).

An effective, durable therapeutic strategy of quality and value to a significant number of patients with psychosis in any community will develop only if those involved at the different levels of the mental healthcare system have a fuller and deeper understanding of the disturbing individual, group and society-wide psychological forces likely to be elicited when there is contact with very seriously disturbed people. We need to be able to identify and understand these powerful forces. We also need to be able to create the means to stand up to them, without denying their existence, being overwhelmed by them or pushing them back on to the patients in whom they are already visibly rife. How are we to achieve this? History can come to our aid. We need to create organizational structures that will resist attempts to circumvent this hard-won knowledge about the inherent nature of mental disturbance; structures that will operate efficiently and in optimal conditions be mutually supporting across local, regional and national levels. Templates and examples of these have already been established by workers in this field, from whom, I shall suggest, we may have much to learn.

Our continuing lack of attention to, and use of, existing and available knowledge, particularly of the mental processes that take place between patients and groups of staff at different organizational levels, accounts for much of our present inability to provide consistent, quality services and care for schizophrenics. In particular, failure of utilization of existing knowledge in the realm of psychodynamics is far more relevant to our contemporary treatment situation than a lack of useful scientific knowledge. A serious and destructive negative reinforcing system (much of it related to the use and fate of projective identification and closely related phenomena) commonly arises in many mental health settings, and it is not difficult to see why. The very nature of psychotic processes implies disturbed individual and interpersonal dynamics that seek to distort our relationship to reality. Unfortunately, this central, defining fact of psychosis is not given the consideration it needs, not least because of the psychic pain that can be experienced when the matter is addressed. To pay attention to the ways in which one's view of reality is being distorted is inherently difficult and disturbing. Inevitably, organizations and institutions malfunction when these essential aspects are not given adequate consideration. The very existence of interpersonal psychotic processes is often subject to levels of institutional denial which can themselves assume 'psychotic' proportions. The consequences of persistent denial of the impact of psychosis are considerable, and can include an organization-wide refusal to acknowledge the pain of working with patients suffering psychosis, poor staff support, high staff sickness rates and a tendency towards authoritarian and custodial forms of patient and staff management, in an effort to 'control' the impact of the powerful psychological forces at work.

Some 'psychotic' mechanisms at work

In this brief contribution it is possible to indicate only some of the processes that depth psychologists have discovered and rediscovered in recent decades and that constitute extremely potent intra- and interpersonal psychological processes in psychosis:

- fragmentation and splitting of self and objects
- pathological reorganization of self and its boundaries
- idealization, omnipotence and denigration
- denial, isolation and other transformations of affects by disturbances in

the balance of primary and secondary process thinking
* projection, introjection, and projective identification.

These unconscious, so-called 'primitive' processes, together with their consequences, come into play in particular to deal with human affects that are felt to be too threatening to psychic stability, or are unbearably painful for the person who is vulnerable to psychosis. The social impact of such phenomena has come to be realized from studies of these processes that have examined transference and countertransference activity in individuals, groups, families and organizations. If we accept that such phenomena are an inevitable part of the dynamics of interpersonal processes when psychosis is present then it must be both legitimate and indeed essential for us to keep them in mind constantly, as a *primary task*. It follows that the fate of these processes will affect all levels of the work of individuals and organizations that have any bearing on patients with severe mental disturbance. Monitoring is of course no easy matter as these mental mechanisms operate unconsciously, and their very aim may be to secretly disown, distort reality or pollute the primary task. The fact that pollution of the primary task has taken place may not always be easily visible.

Examples

One of the best-known studies of the phenomena outlined above is Menzies Lyth's classic account of nursing on general medical wards. Menzies Lyth found that nurses' routine procedures in general hospital wards often developed into rigid systems that were organized by senior staff in a way that served the hidden, additional purpose of protecting nurses from having any opportunity for significant emotional contact with their suffering patients. This emotional contact and support was, of course, originally intended to be one of the primary tasks of nursing (Menzies Lyth, 1960). Further scientific studies are taking place today to demonstrate what many clinicians know from first-hand experience – namely, that pre-operative counselling or psychotherapy improves the speed with which patients get better and leave hospital after surgical operations, for example. These 'new' studies are, of course, a rediscovery that patients are harmed and take longer than necessary to recover if nurses neglect their patients' anxieties and emotions.

A further example, which is very common in contemporary mental health practice, concerns the dyadic relationship of psychiatrist and patient. The strain of integrating both the biological and psychological approaches to the patient's condition can lead to splitting processes by staff, leading to a polarization of thinking amongst the staff group. Where there is professional insecurity at individual or group level in any one area of knowledge or skill, it is commonplace to find splitting, leading to idealization of the easier form of therapy and denigration of the other. For example, a psychiatrist, Dr Smith, talked about John, a patient with schizophrenia, in a joking and rather dismissive manner. He told of John's pleasure in entertaining Dr Smith by demonstrating his capacity to hallucinate and converse at any time with the voice of a famous female pop star. Dr Smith was a biologically biased psychiatrist and seemed very insecure in dealing with schizophrenic communication – essentially, fearing it. He had not given any consideration as to why John needed to entertain him, nor as to the reasons for John's preoccupation with the pop singer. He had ignored the fact that John had become manifestly psychotic and preoccupied with the singer when a girl at his work, with whom he had become infatuated, had refused his offer of a date. Dr Smith had succeeded in reducing the pleasurable hallucinatory voices of the pop star through the use of medication but this had also left John profoundly depressed and feeling empty (as a consequence of which Dr Smith was inclined to prescribe antidepressants). Dr Smith showed no initial insight into John's premorbid insecurity with girls and of the unconsciously defensive function of the pop star, nor of his own way of attempting to conceal his personal insecurities by exhibiting John in a way that disparaged his symptoms. From another doctor, it is quite possible that one could have heard the reverse of this story. For example, there might have been a Dr Brown who was so obsessed and excited with psychoanalytic understandings that he demonstrated bias against the use of medication that might well play an important part in the rehabilitation of John. In both examples we can discern the impact of splitting processes.

The fate of 'expressed emotion' discoveries

I would like to offer a further example of the impact of psychotic processes on individuals and groups taken from larger organizational contexts concerned with the treatment of schizophrenia. In Britain much pioneering work has been done evaluating and unequivocally confirming the high relapse rates of schizophrenic patients when exposed to highly critical family atmospheres (euphemistically referred to as 'high EE' or expressed emotion). This knowledge is well established and it has been repeatedly shown that the incidence of relapse can be greatly reduced by therapeutic work with the family – work that can be taught readily to mental health professionals (Leff et al., 1990). Yet the stark fact remains that, in Britain, very little family work takes place with schizophrenic patients and very few psychiatric services in the UK have staff trained in these methods, let alone psychiatrists and psychotherapists. One might imagine the consternation that would follow if it were to be noticed that, in 1998, cases of active tuberculosis were coming to the attention of doctors but were being sent away as if there were no anti-tubercular medication. I proffer that a comparable situation does exist in the area of family treatment of schizophrenia. This lack of training for mental health professionals in proven family therapies would seem to merit serious enquiry at many levels of our psychiatric organizational structure in Britain, but I know of no such enquiry and more disturbing still, little consternation or interest in the question. Why is this? I would suggest that a central finding of any such enquiry would probably indicate a widespread resistance to, and fear of, greater involvement with disturbing family settings, settings that the 'EE' research has shown to be capable of tipping vulnerable family members into psychosis.

A closely related observation is that patients in a psychotic state are often put into 'modern' mental hospital wards that are characterized by a very high level of disturbance and expressed emotion. Why does this occur when it has been demonstrated clearly that such environments can have a damaging effect on patients with psychosis? It would take very detailed analysis to explain the reasons for these types of facilities. We should need to ask why it is that professionals who work in this area and who already know about expressed emotion and how it may be addressed rarely raise objections to the building of such wards or involve themselves in more appropriate designs of suitable environments for psychotic patients.

Asylums

I have illustrated some common examples of ways in which health professionals can organize or not organize their local, regional and even national practices in highly subtle and well-rationalized ways in order to protect themselves from the most pressing problems of their patients, without consciously being aware of how or why they are doing it. Many years ago, Erving Goffman (Goffman, 1968) identified the centrality of splitting processes to the functioning of mental health asylums throughout the Western Hemisphere. He demonstrated that the way these were maintained depended upon a rigid division between inmates and staff, each viewing the other in pejorative terms in order to protect themselves from various anxieties aroused by communicating with one another. From our knowledge of these classic studies by Goffman, Menzies Lyth and others, it might be expected that contemporary mental professionals would be aware that our institutions, professions and professionals can come to be organized in such a way as to protect or defend staff from certain anxieties – at the expense of patients' mental health. However, it is essential to bear in mind that the defences that I have described are motivated by a need to disguise some of the very therapeutic goals that the institution has set out to achieve. For example, the general tendency (since Goffman's time) has been to close the mental hospitals as though the buildings were the main source of the problem. The buildings and their location may have been part of the problem, but infinitely more important than any building has been the need for psychological changes in staff in order to work successfully with patients either in hospitals or in the newer forms of community psychiatry. In fact, modern psychiatric settings are probably far more stressful environments than those of the old mental hospital with its asylum function: it is for this reason that many psychiatric patients related to older hospitals as 'brick mothers'. Asylum is a process that contains patients' anxieties whilst they are ill: this was the underlying principle of the asylums, despite their many disadvantages. Containment is ideally provided by individuals, staff and family groups and by society at large – by people prepared to forgo denial of the impact on them of their disturbed relatives and patients. With the asylums gone, patients placed in the community and most professionals demonstrating an unwillingness to recognize disturbing psychological forces present in their daily work, the situation for patients has deteriorated despite our growth in scientific knowledge. If there were increased awareness of the processes that I have been describing, then at least there would be the possibility that, as future therapeutic strategies are planned, we might minimize the likelihood that our labours often actually militate against our primary task – the creation of therapeutic strategies.

A counsel of perfection?

It might be argued that given the ubiquity of the processes of denial in the ordinary human psyche when faced with the impact of madness, there is little hope of any significant change and that what I have advocated is an unattainable counsel of perfection. The reality is that in societies where these problems have been addressed in a systematic way, impressive improvements in patient care have followed. For example, it may be worth considering the experience of Finland, a country that seems to be further along the road than most in putting into practice a mature, well-integrated multi-system approach for schizophrenic patients that operates from local through to national levels. First, all psychiatrists in Finland have a 2.5 year training in psychoanalytic psychotherapy (Lindhardt, 1995). There is also a popular two-year speciality training in administration: as a result, these two vital fields are not treated as alien disciplines and are less subject to denigration by psychiatrists. Economic knowledge has been integrated into planning in Finland. It was noted in the 1980s that schizophrenia was the single biggest cause of early retirement. Twenty per cent of all disability pensions were the consequence of schizophrenia (between the ages of 16 and 45 years) and schizophrenia accounted for 12.5% of all hospital costs (Alanen, 1997). Two thirds of the costs of mental illness were due to its secondary consequences (for example, disability pension payments, rehousing, loss of productivity and so forth). Medication accounted for only 5% of direct treatment costs. The most expensive treatment would be no treatment or ineffective primary treatment (Pylkkänen, 1993): this is because of the huge costs to society of the social consequences of chronic psychosis. The chronic patient group (those still needing more than 2.5 years of assistance) consumed 97% of direct treatment costs and 99.5% of total costs. These facts were gathered and faced squarely. A good deal of planning went into thinking where material resources were most needed, but more importantly still, where *thinking* about these patients was most needed. This emphasis on thinking about all aspects of the problem led to a range of findings, including that the rate of new cases of schizophrenia was fairly similar in all parts of the country (Pylkkänen, 1993) but that the incidence of long-stay schizophrenics varied by a factor of four between different regions. This indicated that the treatment situation (an iatrogenic component) was far more influential on outcome than the illness itself. The Finns discovered that many institutions had seriously lost touch with their primary tasks of therapeutic care and rehabilitation. The Finnish National Board of Health initiated a study in six districts that altered the treatment focus to include a much greater, more active psychotherapeutic approach for new cases of schizophrenia in order to try to prevent new chronicity. Even with staff who, at that time, were poorly trained in psychotherapy, this new active approach had dramatic results – only 9% of 219 new patients treated needed hospitalization, although many patients were nevertheless still incapable of work and were given disability pensions. The rate of chronicity remained high.

The next stage was a national project to develop the psychotherapeutic skills of local psychosis teams. These teams would intervene long *before* secondary intra-psychic and interpersonal changes such as family breakdown occurred. They were encouraged to make a full psycho-dynamic formulation of the total family and professional situation and the team would supervise – if not conduct – all subsequent treatment. Interaction and communication replaced the former situation of isolation and rejection. The new therapeutic possibilities this created were based on the relatively well-known Finnish model of the 'need-adapted' approach to schizophrenia in which intervention, for example with the family, therapeutic milieu or individual is based on what is best suited to the patient at a particular point in their difficulties and the intervention is often modified as the situation evolves (Alanen, 1997). The Finnish National Schizophrenia Project created a strategy for change at all levels of the treatment situation – from national to local. The national committee included those responsible for providing finance, representatives of all the main professional organizations and senior representation from the psychosis teams. A 25% reduction in beds over six years was accompanied by a 70% increase in outpatient resources. In some districts 90% of all mental health staff have undergone psychotherapy training, and neuroleptic medication is used in only a minority of cases of psychosis rather than the majority, and the use of hospitalization has reached minimal levels. The incidence of schizophrenia is falling as a result of cases being detected in pre-psychotic states. More detailed results of this Finnish research project have recently being published (see Alanen et al., 2000).

Summary

- A great deal of knowledge from diverse approaches exists that is relevant to psychosocial and psychotherapeutic recovery from schizophrenia. These approaches include economics, health administration, biology, psychopharmacology, family and psychoanalytically informed therapy.
- Depth psychology has demonstrated unequivocally the processes by which painful realities are often distorted and disguised in all parties when faced with the impact of a psychotic condition. These distortions of painful realities do not permit the full therapeutic use of knowledge about psychosis outlined in the first point. Rather, the knowledge itself is often used (and abused) to assist in the distortion of the therapeutic task and to assist pathological or anti-therapeutic organizational structures and processes. Entire organizations of professionals may become bound up in structures that maintain chronic avoidance of painful realities.
- If it were possible to find ways of consistently holding on to the (painful) knowledge that working with patients with psychoses will, by its very nature, *always* lead to a vulnerability to distortion of interpersonal processes affecting staff and their organizations, then far more rational and realistic therapeutic strategies could be developed as a result of taking these fundamental features into account.

References

Alanen Yrjö (1997) Schizophrenia. Its Origins and Need-Adapted Treatment. Karnac Books.

Alanen, Yrjö, Lehtinen V, Lehtinen K, Aaltonen J, Räkköläinen V (2000) The Finnish Integrated Model for Early Treatment of Schizophrenia and Related Psychoses. In Martindale B, Bateman A, Crowe M, Margison F (eds) Psychosis: Psychological Approaches and their Effectiveness. Putting psychotherapies at the centre of treatment. London: Gaskell Press.

Clinical Standards Advisory Group (1995) Schizophrenia. Vol 1. London: HMSO.

Freud S (1914) Remembering, Repeating and Working Through (Further recommendations on the Treatment of Psychoanalysis, II) SE 12. London: Hogarth Press and the Institute of Psychoanalysis.

Freud S (1958) Remembering, Repeating and Working Through. Standard Edition. Vol 12. London: Hogarth Press, pp. 150–4.

Goffman Erving (1968) Asylums. Aldine: Penguin Books.

Hinshelwood Robert (1987) The psychotherapist's role in a large psychiatric institution. Psychoanalytic Psychotherapy 2(3): 207–15.

Jablensky A, Sartorius N, Ernberg G, Anker M, Korten A, Cooper JE, Day R, Bertelsen A (1992) Schizophrenia: Manifestation, Incidence and Course in Different Cultures. Psychological Medicine Monographs (Suppl.20). Cambridge: Cambridge University Press.

Jones E, Alexander J, Howorth P (1996) Out of hospital: after-care for people with schizophrenia. Health Trends 28(4): 128–31.

Leff J, Berkowitz R, Shavit N, Strachan A, Glass I, Vaughn C (1990) A trial of family therapy versus a relative's group for schizophrenia, two year follow-up. British Journal of Psychiatry 157: 571–7.

Lehman AF (1998) The role of mental health research in promoting effective treatment for adults with schizophrenia. Journal of Mental Health Policy and Economics 1(4): 161–72.

Lehman AF, Steinwachs DM and the Schizophrenia PORT Co-investigators of the Project (1998) Patterns of usual care for schizophrenia: initial results from the Schizophrenia Patient Outcomes Research Team (PORT) client survey. Schizophrenia Bulletin 24: 11–20.

Lindhardt Anne (1995) Psychotherapy in the Training in Psychiatry. Report to the UEMS (European Union Medical Mono-Specialties) Section for Psychiatry.

Menzies Lyth, Isabel (1960) The functioning of a social system as a defense against anxiety. Human relations 13: 95–121. Republished 1970 as Tavistock Publication No 3. London: Tavistock Institute of Human Relations.

Pylkkänen Kari (1993) Promoting commitment for psychotherapeutic treatment approach. Experience of the Finnish National Schizophrenia programme 1981-1991. In Haugsgjerd S, Sandin B, Pylkkänen K, Rosenbaum B (eds) Crossing the Borders Psychotherapy of Psychoses, Nordic Association for the Psychotherapy of Psychoses. Ludvika, Sweden: Dualis.

Searles Harold (1965) Collected Papers on Schizophrenia and Related Subjects. New York, International Universities Press, Chapters 6 and 8.

CHAPTER 3

Psychoanalysis and the treatment of psychosis[1]

MURRAY JACKSON

I shall begin with an anecdote: a psychotherapist with no previous experience of the psychotherapy of psychosis had made good initial contact with a schizophrenic patient and things went well until the first vacation break. Whilst she was away the patient became violent and required intensive care and a large increase in medication. The responsible psychiatrist concluded that the psychotherapy was making the patient worse, and ordered the psychotherapy to be terminated. When the therapist returned she found that she was no longer associated with the case, and the psychiatrist expressed his view that the therapist had damaged the patient by talking, and should be held responsible. My point in quoting this unfortunate example is to illustrate the urgent need for mutual understanding in the 'multi-treater' situation in which most schizophrenic patients find themselves.

In the example cited the psychiatrist had a heavy responsibility, and it is possible that his decision was right. On the other hand it might have been wrong because psychotic patients sometimes have acute episodes of breakdown in the course of even the best-conducted psychotherapy, and in some cases this may even be *necessary* if their basic disturbance is to be reached. The psychotherapist has the responsibility of knowing that separation reactions are common in the course of psychotherapy, are disturbing and are an important focus of the treatment. The nursing and psychiatric staff need to be warned that such reactions may occur, and ways of dealing with them need to be considered. One outcome of the failure to address this problem can be

---

[1] An abbreviated version of this paper was presented to the Twelfth Symposium of the International Society for the Psychological Treatment of Schizophrenia, London, November 1997.

37

that the patient may never have a chance to recover from the experience. Having perhaps been terrified by his response to separation and its consequences, and having had the therapy then labelled as unsuitable, he may never again have the chance of a properly conducted psychotherapeutic treatment. It is perfectly true that incompetent psychotherapy in the wrong setting can harm schizophrenic patients but the same holds true of all other interventions, however well intentioned. In experienced psychotherapeutic hands, in the right setting, the risk of adverse consequences is minimal. I make these comments from the basic assumption that individual psychoanalytically oriented psychotherapy is a suitable method of treatment for well-selected psychotic patients in an appropriate setting. Many well-known studies have reached the opposite conclusion, but it has been argued that their methodology has been seriously flawed (Alanen, 1997).

Working with psychotic patients in the public sector of mental health (Jackson and Williams, 1994) and in psychoanalysis in private practice left me with no doubt that psychotic patients in general and those of the schizophrenic group in particular are poorly served by contemporary psychiatry. One of the most important lessons I learned was the fundamental necessity of helping the staff who manage and treat these patients, particularly the nursing staff. The form of help most required (and most welcomed) is the ability to understand the meaning of the psychotic patient's experiences. This endeavour can have profound beneficial consequences for all concerned (Jackson and Cawley, 1992). Supervising psychosis psychotherapy in Scandinavia introduced me to a level of psychosis treatment that is very different from that to which I had been accustomed in British psychiatry, and of sophistication of methods of research and explication (see Cullberg in this volume). In many Scandinavian centres a psychodynamic approach to psychosis has long been established – particularly in Finland, where a large number of family-centred psychosis teams with a psychodynamic orientation have been functioning throughout the country for many years (Rakkolainen et al., 1991; Lehtinen, 1994; Alanen, 1997). Basic training in the principles of psychodynamics and an integrated model of practice have long been a feature of the education of psychiatrists and psychologists in that country, and receptive governments have supported research and treatment (Pylkkänen, 1989). However, even these centres are not immune to the pressures of the market economy, or to what might be referred to as the practice of 'fast-food' or 'hit and run' psychiatry that ignores psychodynamics and fosters an impersonal, dehumanizing process.

I think that three things are needed to improve the situation, particularly in the UK:

- We need a definition of what it is that psychotic patients have a right to expect from us, the people they turn to for help.
- The contribution of advanced psychoanalytic knowledge to the understanding and treatment of psychotic states needs to be clearly specified.
- Most importantly, greater co-operation is needed between our disciplines if the psychotic patient is to receive the treatment he or she needs and deserves.

The rights of the psychotic patient

I wish to offer a prescription, in the form of a charter of the rights for psychotic patients:

- The patient is entitled to assume that the different mental health professionals that he may encounter during the course of his illness are working together in his best interests, and that although they may not speak the same professional language, they can communicate effectively with each other.
- Mental health workers need to recognize that psychotic experience and behaviour has meaning, and that this meaning may be comprehended in terms of the patient's past and present life, of his internal and external reality, and of his conflicts, conscious and unconscious.
- The content of psychotic thinking needs to be understood as being of informative value, with important implications for the treatment and rehabilitation of patients within the hospital and community.
- Psychotic patients have a right to be listened to and understood in the greatest possible depth. Psychoanalytic knowledge offers a necessary tool for this undertaking.
- All psychotic patients are entitled to the best possible psychodynamic assessment at the earliest possible opportunity.
- All psychotic patients, irrespective of diagnosis or stage of illness, should be presumed to be suitable for analytically informed psychological treatments until evidence emerges to the contary. Psychiatric nurses offer a substantial reservoir of psychotherapeutic skill if provided with training and adequate supervision by experienced psychodynamic practitioners, as Alanen (1997) has shown. Formal psychoanalysis, although appropriate and available for only few, remains the essential basis of understanding for this work.

- Neuroleptic medication should be used to alleviate severe distress and to allow verbal communication and exploration of psychological conflicts to proceed. Those prescribing medication should take into account its meaning, conscious and unconscious, for the patient, and for the prescriber himself. It should be recognized that some first-episode patients might need little or no neuroleptic medication if they can be treated in a high-quality psychodynamic milieu where the patient can be helped to talk about and explore their psychological problems.
- Finally, first-episode patients should be regarded as deserving the same quality of attention as that afforded to life-threatening physical illness.

Many psychotic patients are suitable for psychoanalytic psychotherapy and have a good prognosis if treated under proper conditions (Jackson, 2000). Many more can benefit from a psychoanalytic approach, which can contribute to the aim of bringing them out of their psychosis, even if they remain in need of long-term support. Therapists who engage at this deep level have the opportunity of learning about certain fundamental aspects of mental life, which can also be of great value in their efforts to understand their less ill patients.

The contribution of psychoanalytic knowledge to psychosis

Explaining, understanding and anti-understanding

Psychodynamic explanations can give rise to intellectual understanding, which on its own is not necessarily therapeutic for the patient. 'Understanding', in an emotional as well as an intellectual sense, requires empathy and a capacity for insightful support that is often referred to as 'containment'. Intellectual understanding can be regarded as a prelude to treatment, whereas emotional understanding and 'containment' are likely to be therapeutic in themselves, although long 'working through' of conflicts may be necessarily to achieve stability of change. The acquisition of insight usually brings with it mental pain and, although a patient may wish to be understood, he or she may not wish to understand. Although the more mature or sane aspect of the patient may wish to understand, another 'part' may be actively devoted to preventing reflective thinking, to obliterating any recognition of the need for, or envy of, other people and to maintaining a state of pseudo-independence. This situation plays a part in the familiar process of the 'negative therapeutic reaction'. This 'psychotic part of the personality' (Bion, 1957) has been described as a 'psychotic organization' (Steiner, 1993). It has also been depicted as the consequence of the co-habitation of two separate minds within one body (Sinason, 1993). Such forces of opposition to integration may be partly understood in Kleinian terms as a regression in a person who has begun to move from his fixation in the paranoid-schizoid position to the depressive position but is unable to contain and accept help in working through the anxiety and the mental pain of mourning. However, such a person may prove to have a better prognosis than one who has not proved capable of such a relatively integrated state of mind as depression.

Basic psychoanalytic concepts

The psychoanalytic concepts of the dynamic unconscious, conflict and defence, the inner world of psychological reality and the personal meanings of pathological thinking for the patient are the basis of psychoanalytic thinking about psychosis. Splitting of object and self, and identification (projective and introjective) help in our understanding of many psychotic phenomena. When primitive mental mechanisms and unconscious phantasies find expression in hallucinatory and delusional experience the patient's grasp on rational thinking is undermined, although a sane ('non-psychotic') part of the personality may often be discovered to be intact and capable of co-operating in the therapeutic enterprise. When unconscious phantasies become enacted in the real world they may find expression in bizarre behaviour.

Example

A male patient who insisted that he was pregnant put pepper into his rectum with sufficient determination to cause a chronic inflammation explained that he was trying to bring about an abortion. He was angry with the nursing staff whom he believed were invading his body in order to destroy his sexual organs. During the course of analytic psychotherapy he was found to be enacting unconscious phantasies concerning the pregnancy of his long-dead mother with whom he was identified. The concepts of splitting, of projective and introjective identification, of separation conflicts and of early oedipal dynamics opened the door to further understanding, which eventually permitted long-term individual psychotherapy to proceed to a satisfactory conclusion.

Example

If psychoanalytic thinking is missing, understanding can be lost. A psychiatrist conducting an assessment interview was disconcerted when a psychotic patient handed him a book by the philosopher Descartes, saying that he had been reading it and wondered what the psychiatrist's opinion of it might be. Somewhat taken aback he replied that he appreciated the offer, but thought that he might be able to learn more from it than the patient, because the patient's illness must make learning difficult. Thus the psychiatrist did not learn what the patient might have been asking about his thinking and his sense of identity ('I think therefore I am'), and the patient learned that the psychiatrist had not understood the meaning of his offer and was unable to help him.

Psychosis, meaning and the media

Bizarre and dramatic public behaviour attracts the attention of the media, and it makes depressing reading to realize how little interest is shown in the underlying motivations of many of these often tragic events. Although many patients who have recovered from an acute psychotic episode wish to forget it, or are satisfied with simply biological explanations, others have a strong wish to find a more satisfactory explanation of their deeply traumatic experience. Many live in dread of a recurrence and can be receptive to the idea of exploring the meaning of their experiences in terms of their personal life. Some will remain satisfied with the psychotic explanations that infiltrate their own minds, but others may show an impressive recognition that their experience of madness requires a deeper understanding than they have been able to achieve on their own or have been offered to date.

Example

In the UK there occurred a widely publicized event in which a young man was severely injured in a zoo when he climbed into a lion's cage and fed the lion with a chicken. This event evoked a national outcry about the inadequacy of supportive services for schizophrenic patients in the community. Although this was an appropriate, even effective, response no evidence appeared in the media to suggest any curiosity about what this event might have meant in terms of the victim's personal life, although clues were available, such as his longstanding interest in retrieving or rescuing dead or injured animals. Whilst this admirable characteristic might have been an expression of his emotional maturity, it might also have represented an enactment of an inner drama concerning attempts to control destructive phantasies, attempts that eventually failed and led to his psychotic behaviour in the zoo, where he became the victim of the destructive attack. Whether or not such a speculation might explain his bizarre behaviour, the significant feature is that it had not, apparently, been considered. His own comment was that something terribly powerful had happened to him that he could not understand. Although he was receiving a high standard of conventional care, he added that 'all the experiences and feelings you got at the outset seem to be crushed by the well-meaning staff' (Silcock, 1994).

Psychoanalytic theories of schizophrenia: psychotic breakdown

Although there is debate in psychoanalytic circles concerning the role of organic factors in psychosis and of neurosis and psychosis as a continuum, there is broad agreement about the importance of failure of early psychological development, beginning in the mother-infant relationship, as a basis for the predisposition to schizophrenia in later life. Many potent ingredients are funnelled into the mother-baby relationship, including biological, psychosocial and maternal psychology and psychopathology (Volkan, 1995). Biological factors are neither necessary nor sufficient causes of psychosis, but may play a contributory role. The impairment of ego functions that characterizes psychosis can be traced to degrees of failure to achieve mastery of the capacity to manage affective states in infancy, to differentiate self from object and to form the basis of a secure sense of identity.

Early pathogenic developmental experiences may thus lead to primitive, omnipotent modes of mental functioning, which may persist or be regressively reactivated when mechanisms of maintenance fail. Theoretical developments by Klein, Winnicott, Bion, and by some contemporary psychoanalysts have provided a model of mother–baby interaction, which specifies the establishment of a 'good containing internal object' in the inner world through processes of projection and introjection. It is this structuring of mental life that ensures the basis of future mental stability and the capacity for reflective thinking. Its impairment renders the individual vulnerable to psychosis in later life, rather than to neurosis. Kleinian object-relation theory, for example, represents a revolutionary innovation in psychoanalytic thinking, and the concepts of an inner world of objects and part objects that can be damaged by hatred and repaired by love adds a new dimension to classical libido theory.

When weakly established ego functions are exposed to sufficient psychological or psycho-biological stresses, internal or external, a regressive process can occur in which earlier modes of mental functioning are reactivated, impairing the capacity for rational thought and distorting perceptions. Object relationships may be replaced by identifications, and the capacity to differentiate inner from outer reality is compromised. Space-centred thinking undermines the subject's sense of time and this leads to memories being experienced as immediate perceptions. Wishes and fears assume hallucinatory and delusional qualities and may be experienced as present realities, and rational thinking is distorted by dream-like primary process thinking. At its simplest an acute breakdown can be regarded as the defensive response to life crises in an individual who is both psychologically and perhaps biologically vulnerable. This psychological vulnerability has been considered in terms of the encapsulation of unresolved, overwhelming destructive feelings in part–object relations arising originally in the mother–infant relationship (Grotstein, 1977).

Concrete thinking

Whereas the normal individual experiences his dreams as concrete reality during the period of his sleeping consciousness, his reality sense is restored on waking and his hallucinatory experience vanishes once again into the inner world of the unconscious. The schizophrenic individual could be considered as waking from his dreams only partially and thus living in two worlds at once. His capacity for reality testing is seriously impaired and he confuses inner and outer realities. With the capacity to recognize symbol and metaphor weakened, his thinking assumes a concrete quality and he experiences varying degrees of difficulty in differentiating the symbol from that which it signifies. As Freud expressed it, 'word-presentations' are replaced by 'thing-presentations'.

Example

A young professional golfer found himself inexplicably reluctant to use a particular golf club, the driver, the metal shaft of which was attached by insertion into its wooden head. This inhibition ushered in an acute psychotic episode of some severity. Upon recovery he was able to use the club again, and to explain that he now realized that the club had reminded him of his parents' sexual relationship, a matter that had for many reasons profoundly disturbed him. In the course of psychotherapy it emerged that hitting the golf ball aggressively represented his unconscious destructive feelings towards the parental couple. In such a case, objects, whole or part, are being equated on the basis of a single characteristic, impairing the capacity for symbol formation, which depends for its success on the mechanism of displacement from an object of primary interest to one that is recognized as different but in an important sense equivalent. As this patient recovered from his psychotic episode he regained his capacity for symbolic thinking and was able to realize that the activity of striking the golf ball *represented*, that is to say reminded him of, his own internal destructive feelings, rather than actually *being* (presenting) them concretely in the form of a 'symbolic equation' (Segal, 1981).

The paranoid-schizoid and depressive positions

The Kleinian concept of a developmental pathway of integration from the paranoid-schizoid to the depressive position helps to clarify the dynamic relationships between the least integrated schizophrenic psychoses, the more integrated schizo-affective conditions and the least disintegrated (albeit no less devastating) manic-depressive psychoses. Obsessive-compulsive, claustro-agoraphobic, and some severe anorexic states can be located within this context (Rey, 1994). A psychotic person may no longer experience his own thoughts, feelings and impulses as inhabiting his own mind. The fear of losing a sense of personal identity may find expression as sensations within the body, or a belief in imminent destruction by alien forces. Lethal rays may be thought to be melting the brain, or a computer bug implanted in the patient's skull keeps him under constant surveillance. Extreme anxiety may reactivate defence mechanisms of splitting and projective identification, with the consequence that the patient may come to identify with the object of his own unconscious destructive feelings, which he projects into some containing object. In the course of psychotherapy this may lead to a psychotic transference or impulsive acting-out.

Self-destructiveness – which self?

Some forms of apparently self-destructive behaviour in psychotic or borderline patients may be understood in this way. If a patient forms a deep emotional attachment to a psychotherapist, or to a staff member in 'multiple-treater' settings, a regressive revival of deep and unresolved conflicts concerning separation may take place. One disturbing way in which this can find expression is in the form of command hallucinations – for example, an instruction to the patient to run into traffic and throw himself under a car. The reversal produced by projective identification (expressed as 'aggression turned against the self') does not fully explain this phenomenon. The patient's self becomes identified with the offending object, perhaps the therapist or a staff member. The latter is spared the patient's anger (which the patient fears to be omnipotently destructive) by projection of the aggressive aspects of the patient's self into a lethal container, in this instance a passing car. What is projected violently returns, boomerang fashion, to its origin. Understanding the process whereby the needed staff member has become, for the patient, an 'abandoning' mother can help all concerned. If this dynamic is not understood treatment may break down, staff may be forced into prolonged intensive surveillance of an apparently acutely suicidal patient, and at the worst the outcome may be fatal.

Assessing prognosis

The prognosis of acute psychotic illness will depend on many factors, past and present, of benign or malign influence. The work of Ping-Ni-Pao (1979) and others has illuminated the complexity of this situation. Purely symptomatic treatment will usually bring about remission. Good clinical psychiatric practice that investigates personal problems and family relationships will sometimes achieve a sufficient resolution of more obvious problems and achieve a good outcome: the support offered by a sufficiently mature family can also help to bring this about. However, the patient may continue to remain vulnerable to further breakdowns if the unconscious conflicts related to his relevant life problems have not been sufficiently explored and resolved. The 'sealing over' of psychotic material may be the best possible solution in some cases, but here again psychodynamic exploration itself can help to decide when deeper conflicts should be left alone, at least for the moment. In selected cases long-term individual psychoanalytic psychotherapy undertaken in the right circumstances can promote new personality growth and integration. Motivation and what Alanen has called a 'grip on life' may at times be as important a prognostic indicator as psychopathology.

The relevance of genetics in assessment

Spectacular progress in biomedical research and into genetic aspects of psychosis should not mask the dangers of its overuse in the assessment of individual patients. Genes represent tendencies, no more and no less, and early experience may play a great part in determining whether or not genetic endowment becomes manifest (Tienari, 1992). Biological factors are most appropriately considered as sometimes contributing to vulnerability to later psychosis, but not as necessary or sufficient causes. Emphasis on genetic factors in the psychiatric assessment of a psychotic patient may easily be misused as a defence against emotional contact, and to bypass thought and curiosity about early environmental experiences. Such idealization of bio-medicine and relegation of psychodynamics can seriously mislead worried patients and their relatives. Adequate early career training in psychoanalytic concepts relevant to psychosis can prevent clinicians from making such mistakes.

Projective identification

The concept of projective identification has had revolutionary consequences for the understanding of psychotic psychopathology. It refers to an unconscious belief that a part of the self or inner world, usually unwanted, can be disposed of by relocation into a mental representation of another object (person). It can be regarded as a primitive precursor of the familiar mechanism of projection. Thus 'projection into' has a deeper implication than 'projection on to' in that it refers to space-centred processes and conceives of a 'containing' object as the recipient. Different aims have been ascribed to projective identification: to expel good or bad parts of the self or inner world: to control or damage the object: or as an infantile method of communicating with the object (which Bion regarded as a normal feature of mother–baby communication). Although the term has been used in different ways, it throws light on intra-psychic and inter-personal transactions and can be regarded as an important bridge between psychiatric and psychoanalytic concepts, with considerable relevance for work in the field of expressed emotion in particular.

Transference and countertransference

Projective identification can be deeply involved in the processes of trans-ference and countertransference that influence significant relationships. Those between patient and family, and between patient and therapist, are regarded as being of the greatest importance in contributing to processes of understanding and misunderstanding. It is not only psychotherapists who should be aware of their countertransference responses: they may be mobilized in everyone who makes contact with a schizophrenic patient. A familiar example concerns the projection of guilt into therapists and other staff members. A less well known but disturbing situation can arise when a patient projects his sane capacity to doubt his psychotic explanations of his experience into another person, and then proceeds to exert pressure on the person to make him agree that the patient's delusional ideas are sane and normal. This dynamic, a version of what Searles (1965) called 'the attempt to drive the other person crazy' may be far more common than is usually recognized. Psychotic patients have a disturbing effect on staff, and this may lead to inappropriate responses (see Martindale, this volume). Such disturbances may have a rational origin, in which case discussion and support may bring relief. However, disturbances produced by projection at an unconscious level require special skills to resolve, for which training in psychodynamics and supervision is essential. Even with this experience it remains highly stressful to be used as a container for parts of the patient's world of internal object relations. In the course of individual psychotherapy, and within a ward milieu, delusional transfer-ences may emerge, and considerable skill may be needed to deal with such events. If they are successfully managed important integrative conse-quences may follow.

Reparation

The concept of reparation is central to much psychoanalytic thinking. Some psychotic patients reveal a history of onset at a point where they were unable to bear the mental pain and potentially constructive guilt associated with a belief in having damaged a loved object. The normal pathway to integration, which involves the emergence of the capacity for symbolic expression, of reparative wishes and the process of mourning, is thereby closed. The concept of the manic defence has led to recognition of methods of escape from the pains of integration and has shown how frequently such potentially integrative processes come to a halt, particularly in the case of psychotic patients. Defensive processes, variously described as false reparation, manic, concrete or psychotic reparation may assume a variety of disguises and it may be difficult to recognize the progress towards integration that may have generated them. So strong is the denial of loss by damage or death that many patients are impeded through the unattainable belief that the object of reparative wishes must be completely and perfectly restored, a task equivalent to raising Lazarus from the dead. Psychotic reparative attempts can assume extravagant and bizarre forms.

Example

A young man caught in the confusion of a schizophrenic episode committed homicide, killing his mother in the delusional belief that she was about to murder him. When engaged in psychotherapy he said that this event presented no problem for him. Whenever he began to think that his mother was dead he discovered that he had a big lump protruding from his skull. He was then able to function in the role of rewriter of a type of film script in which his mother was alive and well – whereupon the protruding lump immediately disappeared. An even more complex form of concrete reparative attempt has been described by Rey (1994), in which the patient may suffer in identification with a loved and damaged object, and will not get better until the underlying preoccupation is dealt with. In this sense the patient may be considered to be bringing his damaged objects to the therapist to be repaired.

Inter-disciplinary co-operation: convergence and divergence of approaches

There are many points of convergence between psychodynamic, psycho-educational and cognitive ways of understanding and methods of treatment in the field of psychosis. In the cognitive-behavioural sphere in

Britain there has been a dramatic investment in recent years in attempts to alleviate the distress caused by delusional thinking. Contemporary research by psychologists into the nature of auditory hallucinations and delusional thinking, and the therapeutic application of cognitive-behavioural methods of treatment in psychotic conditions is of considerable interest and importance (Fowler, Garety and Kuipers, 1995; Chadwick, Birchwood and Trower, 1996). Such investigations of the function of hallucinatory voices and the willingness to listen to patients in detail are a great advance on the practice of some psychiatrists that may centre on the collecting of data in order to make a diagnosis without, however, managing to relate to the patient as a person, or trying to understand what is going on in his mind and to assess how he might be helped to deal with his personal and emotional conflicts.

Although there are important points of contact between cognitive-behavioural and psychoanalytic perspectives, there are also major differences. Perhaps an essential difference lies in the stance that the therapist adopts to the patient – the one educative and the other insight-oriented. Milton (1997) has pointed out that education has its limits and beyond these the unconscious is likely to have its intrusive and compelling say sooner or later. Constructive debate is certainly needed on the merits of educative and insight-oriented approaches and how to bring them together without damage to either. In the field of expressed emotion there is a new interest in the role that projective and introjective processes may play in the interpersonal relations between the patient, the patient's family and the therapist or therapeutic team. Consideration of the part that the patient may play in producing high 'expressed emotion' in relatives involves careful scrutiny of the psychodynamics underlying the beneficial changes that this approach can release.

Example

One interesting process concerns the improvement in the patient's state of mind that may follow a successful attempt at helping the family to lower expressed emotion levels. If the patient has been projecting forcibly into the family, and acting in such a way as to 'make' them play the role he is pressing upon them (a process that has been described as the inter-personal phase of projective identification) a high expressed emotion level is likely to ensue, and this may involve counter-projection by family members (as for instance in the common practice of mutual evacuation of feelings of guilt). If the family can be helped to abandon this designated role in a genuinely tolerant manner, a considerable ameliorative psycho-dynamic shift may take place. This could be explained in psychoanalytic terms as the introjection by the patient of a 'containing' object, as occurs in successful psychotherapy, with an associated benign structural improvement in the patient's inner world. Although work in the psychosocial perspective has proved to be a powerful and effective therapeutic tool it has limitations if applied outside a psychodynamic context. For example, attempts at alleviating the guilt of relatives may be more controversial. It is not uncommon to find that relatives have a better understanding of the nature of the disturbance than their professional advisers. An explanation of the illness as being of essentially a biological nature may relieve many, but it may also frustrate the genuine curiosity and the search for deeper understanding of others (see Anon, 1994).

Partnership or conflict?

A small number of British psychoanalysts have made profound contributions to the understanding and treatment of schizophrenia, much of which are based on the work of Melanie Klein. However, relatively few contemporary psychoanalysts have had the opportunity of encountering the range of seriously ill schizophrenic patients found in a public hospital setting or of psychotic conditions encountered in the course of clinical psychiatric practice. As a result, these analysts may derive their knowledge of the field from the study of psychotic mechanisms in patients with borderline personality disorders. As Freeman (1986, 1988), an important British contributor, has pointed out, there is much that such analysts could learn from psychiatrists about psychosis. The outcome of this dissociation of labour is that the skills of the most highly trained psychotherapists, who do not have the supportive psychiatric resources that are essential to the psychoanalytic psychotherapy of psychosis, are usually beyond the reach of those schizophrenic patients who might derive the greatest benefit from them (Lucas, 1986). However, there are a great many Scandinavian psychotherapists of varying disciplines with different degrees of experience and training who currently do valuable and effective individual psychoanalytic psychotherapy with psychotic patients, often under difficult conditions (Alanen, 1997; Hansen, 1993). The fact that such workers may achieve good results raises the question of how much skilled psychoanalytic treatment might achieve in selected cases, given the necessary partnership with experienced psychodynamic psychiatrists.

The future

The 'need-adapted' Finnish model, increasingly cited as an example of good practice, could certainly help psychiatrists, psychologists, psychotherapists, nurses and other professionals to learn from their own and others' experience with psychotic patients by working together and using the insights gained by psychoanalysis. Such co-operation could support the growth of a climate wherein new learning develops through rational dialogue and constructive assessment of the merits and limitations of collaborative work. These benign changes would be in the interest of psychotic patients and of recruitment into psychiatry and psychiatric work of nurses who have left the profession in ever-increasing numbers. The benefits for over-stressed clinical psychiatrists, themselves sometimes regarded nowadays as an endangered species, are obvious (Deahl and Turner, 1997). The training of the next generation of health professionals would be enriched by this collaboration and by an understanding of the place of psychoanalytic thinking in work with psychotic patients.

Despite an urgent need for improved funding for the treatment of psychosis I believe that the main obstacle is not financial alone. Psychiatrists are already free to work towards creating a 'need-adapted' setting in their own personal practice. In this setting, specialist psychotherapists can be recruited to contribute effectively to the team by making psychodynamic assessments, by helping staff groups with counter-transferential and other stresses, by supervising the work of other psychotherapists – in particular that of nurse therapists – by conducting individual psychotherapy themselves and by working alongside and with other psychological therapists.

Cognitive-behavioural psychotherapy

I think that the long-term future of cognitive-behavioural work with psychotic patients without a psychoanalytic input is uncertain. At present these practitioners are attempting to help patients for whom analytic treatment is rarely available, or even useful, and they have the research procedures, academic status and sometimes financial resources that long-term psychotherapy does not attract. However, such work is vulnerable to the criticism that it attempts ultimately to manipulate the patient in order to make him or her stop having delusions, without investigating the person who suffers the delusions or the dynamic reasons why he or she has found it necessary to prefer psychotic explanations to rational ones. At worst it could become a purely empirical and sterile exercise with disappointing long-term results. At best the enormous investment that has gone into understanding conscious mental processes could link up with established psychoanalytic knowledge to produce something original and valuable. Some of the work done by contemporary cognitive-behavioural therapists might be regarded as techniques for supporting the sane part of the personality and, as such, is comparable to analytically oriented supportive psychotherapy. Yet there are crucial differences such as a lack of focus on transference, countertransference and separation reactions. If such deficiencies can be addressed I can conceive of a vigorous partnership. A recent report by cognitive therapists, which contained a psychoanalytic commentary, illustrates how this can be done (Turkington and Siddle, 1998).

To change polarized attitudes and reduce poor-quality work clinicians must, as Michael Balint recommended, work together to distinguish, in each case, between what we can do, what we might do had we the resources, what we must not do, and what we are, under the circumstances, going to do. All improvements begin with the clinician. He can elect to listen to his psychotic patients carefully and empathetically and, in the light of his increased understanding, help to construct a setting within which psycho-analytically informed psychotherapy, cognitive-behavioural therapy, group or individual therapy (supportive or exploratory) may contribute to achieving effective results. There are many settings within which good integrated work can be carried out. The most obvious is the psychiatric hospital, recently devalued but still the best basis for work with the severely psychotic person. In that setting emergency response teams in the community can find a home, specialized treatment homes can find a supportive base and community care can find a source of knowledge. I believe that the starting point for a framework of collaboration between the psychoanalytic and other perspectives is to be found in the area of first-episode psychosis. An early psychoanalytic evaluation of the patient's outer and inner life, past and present and his family context can provide a psycho-dynamic rationale for subsequent family, psychosocial, psychoanalytic psychotherapeutic and cognitive-behavioural interventions. Learning to think along these lines will help to build theoretical as well as technical bridges, and this will help to improve the quality of care for the psychotic individual.

References

Alanen YO (1997) Schizophrenia: Its Origins and Need-Adapted Treatment. London: Karnac Books.

Anon (1994) Worse than the worst nightmare. British Medical Journal 308: 1995.

Bion WR (1957) The differentiation of the psychotic from the non-psychotic personalities. In Bion WR (1957) Second Thoughts. London: Karnac Books.

Chadwick P, Birchwood M, Trower P (1996) Cognitive Therapy for Delusions, Voices and Paranoia. Chichester: Wiley.

Deahl M, Turner T (1997) General psychiatry in no-man's land. British Journal of Psychiatry 171: 6–8.

Fowler D, Garety PA, Kuipers L (1995) Cognitive Behaviour Therapy for Psychosis: Theory and Practice. Chichester: Wiley.

Freeman T (1986) Psychotherapy and general psychiatry – integral or separable? Psychoanalytic Psychotherapy 1(1): 19–30.

Freeman T (1988) The Psychoanalyst in Psychiatry. London: Karnac Books.

Grotstein JS (1977) The psychoanalytic concept of schizophrenia. 1.The dilemma. 2. Reconciliation. International Journal of Psychoanalysis 58: 403–52.

Hansen JB (1993) Crossing the Borders: Psychotherapy of Schizophrenia. Ludvika. Dualis.

Jackson M, Cawley R (1992) Psychodynamics and psychotherapy on an acute admission ward: the story of an experimental unit. British Journal of Psychiatry 160: 41–50.

Jackson M, Williams P (1994) Unimaginable Storms: a Search for Meaning in Psychosis. London. Karnac Books.

Jackson M (2001) Psychotherapy for Psychosis: weathering the storms. London: Karnac Books (in press).

Lehtinen K (1994) Need-adapted treatment of schizophrenia: family interventions. British Journal of Psychiatry 164 (Supp. 23): 89–96.

Lucas R (1986) On the contribution of psychoanalysis to the management of psychotic patients in the NHS. Psychoanalytic Psychotherapy 1(1): 19–30.

Milton J (1997) Psychoanalysis and the Limits of Education. Paper Delivered to the Psychotherapy Section of The British Psychological Society in Conference On Meanings, Cognitions and Feelings: Dialogue between Analytical and Cognitive Psychotherapies.

Milton J (2001) Psychoanalysis and cognitive-behavioural therapy. International Journal of Psychoanalysis (in press).

Pao P-N (1979) Schizophrenic Disorders. Theory and Treatment from a Psychodynamic Point of View. New York. International Universities Press.

Pylkkänen K (1989) A quality assurance programme for psychotherapy. Psychoanalytic Psychotherapy 4: 13–22.

Rakkolainen V, Lehtinen K, Alanen YO (1991) Need-adapted treatment of schizophrenic processes: the essential role of family-centred meetings. Contemporary Family Therapy 13(6): 573–82.

Rey JH (1994) Universals of Psychoanalysis in the Treatment of Psychotic and Borderline States. London: Free Association Books.

Segal H (1981) Notes on Symbol Formation. In Segal H (1981) The Work of Hanna Segal. London: Jason Aronson.

Silcock B (1994) The musician's tale. Sanetalk (Summer): 5.

Sinason M (1993) Who is the mad voice inside? Psychoanal. Psychother. 7(3): 203–21.

Steiner J (1993) Psychic Retreats. London: Routledge.

Tienari P (1992) Implications of adoption studies on schizophrenia. British Journal of Psychiatry. Supplement 18: 52–8.

Turkington D, Siddle R (1998) Cognitive therapy for the treatment of delusions. Advances in Psychiatric Treatment 4: 235–42.

Volkan V (1995) The Infantile Psychotic Self and its Fates. London: Aronson.

CHAPTER 4

Treating and studying the schizophrenias

THOMAS FREEMAN

I wish to strike a personal note in my contribution to this collection of papers on psychoanalysis, the psychoses and the importance of acquiring a coherent, useful conceptual and clinical language. This contribution is personal in the sense that it gives an account of my experiences in trying to treat and study patients suffering from acute psychotic attacks and those whose illness reached a chronic stage. My interest in the psychoses began in 1947 when I was a candidate at the London Institute of Psychoanalysis. I was working in psychiatric hospitals when the treatment of the psychoses consisted of electro-shock therapy, insulin coma and barbiturates – administered singly or jointly. Seven years were to elapse before chlorpromazine came into general use (in 1954). At one hospital the medical superintendent gave me the task of running the male ward of the insulin coma unit. After a year I was transferred to the female ward where I remained for further eight months. During the induction of the hypoglycaemic coma one could observe the gradual dissolution of adult nervous and mental life and the emergence of more primitive forms of neurological and psychological functioning. Prior to the loss of consciousness and during recovery from the hypoglycaemic coma patients gave expression to childhood modes of behaviour; for example, to finger sucking. There was misidentification of nurses as sisters or mothers and myself as brother or father, in a manner similar to that found in acute or chronic brain syndromes or in acute psychotic attacks. These manifestations were often accompanied by an intense attachment to a member of the treatment team. A woman of 25 who had been admitted to hospital because she believed that she was being drugged and sexually abused would masturbate freely just as she regained consciousness. When fully awake she repeatedly claimed that one of the nurses was in love with me but was too shy to declare her feelings. She was sure I would marry the nurse and have children by her.

Most significant was the patient's admiration of the nurse: 'What lovely hair she has, what a pretty nose and mouth', she would say. When this nurse took another patient out to tea the patient became violently jealous and remained mute for some hours. The next day she returned to her phantasy of the nurse and myself and persisted with this phantasy until the end of the treatment.

In mis-identifying nurses as siblings or parents, and relating to them as such, the insulin coma patient brings to life and repeats, emotionally, important relationships of the past, just as the neurotic patient gradually does during psychoanalytic treatment. The phenomena observed in the insulin ward were spontaneous transferences whose emergence was facilitated by the psychological regression (dissolution) caused by the hypoglycaemia. They occurred in patients, who, in clear consciousness, were withdrawn and negativistic. The phantasy of the female patient was a repetitive phenomenon but altered through externalization, that is, it was the nurse who was in love, not she. However, here the heterosexual phantasy acted as a cover for her homosexual love for the nurse. The capacity for object love (to relate emotionally to others), though apparently lost during the psychotic attack, is not irrevocably lost. The presence of this potential makes a psychotherapeutic treatment possible.

Although physical methods of treatment predominated throughout the 1930s and 1940s, there were psychiatrists in Germany, Switzerland and the USA who found that patients suffering from psychoses could be helped by a psychotherapy based on psychoanalysis. As early as 1920, Federn (1953), one of Freud's first adherents, was treating psychotic patients by a modified form of psychoanalysis. A mental hospital conducted along psychoanalytical principles was established in Germany by Simmel (1929). About the same time Sullivan (1932) was treating schizophrenic patients by a psychotherapy derived from psychoanalysis at the Sheppard and Enoch Pratt Hospital in Baltimore. Like Simmel, Sullivan recognized that the nursing staff required a special training if they were to contribute to the treatment regime. A few years later serious attempts were being made to treat psychotic patients by psychoanalysis at the Menninger Clinic in Kansas and at the Chestnut Lodge Sanatorium in Maryland (Knight, 1939; Fromm-Reichman, 1948; Hill, 1955).

After 1945 the psychotherapeutic approach to the psychoses flourished particularly in the US and Switzerland. Many new techniques were introduced to facilitate contact with long-standing cases of schizophrenia. Outstanding in this respect was the method of *symbolic realization* devised by Sechahaye (1951) and the technique of *direct analysis* introduced by Rosen (1952). Those who undertook this work either followed a strict technique based on the theories of Melanie Klein or employed modifications of the classical psychoanalytic method. Rosenfeld (1950) and Bion (1957) in London were representative of the former, while Fromm-Reichman (1948), Benedetti (1979) and Muller (1979) in Switzerland were representative of the latter. One of Fromm-Reichman's pupils, Searles (1963), was later to become well known for his work with long-standing cases of schizophrenia. The clinical experiences of these psychoanalysts led to revisions of the classical psychoanalytical theory of the psychoses. In the post-war years the schizophrenias posed a stimulating challenge to the psychoanalyst who found himself working in a mental hospital. In 1952, having completed my psychoanalytic training, I moved to Glasgow Royal Mental Hospital, now known as Gartnavel Royal Hospital. Both the physician superintendent, the late Dr Angus McNiven, and the newly appointed Professor of Psychological Medicine, the late T Ferguson Rodger, had been pupils of Adolf Meyer at the Phipps Clinic in Baltimore. Like Meyer, they regarded mental illnesses as reactions of vulnerable personalities to adverse life circumstances. There was therefore nothing fixed or immutable about the symptoms of mental illnesses. The form of expression and the content of the illness followed from current and past life events. Psychoanalysis appeared to McNiven and Rodger as a development of Meyer's psychobiology. It was not surprising that they believed that psychoanalysis had much to contribute to clinical psychiatry.

During my first year at the hospital, whilst working with the late JL Cameron, we attempted to treat, in a group-analytic setting, seriously depressed patients who had failed to respond to electro-shock therapy (Freeman and Cameron, 1953; Cameron and Freeman, 1955). Professor Rodger suggested, in view of the current interest in the psychotherapy of the schizophrenias, that we investigate how far this group of illnesses might respond to a group psychoanalytic approach. Having obtained financial assistance from the Scottish Hospitals Endowment Trust in 1954, JL Cameron was appointed research psychiatrist, and Andrew McGhie research psychologist. The first matter to be settled was the category of schizophrenic patient to be included in the study. The question of what constitutes a schizophrenic psychosis was as controversial an issue in 1953 as it is today. As the symptom complexes that appear at the onset of an illness give no indication of the course it will follow – whether remitting or non-remitting – it was and is very difficult to argue against those who claim that patients who improve or recover after psychotherapy would have done so spontaneously. We decided to select only established cases where there were unequivocal signs of a chronic autistic development. In retrospect I can think of no more daunting task that the one we proposed to undertake. Fourteen patients were chosen – seven men and seven women. A male group of six patients and a female group of six patients were seen daily over two years. One man and one woman patient were seen daily on an individual basis. McGhie acted as the observer in the groups, compiling a verbatim note of the verbal and as far as possible, the non-verbal behaviour of patients, nurses and psychiatrists. The separate statements made by patients during the group sessions were typed on individual cards in order to facilitate the comparative matching of the reactions of different patients and to record changes in patients' behaviour. An important aim of the project was to evaluate the role of the nurse in the treatment and management of the schizophrenias. To this end a nurse attended the group sessions. At the suggestion of JL Cameron a room was set aside where two nurses spent the day with five patients of a type similar to those in the group. JL Cameron spent an hour a day in this room. Additionally, he spent several hours daily in the ward where the female group patients resided, observing the behaviour of the patients and the nursing staff. Regular meetings were established with the nurses involved in the project. The purpose of these meetings was to increase the nurses' sense of security and to encourage them to report their observations.

It is important to remember that the study took place prior to the introduction of the phenothiazine drugs. Patients were neglectful of themselves, impulsive and frequently acting under the influence of delusions and hallucinations. At the beginning we were confronted with the important issue of technique. Many patients were mute and apparently inaccessible. The speech of others was incomprehensible. Some were restless and wandered aimlessly about the room. How were we to approach them? We were fairly familiar with the interpretative techniques of those who had published accounts of their therapeutic work. We decided to forgo instant interpretations of, for example, what might have been a possible transference reaction, in favour of an observing and an 'expectant' role. However, we did not remain silent. We were reasonably friendly and took every opportunity to indicate that we recognized that the patient must feel anxious and bewildered about what was happening. There was never an immediate or direct response to this.

We were interested to find out whether what was observed supported or refuted the several revisions of the classical theory of the schizophrenias. Did transferences arise in cases of schizophrenia? If they did, could they be employed for therapeutic ends – in other words, were they 'working transferences'? It was Freud's view that such 'working transferences' were not available to the patient suffering from a non-remitting schizophrenia. A further question concerned the cognitive disorganization found in so many of these patients. Was this a defensive psychological manoeuvre, as some psychoanalysts maintained? Our hope was that by studying the patient in his or her relationship to other patients, to nurses and doctors, it would be possible to observe the conditions attendant upon the emergence, persistence and disappearance of clinical phenomena. We were not disappointed in this respect. I do not intend to give an account of what happened in our group meetings, in individual sessions or what took place between patients and nurses, as there is no space here and these data have been described in a number of publications (Cameron and Freeman, 1956; Freeman et al., 1958). However, we did confirm the fact, described originally by Bleuler (1911), that patients who suffer from long-standing schizophrenias are acutely sensitive to their immediate environment. Acute attacks occurring in the chronic state provoked by events of an interpersonal nature in patients who had been withdrawn and unresponsive for years, gave expression to delusional ideas that had occurred at the onset of the illness. During our work with these cases of non-remitting schizophrenia, we were impressed by their tendency to act similarly to those who were around them. This 'identificatory' behaviour was usually transient but achieved some degree of permanency if they remained continually with others, for example the nursing staff. The patients appeared to be uncertain of their own identities. They frequently referred to themselves in the third person. It was this loss of the ability to clearly differentiate themselves from others and the 'identificatory' behaviour that led Federn (1953) to formulate his theory of the loss of the ego boundary in the schizophrenias. These long-standing cases provided an excellent opportunity to demonstrate and to understand that the significant effect of the morbid process lies in the loss of those functions that ensure healthy mental life. We hoped that dealings with the nursing staff in the groups and in the treatment room would encourage in the patient the growth of positive 'identificatory' behaviour and strengthen what remained of healthy mental life (Bleuler, 1978). Unfortunately these identifications were vulnerable to the state of the patients' relationships with nurses and psychiatrists. A disappointment or frustration easily led to the loss of the identification.

Transitivism is a well-known sign of schizophrenic psychoses at onset and in chronicity. It reflects the loss of the ego boundary. Transitivism describes the way in which a patient consciously experiences and expresses elements of his/her physical or mental self in someone else and vice versa – for example one female patient shouted 'That woman is cursing me with my voice'. In his theory of the loss of the ego boundary, Federn (1953) followed the Jacksonian principle (1884) which states that the loss of nervous and mental functions follows from their dissolution caused by a morbid process. Transitivism is thus the direct result of the loss of the ego boundary. An alternative explanation is advanced by Kleinian psychoanalysts who propose that transitivism follows from a process of expulsion (projective identification) and assimilation (introjection) of aspects of the self and objects. Transitivism thus gives expression to an object relationship – a transference psychosis. Other phenomena such as disinterest, negativism and withdrawal are also explained on the basis of projective identification and introjection.

I was not satisfied with what I could discover in the group work. The individual patient's personality tended to get lost in the group. I needed to find out more if I was to understand and recognize the action of the transference psychoses claimed to be present in schizophrenic patients under treatment. I had little difficulty in perceiving the random and unpredictable transferences that were always making their appearance (Freeman et al., 1958). I decided, therefore, to spend a good deal more time with individual patients, which I did over the ensuing years. Working with individual patients over an extended period (Freeman, 1969) as well as short-term studies enabled me to recognize the great variation in symptoms and courses of illness which occur within the group of schizophrenias. In my view, *attention to this variation is a pre-requisite for a therapeutic outcome.*

As other contributors to this volume have emphasized, winning a patient's confidence and being permitted to glimpse something of his or her inner life is not the prerogative of the psychiatrist who may be treating the patient. Indeed, there are psychiatrists who take scant interest in the patient's internal life at all, to the detriment of both. The need for collaboration between staff had been forcibly impressed on me during my early work with the chronically ill patients. The co-operation of nurses and all those dealing with the patient was essential for both investigation and therapeutic purposes. Regular meetings permit the exchange of observations about patients' behaviour and their complex responses to treatment.

In pursuance of my interest in systematically recording psychotic phenomena I constructed a schema that I hoped would serve two purposes. First, it would accommodate the clinical data and second it would provide a comprehensive explanatory account of these phenomena. The stimulus for this came from Anna Freud's profile schema for the adult psychoneurotic patient (Anna Freud et al., 1965). It was at her suggestion that I tried to adapt her schema to the psychoses. In Anna Freud's schema the clinical phenomena are ordered in terms of Freud's metapsychological concepts (Freud, 1900; 1914; 1915a, b, c) – that is, from the dynamic, economic, topographic and developmental aspects. Anna Freud emphasized that her schema was not to be used as a questionnaire but, rather, to help in conceptualizing clinical observations from a metapsychological standpoint – forming a conceptual language (Anna Freud et al., 1965). After recording the reason for referral, description of the patient, family background, significant environmental circumstances, the principal headings of the adult schema (Anna Freud et al., 1965) were, respectively, Assessment of Drive and Superego positions.

A The drives
   1 Libido
      a Libidinal position,   b libido distribution
         i   Cathexis of the self
         ii Cathexis of object

   2 Aggression

B Ego and superego

C Assessment of fixation points and regression

D Assessment of conflicts

E Assessment of general characteristics with a bearing on the need for analytic therapy and the ability to profit from it.

My modification of Anna Freud's profile schema and how I used it with schizophrenic patients has been described elsewhere (Freeman, 1972a, 1972b, 1973, 1988). Although I used the schema over a long period I was never entirely satisfied with it in one particular respect. The concepts that were employed to classify the clinical data were themselves of an explanatory kind. I decided on an alternative approach and constructed a second schema, which dispensed with the purely psychoanalytic classification without discarding the need for explanation based on psychoanalytic concepts. The first part of this schema (Freeman, 1969) consisted of seven sections:

- the status of the patient's interpersonal relations;
- perception of the self, self-regard, autonomy of the self and personal identity;
- status of the cognitive functions;
- motility (voluntary and automatic movement);
- sensori–motor organization (I should mention that I was interested in assessing the neurological status of both recent and long-standing cases of schizophrenia);
- the affective state; and

- overt instinctual expressions, such as masturbation and anal and oral phenomena.

Under the heading 'interpersonal relations' I recorded the ways in which the patient perceived and related to me, to nurses and to others. I distinguished between these relationships and those with delusional figures, such as known and unknown persecutors, and other figures who might be part of the patient's delusional reality. As to the former, I recorded whether the patient regarded myself or the nurse solely as a means for the satisfaction of a need, for example for cigarettes or help to obtain discharge from hospital, or to help fulfil a delusional wish phantasy. This need-satisfying behaviour is characteristic of long-standing cases of schizophrenia where there is withdrawal, inattention and often negativism. Such behaviour reflects the presence of an emotional egocentrism akin to that of the infant and young child (Anna Freud, 1966). Signs of interest in or concern for myself and others were noted, and were most evident in schizophreniform and in remitting schizophrenias, and in manic depressions. If such an interest were present, did it vanish following anger, disappointment or separation? Was the patient envious or jealous? Was there an inappropriate anxiety and concern for others or myself? Was I irrationally overvalued? Did the patient perceive others or me as an agent of the persecutors, or a victim of the persecutors like himself? Was there an overt indication of heterosexual or homosexual wishes or behaviour? As far as delusional figures were concerned, did they find representation through mis-identifications, through hallucinatory experiences or through effects on bodily or mental sensibility? An account of the patient's attitude to the delusional figures was recorded. Was the patient friendly, hostile or dependent on these figures? What was the attitude of the delusional figures? Were they advising, friendly, reassuring, critical or persecutory? Were these figures related or connected to real persons existing in the present or in the past?

In the section dealing with the self and self-regard, a note was made as to whether or not there was adequate investment in the boundaries of the self. Was there loss of autonomy of the self as reflected in disturbances of self-object discrimination, resulting in transitivistic phenomena? Was there disturbance of personal and sexual identity? Was there overvaluation of the self? Was there an increase in the intensity of bodily sensations? Were there changes in the body image? As to cognitive functions, I shall omit questions about thought processes, verbalization, perception and memory. I should, however, like to refer briefly to the function of attention, as it is always disturbed in the schizophrenias. Was the patient able to sustain attention for ordered thinking and speech and for appropriate reactions to environmental stimuli? Were there signs of distractibility? Did this distractibility emanate from the patient's attempt to understand his conscious experiences or was the external stimulus assimilated outside consciousness, only secondarily making its appearance in speech? Was a change to normal attention related to the anticipation of the satisfaction of a need or to an affect or hallucinatory experience? There are those who suggest that a disorder of selective attention plays a decisive role in creating the disturbance of thinking and perceiving that occurs in the schizophrenias. My former colleague, McGhie (1965), arrived at this conclusion on the basis of experimental studies.

Under the heading 'motility disorder' I hoped to note such disturbances of voluntary movement as ambitendency, motor perseveration, repetitive movements and postural persistence (catalepsy). Were these phenomena associated with particular mental contents? As to sensorimotor organization I looked for signs of hypotonia, hypertonia and asymmetrical tonus states. Was there a tonic reflex response particularly in cases presenting with hypertonia of the upper limb musculature? Were there signs of inattention to tactile and painful stimuli? Were there indications of displacement (disturbed localization) of sensation from one body part to another? Was there evidence of face dominance? With respect to instinctual drive activity, it was a matter of noting the occurrence of masturbation, genital or anal, and bodily exhibitionism, and overt heterosexual or homosexual behaviour. As far as aggression was concerned – was there overt aggression? What was the cause of this? Was there an association between the expression of aggression and changes in motility such as catalepsy, motor blocking, ambitendency? Was aggression directed to the body or to the mental self in the form of self-reproaches? Affects were recorded – particularly envy, jealousy and anger. Of particular importance were the affects the patient attributed to real and delusional figures.

The final completion of a schema depended on observations made by the nursing and ancillary staff quite apart from myself – hence the vital importance of the regular meetings that I had with all those involved in the treatment of the patient (Freeman, 1969). The descriptive section of my amended schema was followed by an interpretation – an explanation – of the clinical phenomena, in psychoanalytic terms. Thus a formulation was arrived at of the causes of the prodromal symptoms (the pre-psychotic phase – Katan, 1954) of the immediate causes of the acute attack, of the content of delusions and hallucinations and of the cognitive disturbances. A picture was drawn of the way in which the patient had met the danger provoked by the derivatives of instinct (libidinal and aggressive phantasies) during the pre-psychotic phase and during the attack itself (Freeman, 1988). These defensive manoeuvres were seen as playing an important, if not decisive part, in creating the content of the symptom-atology. For this reason this section of the schema was called 'defensive organization'. The schema that I have described represents an ideal as far as its explanatory component is concerned. It cannot provide an objective verifiable account of the unconscious mental processes that underlie the phenomena of a psychotic illness. These psychopathological events lead to different hypotheses. The schema, in its explanatory aspect, is far removed from the physical investigations undertaken in organic disease, which provide objective data on which diagnoses and treatment may be based. As far as mental illness is concerned the best that can be done, as in the schema, is to ensure that the explanatory hypotheses remain as close as possible to the descriptive data. Today there are different 'maps' that claim to provide direction to the sites of psychopathology in mental disorders. The schema I have described offers the information for one such 'map'. When completed it can contribute usefully to the management and treatment of patients.

Chemotherapy of the schizophrenias

I should now like to comment on the chemotherapy of the schizo-phrenias, because it is so freely used in the treatment of these illnesses. There is general agreement that chemotherapy is a symptomatic treatment. It does not eradicate the morbid process – hence the refractory response of many patients whose illness proceeds to a chronic state (the non-remitting schizophrenias). Chemotherapy relieves the patient of the pressure of delusional and hallucinatory experiences. This applies equally to delusions and hallucinations that have a pleasurable, wish-fulfilling content and to those that cause anxiety and distress. There are hazards attendant on the use of long-acting neuroleptic drugs. These are not confined to the physical sphere (dyskinesias, and so forth). It is estimated that a large percentage of patients treated by maintenance (depot) drug therapy suffer from severe bouts of depression (McGlashan and Carpenter, 1976; Johnson, 1981). Why does this happen? Are the depressive symptoms simply a manifestation of the illness as it proceeds on its course? Are they an expression of the patient's awareness of his psychical infirmity? Or are they connected with the chemotherapy? Psychotherapeutic work with established cases of schizophrenia suggests that the depressive symptoms are closely related to the fate of aspects of the patient's delusional reality (Freeman, 1962; Burnham et al., 1969; Fort, 1989). It may be hypothesized that schizophrenic patients who become depressed during treatment by depot medications do so because these drugs abolish delusions and hallucinations, which act to dispel real-life circumstances. This hypothesis cannot lightly be dismissed. In some cases it is possible to observe the presence of a wishful psychotic reality and its disappearance under the influence of depot medications (Freeman, 1994). Although the oral administration of neuroleptics may present difficulties with regard to non-compliance it offers a flexible method of administration. As in the case of physical disease whose etiology is unknown, the treatment of the non-remitting schizophrenias is symptomatic. This applies as much to psychotherapeutic intervention as it does to chemotherapy. Symptomatic improvement in long-standing cases often follows the introduction of a psychotherapeutic approach but it rapidly disappears for obvious or unfathomable reasons. The remitting cases can be compared to the paranoiac psychoses (Batchelor, 1964) that occur in and after the fifth decade of life. They tend to remit spontaneously or respond either to chemotherapy or psychotherapy. In these groups of psychosis (remitting and paranoiac) modest doses of neuroleptics facilitate the development of a therapeutic alliance, which enables the patient to make use of insight-providing interventions.

A case of remitting schizophrenia

I shall conclude this account, which has tended to concentrate on the non-remitting schizophrenias, with an example of psychotherapeutic work with a patient whose psychosis could be categorized as schizophreniform or remitting schizophrenia. The psychotherapy was facilitated by small amounts of an anti-psychotic medication. The patient, a male student aged 20, complained that a fellow student was spreading a rumour that he was a homosexual: in particular, that he was having a sexual relationship with a chemistry lecturer. These persecutory ideas were accompanied by wish delusions. He claimed that he had designed original pieces of scientific equipment. With their aid he was about to demolish a theory advanced by a famous chemist who was evil and intending to dominate or destroy mankind. Now that his (the patient's) name was being slandered he would be despised instead of acclaimed. This patient was seen daily in hospital by me, for several months. He talked freely. Soon after the psychotherapy began he revealed that he had been attracted to a female biology student. He was shy and ill at ease in her company, believing that his knowledge of sexual matters was inadequate and must be far inferior to hers, as she was a biology student. He had the impulse to change his course to biology. Instead, he joined a student society, the Sexual Reform Society, in the hope that he might learn how to approach the girl and initiate a relationship with her. Interestingly, he had the idea that she was the daughter of the chemistry lecturer, because there was a facial similarity. In the course of the psychotherapy he referred to the way he felt about older men – in particular the chemistry lecturer, whom he admired, and to his admiration of his father. His mother, however, was the chief object of his criticism. He blamed her for his lack of self-confidence and his timidity. At school he had liked the male teacher who taught him geography; it was he who had advised him to take the course that he was now following at university. During his last years at school he was convinced that this teacher was 'synchronized' with him – that is, the patient always 'knew' what this man thought, and he 'knew' whatever questions he was going to be asked. He had concluded that the reason for his closeness with the teacher lay in the fact that his mother had told him that he (the teacher) had been in love with her sister. The patient's delusional ideas gradually receded *pari passu* with the ventilation of his fears about heterosexual intercourse and with the acknowledgement of his masturbation conflict, which had been exacerbated by the separation anxiety consequent on leaving home for university. He now recognized the irrationality of the ideas that had led to his hospitalization. The clinical improvement was accompanied by an increasing silence in the psychotherapeutic sessions. He expressed the wish to be discharged. This was also his parents' wish and it was agreed to. He was seen as an outpatient for several months. Following this he resumed his studies. More than four years later there was no sign of a recurrence of the illness.

It may be hypothesized that this patient's acute psychotic attack was preceded by a phase, during his first university term, when he was sexually aroused by a girl and wanted to act on this. The love object had a homosexual association in that the girl appeared to possess physical characteristics of the chemistry lecturer. He turned to the group that called itself the Sexual Reform Society to help strengthen his heterosexuality, for the arousal of his sexuality had made him anxious. He had said to me that he feared the girl would be 'too fast for him'. A regression of the libido to unconscious homosexual phantasies may be suspected. Heterosexual object choice was abandoned in favour of identification with the girl student. This type of identification, which sometimes leads to overt homosexuality, may have contributed to the heightening of an unconscious wish to be a woman. Such a wish phantasy of acting the woman with the chemistry lecturer led to acute homosexual anxiety and to psychical dissolution. It is possible that the treatment led to a strengthening of his masculinity through identification with me, on the basis of a strong positive transference deriving from his father and father substitutes (the geography teacher). This could have resulted in the successful repression of the passive-feminine wishes. Once the threat they posed was removed the libido could return to invest heterosexual phantasies and have an outlet in masturbation. In this case remission of the psychotic attack did not coincide with the patient obtaining full analytic insight into his masculinity–femininity conflict. Resolution of the symptoms was accompanied by a resistance against further psychical exploration. This was relatively unimportant from a purely practical point of view. However, in so many cases such resistance can have the effect of disrupting the treatment, often with an exacerbation of symptoms. What is the cause of this? Is it entirely due to a terror of instinctual derivatives, whatever their content? There is another factor that is not always given sufficient emphasis, namely, dread of reliving the experiences of the acute psychotic attack. There is much to commend the view that a patient's ability to persevere with a therapeutic relationship depends on his capacity to overcome the memories of such attacks. This fear is enhanced by the very means by which it is hoped to cure the illness, for the analytic method encourages psychical regression. In non-psychotic patients it is this regression that permits the repetition of pathogenic conflicts as transferences, whereas in the psychoses the regression accentuates the destabilization of psychic structures.

As the patient emerges from the acute attack there is a constant dread of the consequences of this destabilization – a dread of the return of the mental state caused by the confusion that existed between phantasy and reality, and between self- and object-representations. This indeed may be the principal cause of the 'resistance' that so many schizophrenic patients manifest.

Controversy still exists as to what constitutes a schizophrenic illness. Are the patients who respond to chemotherapy and/or psychotherapy suffering from the same morbid process as those who fail to remit? At present there are no means available to accurately forecast which patients will respond favourably to either chemotherapy or psychotherapy. There is a need for a systematic long-term audit into the results of treatment that has both psychotherapeutic and chemotherapeutic components. The profile schema described above was one such attempt to initiate this type of research.

References

Batchelor IRC (1964) The diagnosis of schizophrenia. Pro. Roy. Soc. Med. 57: 417–19.

Benedetti G (1979) The structures of psychotherapeutic relationship in the individual treatment of schizophrenia. In Muller C (ed.) Psychotherapy of Schizophrenia. Amsterdam: Excerpta Medica Press.

Bion WR (1957) Differentiation of the psychotic from the non-psychotic personalities. Int. J. Psychoanal 38: 266–72.

Bleuler E (1911/1955) Dementia Praecox or the Group of Schizophrenias. New York: International University Press.

Bleuler M (1978) The Schizophrenic Disorders. New Haven: Yale University Press.

Burnham DL, Gladstone AI, Gibson RW (1969) Schizophrenia and the Fear-Need Dilemma. New York, International University Press.

Cameron JL, Freeman T (1955) Observations on the treatment of involutional melancholia by group therapy. Brit. J. Med. Psychol. 28: 224–38.

Cameron JL, Freeman T (1956) Observations on chronic schizophrenia. Psychiatry 19: 271–80.

Federn P (1953) Ego Psychology and the Psychoses. London: Imago.

Fort TP (1989) Present day treatment of schizophrenia. In Silver ALS (ed.) Psychoanalysis and Psychosis. New York: International University Press.

Freeman T (1962) The psychoanalytic observation of chronic schizophrenic reactions. In Richter D, Tanner JM., Taylor L, Zangwill OL (eds) Aspects of Psychiatric Research. London: Oxford University Press.

Freeman T (1969) Psychopathology of the Psychoses. London: Tavistock.

Freeman T (1972a) A psychoanalytic profile schema for the psychotic patient. Brit. J. Med. Psychol. 42: 243–52.

Freeman T (1972b) The use of the Profile Schema for the Psychotic Patient. In Freeman T (1972) Studies at the Hampstead Child Therapy Clinic. New Haven: Yale University Press.

Freeman T (1973) A Psychoanalytic Study of the Psychoses. New York: International University Press.

Freeman T (1988) The Psychoanalyst in Psychiatry. London: Karnac.

Freeman T (1994) On some types of hallucinatory experience. Psychoanal. Psychotherapy 8: 273–81.

Freeman T, Cameron JL (1953) Anxiety after electroshock therapy in involuntional melancholia. Brit. J. Med. Psychol. 26: 245–61.

Freeman T, Cameron JL, McGhie A (1958) Chronic Schizophrenia. London: Tavistock.

Freud A (1966) Normality and Pathology in Childhood. London: Penguin.

Freud A, Nagera H, Freud WE (1965) Metapsychological assessment of the adult personality. Psychoanalytic Study of the Child 20, 9–41.

Freud S (1900) The Interpretation of Dreams. Standard Edition. London: Hogarth.

Freud S (1914) On Narcissism: An Introduction. Standard Edition. London: Hogarth.

Freud S (1915a) Instincts and their Vicissitudes. Standard Edition. London: Hogarth.

Freud S (1915b) Repression. Standard Edition. London: Hogarth.

Freud S (1915c) The Unconscious. Standard Edition. London: Hogarth.

Fromm-Reichmann F (1948) Notes on the Development and Treatment of Schizophrenics by Psychoanalytic Psychotherapy. Psychiatry: II, 46–60.

Hill LB (1955) Psychotherapeutic Intervention in Schizophrenia. Chicago: University of Chicago Press.

Jackson HJ (1884) Remarks on evolution and dissolution of the nervous system. J.Ment Sc 33: 25–48.

Johnson DAW (1981) Studies of depressive symptoms in schizophrenia. Brit J Psychiat 139: 89–101.

Katan M (1954) The importance of the non-psychotic part of the personality. Int.J.Psychoanal. 35: 119–32.

Knight, R.P (1939) Psychotherapy in acute paranoid schizophrenia with successful outcome, a case report. Bull. Menninger Clinic 3: 97–105.

Muller C (1979) Intuition in psychotherapy of schizophrenia. In Psychotherapy of Schizophrenia (ed) Muller C. Amsterdam: Excerpta Medica Press.

McGlashan TH, Carpenter WT (1976) Post-psychotic depression in schizophrenia. Arch. Gen. Psychiat. 33: 231–39.

McGhie A (1965) Psychological Studies of Schizophrenia. In Freeman T, Cameron JL, McGhie A (eds) Studies on Psychosis. London: Tavistock.

Rosenfeld H (1950) Notes on the psychopathology of confusional states in chronic schizophrenia. Int. J. Psychoanal. 31: 132–7.

Rosen J (1952) Direct Analysis. Newark: Grune & Stratton.

Searles H (1963) Transference psychosis in the psychotherapy of chronic schizophrenia. Int. J. Psychoanal. 44: 249–65.

Sechahaye M (1951) Symbolic Realization. New York: Int. Univ. Press.

Simmel E (1929) Psychoanalytic treatment in a sanatorium. Int. J. Psychoanal. 10: 70–82.

Sullivan HS (1932/1962) The modified psychoanalytic treatment of schizophrenia. In Schizophrenia as a Human Process. New York: Norton.

CHAPTER 5

The unconscious and psychosis
Some considerations of the psychoanalytic theory of psychosis

FRANCO DE MASI

> At that time almost the whole of my life was not experienced as such but as a film or as a reflection of the film projected by my mind on to the screen of my unconscious. Unfortunately, the unconscious can only feel and does not see, just as the eyes can only see and do not feel, and because the unconscious does not have eyes of its own to see inside, into its fantasies, but can only feel itself, it sees the internal images as delusions outside through eyes it lacks inside.

These words were written to me a year after the end of his analysis by a patient whose case I described in a contribution on the transference psychosis (1992) and refer to a long period of the treatment that was dominated by a psychotic state. What was the patient telling me? Why was he talking about the unconscious that had no eyes to see inside itself? Which unconscious was he referring to? His words seemed to me to provide a suitable opening for this chapter on the unconscious, the aim of which is to examine some of the relations between analytic theory and psychosis. Which unconscious, then, is relevant to psychosis? Does the unconscious have no eyes to see, or is it blinded?

The meeting between psychoanalysis and psychosis took place very early on: many analytic intuitions stemmed from the observation of psychotic states or were used to explain them. For example, the theories of primary narcissism, auto-erotism and withdrawal of libido from the relationship with the outside world owe their existence to the study of psychotic processes. The analogy between the unconscious and psychosis – the latter understood as an invasion of the ego by the unconscious whereby the links with reality are broken – was put forward to explain many of the characteristics of the unconscious, such as the primary process, timelessness and the absence of contradiction. The idea of hallucinatory wish fulfilment in children is also based on this similarity.

In his description of the unconscious processes that underlie dream production, Freud uses psychotic phenomenology as his model. He writes that a dream is basically nothing but a minor psychosis that occurs every night: 'A dream, then, is a psychosis, with all the absurdities, delusions and illusions of a psychosis . . . an alteration of mental life [that] can be undone and can give place to the normal function' (1940a, p. 172) (cf. Eigen, 1986). However, the passage from theory to clinical practice proved highly complicated. On the one hand, as in the case of Senatspräsident Schreber, Freud applies a psychoanalytic model to the explanation of the patient's symptoms, but, on the other, he declares that analytic treatment is unsuitable for psychotic patients. For the rest of his life, Freud deliberately avoided penetrating systematically into this field and undertaking the analytic treatment of psychotic cases, but he did ultimately come to believe that they could be treated advantageously. Sometimes he states explicitly that the interpretation of psychosis does not differ substantially from that of neurosis:

> The same research workers who have done most to deepen analytic knowledge of the neuroses, such as Karl Abraham in Berlin and Sandor Ferenczi in Budapest (to name only the most prominent), have also played a leading part in throwing analytic light on the psychoses. The conviction of the unity and intimate connection of all the disorders that present themselves as neurotic and psychotic phenomena is becoming more and more firmly established despite all the efforts of the psychiatrists. (Freud, 1924, p. 204)

Whereas Freud, in emphasizing the coincidence of psychoanalytic method and theory, asserts the legitimate right of psychoanalysis to study and understand psychotic states, we today no longer share the idea of a profound unity between neurosis and psychosis. This chapter seeks to show that, on the basis of the study of the unconscious, the difference between neurosis and psychosis can be clarified and a better analytic approach to the psychoses can be constructed. The nub of the problem probably lies in the fact that the unconscious, the first object of analytic study, is not described unequivocally in the theory.

The unconscious: singular or plural?

The French philosopher Michel Henry (1985) contends that, although Freud was the first to deny the philosophical assertion that 'psychic' coincides with 'conscious', he did not delve in sufficient depth into the nature of the unconscious. Henry wonders if it is possible to describe something without a simultaneous detailed consideration of the significance of the antithetical concept: in his view, the characteristic aura of indeterminacy surrounding the psychoanalytic unconscious is due in part to Freud's failure to undertake a parallel investigation of the nature of consciousness. For Henry, the Freudian concept of the unconscious, which is at once ontic and ontological, is for that reason ill defined. In the ontic sense, it represents the seat of the drives, of their representations, of the primary process, of the mechanisms of displacement and condensation, and of the symbolic contents of the infantile and phylogenetic past whereas, in ontological terms, it is described as the negative of the conscious. The unconscious thus appears as an ontologically indeterminate term, so that psychoanalysis is liable to lapse from the ontological level into ontic naturalism. Besides the difference of opinion between philosophers and psychoanalysts as to the nature and importance of the unconscious in mental life, psychoanalysts themselves disagree on the matter. Klein's unconscious is not the same as Lacan's or Jung's, and differs again from that first described by Freud. In recalling that Freud defined the work of analysis as making the unconscious conscious, Baranger (1993) notes that the term 'unconscious' is not devoid of ambiguity, even in Freud himself. As we know, the unconscious of 1915, the correlate of which is repression, takes on a wider connotation in the paper on splitting of the ego and the mechanisms of defence (Freud, 1940b). As Baranger says, behind one and the same word, 'unconscious', lie the different concepts of the principal analytic schools. By the 'deep layers of the unconscious', Klein means an organized mass of archaic fantasies that are present and active at every moment of life. Conversely, when Lacan tells us that the unconscious resists any ontology, he means that the unconscious is not a thing.

Following this brief introduction, I should like to develop three propositions. First, psychoanalytic theories and the techniques derived from them differ from each other because they are based on different conceptions of the unconscious. Second, the unconscious is not a unitary structure: the various theoretical models refer to different unconscious realities, describable as different functions of the mind. Third, the various models are not interchangeable: each calls for confirmation in the specific clinical situation and in analysis of a specific unconscious function. Let me stress in particular that the various theoretical approaches, based on different functions, all of which are present in the unconscious, may correspond to different areas of human psychopathology. To determine the correct analytic technique it is therefore necessary to identify the model of the unconscious that is most appropriate for an understanding of the nature of psychosis.

I shall now describe the views of the unconscious presented to us by Freud, Klein and Bion. My elementary account admittedly fails to do justice to the complexity and profundity of the authors' thought, but my aim is to compare and contrast the various approaches rather than to discuss the individual models in depth.

Freud's dynamic unconscious

Freud uses the term 'unconscious' to refer to two different kinds of psychic experiences of which the subject is unaware: thought processes that have easy access to consciousness (the preconscious), and ones that can enter conscious awareness only with great difficulty (the unconscious proper). Because human knowledge is invariably bound up with consciousness, the tension between the unconscious and consciousness is of fundamental importance. Whereas, from the descriptive viewpoint, there are two types of unconscious, in dynamic terms there is only one (Freud, 1923). Topographically, the unconscious denotes a system of the psychic apparatus made up of contents that are barred from access to the preconscious/conscious system by repression. Objects are stored as unconscious representations linked by memory traces. The Freudian unconscious is therefore a psychic locus possessing specific mechanisms and contents. The contents are the 'undisguised' instincts, drives and affects: these are regulated by the primary processes, condensation and displacement. They are therefore recognizable only through derivatives that have access to the preconscious/conscious system in the form of compromise formations distorted by the censorship. Fantasies are the unconscious mental representations of the drives. The unconscious is the reservoir of unconfessable wishes and of the primitive instincts, of the personal and phylogenetic past – but it does not consist solely of the repressed and of wishes from infancy that have undergone fixation. There are primal fantasies that structure the subject's infantile experiences. The first split between unconscious and preconscious is effected by infantile repression. The characteristics of the unconscious system are those of the primary system, involving the absence of negation and doubt, indifference to reality and regulation by the pleasure-unpleasure principle. In the second topography, the unconscious comprises not only the id but also part of the ego and superego. Alongside the dynamic unconscious, whose basis is repression and the conflict between instinct and culture, Freud described other forms of unconscious functioning.

Repression is merely one mode that is characteristic of neurotic functioning, but not the only system in which the unconscious is embodied.[1] Much of the unconscious operates in other ways. Splitting, negation and disavowal are all defence mechanisms that sustain and mediate conflicts between different psychic structures or between the ego and reality. They contribute to the formation of the unconscious and are themselves unconscious mechanisms. In the splitting of the ego that occurs in perversion, for example, two conceptions of reality, each unaware of the other, coexist and can never be integrated.

The Kleinian unconscious

While continuing to espouse Freud's theory of the unconscious, Klein contributed two significant innovations: the notion of unconscious fantasy and the introduction, alongside repression, of the concept of splitting of the object and, later, of splitting and projection (projective identification). Unconscious fantasy differs from unconscious representation: it is not only the psychic representative of the drive but also a mental representation that includes physical perceptions interpreted as relations between objects, and the corresponding anxieties and defences. The Kleinian unconscious is made up of relations between internal objects perceived concretely (Isaacs, 1952) and fantasies about them. The fantasies may be elaborated or modified by manipulation of the body (masturbatory fantasies), or produced actively through the imagination. They are said to be unconscious because they are knowable indirectly, in accordance with Freud's view, through clinical material (interpretation of tics, oral fantasies or fantasies of parental intercourse).

Unlike Freud, for whom fantasies are gratifications of instinctual impulses that cannot find pathways for discharge, Klein holds that the child is always able to achieve hallucinatory fulfilment of the wish and accompanies the relationship to reality with continuous fantasy activity. Innate fantasies, derived from the instincts, are primarily unconscious. They include knowledge of the nipple and the mouth and represent all mental activities: for instance, perceptual activity is represented as incorporation of external reality through the sense organs. In unconscious fantasy, the relations between and significance of the mental objects (good and bad) are structured by splitting according to the quality of the subject's bodily sensations.

The geographical metaphor is accentuated in Klein's description of the unconscious: in projective identification, the unwanted contents, including parts of the self banished from consciousness, are projected to the outside, deposited in and confused with an object, and subsequently reintrojected. The concept of the unconscious is extended through projective identification to the bi-personal field: the projection into another person modifies the perception of the subject, who projects and distorts the perception of the object that receives the projection. In one of her last contributions, Klein (1958) describes an unconscious that is inaccessible and incapable of elaboration; she postulates the existence of separate, split-off areas of the unconscious that are not amenable to normal transformations – namely, cruel and primitive aspects of the mind, thrust down into very deep layers of the unconscious (again the spatial metaphor!) where they remain as potential and inaccessible generators of madness.

Bion's unconscious

Whereas Descartes had seen the mind and consciousness as a unity and excluded the experience of animals, Freud's formalization of the unconscious as the seat of the instincts and primitive emotions helped to re-establish the link between animals and human beings. Where is the animal heritage to be found in Bion's unconscious?

In Bion, the unconscious loses the ontic connotation of place: it is a function of mind and not a space for depositing the repressed. Thus, when walking we are conscious of doing so but unaware of how we perform the walking function. If we were so aware, our minds would be clogged up with perceptions and we should not be free to walk.

The contact barrier and the alpha function serve to free the mind from excess sensory stimuli or to transform it. Dreams are the way the psyche works in waking life: their function is to establish the contact barrier through which beta elements are transformed into alpha elements and sensations become emotions. At the beginning of life this function was performed by the mother through her capacity for reverie. The concept of repression is replaced by that of a semi-permeable membrane, a kind of unconscious organ of consciousness, which helps in the processing and knowledge of the world and emotions. For Bion there is no antithesis between conscious and unconscious (the latter defined as a complex of primitive, archaic contents that can be uncovered and understood), but instead he emphasizes relations between objects and functions whose fields and relations can be intuited but of which we are not aware. Bion's grid, like the Mendeleyev table of chemical elements, investigates relations between the elements of psychoanalysis, the structure of which is not directly accessible. In Bion, the antithesis is not between the unconscious as repressed (Freud) or split off (Klein) and consciousness, but between waking and sleeping, between what is and what is not conscious on the level of awareness. As the metabolizer of psychic experiences, the unconscious must function satisfactorily if the mind is to produce thoughts (via the semi-permeable membrane and the alpha function). In this conception the spatial metaphor has been dropped and with it the notions of repression and splitting, together with guilt and anxiety at what has been done to objects. The patient may be conscious but unaware, in accordance with Bion's theory of thoughts without a thinker. In psychotic states, thoughts lack a thinker owing to the damage sustained by the alpha function. 'Thinking' coincides with the possibility of 'dreaming'. The dream is not only the process whereby the unconscious is made conscious, but also the means of transformation into material suitable for storage; the subject moves on from the paranoid-schizoid position (expulsion) to the depressive position (assimilation). Preverbal unconscious material must be constantly subjected to dream work, which operates outside consciousness. Bion is concerned with the birth of the emotions, of affective symbolization and of the foundations of psychic life. He distinguishes Freud's concept of 'dream work' from his own. He writes: '[Freud] took up only the negative attitude, dreams as "concealing" something, not the way in which the necessary *dream is constructed . . . Freud . . .* states that a dream is the way the mind works in sleep: I say it is the way it works when awake' (Bion, 1992). Dreams, like the unconscious, are intrapsychic and interrelational communications and not constructions to be interpreted. The unconscious, through dreaming, provides new supplies of symbols and images that transform sensory experience into thought. Far from being the product of repression, the dream, like the unconscious, is a function that moulds and records emotions – a daytime activity that is always present on a subliminal level.

The unconscious of the neurosciences

It seems to me that psychoanalysts, who concentrate on the emotions of the unconscious and the reconstruction of early affective relations, might do well to acquaint themselves with the findings of the neurosciences. Recent neuroscientific research on emotionality, an area long excluded from the behaviourally inspired discipline of neurobiology, can make a valuable contribution to our consideration of the unconscious. Behaviourism has concentrated on understanding how people resolve logical problems and has sought to eliminate from its research any factor suspected of being misleading by being determined by subjective elements. The psychologist John Kihlstrom (1987) coined the term 'cognitive unconscious' to describe the subterranean processes that are the stock in trade of the cognitive sciences. These processes range over many different levels of complexity: for example, routine analysis of the physical characteristics of stimuli, remembering past events, using grammar or syntax, imagining things that are not present, taking decisions, and so on, all take place outside our field of consciousness (Pally, 1997). However, to what extent does neurobiological research bear out analytic intuitions and in what respects does it differ from or contradict them? And can the objects of the neurobiological discoveries be deemed to be the same as those of psychoanalysis? LeDoux (1996), one of the best known neuroscientists, acknowledges that Freud was absolutely right to define the conscious ego as the tip of an iceberg. The experimental neurobiologists confirm that emotional experience includes much more than the mind knows about. The identity between emotions and the unconscious is one of the most important points of convergence between psychoanalysis and the neurosciences. Having established that the connections from the emotional to the cognitive system are more robust than those in the opposite direction, neuroscientists believe that the unconscious has a preponderant influence over our behaviour, as we tackle the vicissitudes of life. States of consciousness arise only when the system responsible for awareness is put in touch with the systems of unconscious processing, an activity that may remain forever unconscious. The system responsible for the emotions has been identified experimentally and found to comprise important subsystems (located respectively in the amygdala, the mammillary bodies, the striate nucleus, the hippocampus and the thalamus), each of which performs a different function in the triggering of different integrators of emotions. For obvious reasons, the most comprehensively studied emotion is fear. Fear leads back to trauma and its important role in memory, amnesia and repression or, conversely, anxiety. An excessively high level of anxiety can demonstrably block memory and ultimately damage the hippocampus. The experimental data prove beyond doubt the kinship between the emotional unconscious of the neurobiologists and the analytic unconscious. Whereas neurobiologists and psychoanalysts alike now manifestly reject the Cartesian idea of the equivalence of mind and consciousness, the emotional unconscious of the neurosciences nevertheless still appears remote from the psychoanalytic unconscious.

The dynamic unconscious and the emotional unconscious

While the work of the neuroscientists confirms some aspects of Freudian metapsychology, it refutes others. The unconscious of the neurosciences has no place for drives, repression and splitting, and therefore differs greatly from the dynamic unconscious of psychoanalysis. According to the neurobiologists, even when traumatic experiences are stored in memory systems that are not accessible to consciousness – whether or not Freudian repression is involved – an unconscious or implicit memory definitely does exist, or rather a number of memories of unconsciously stored experiences, each operating within different sub-systems. However, neurobiological research bears out some of the data of psychoanalysis, confirming that the emotions have an unconscious life separate from the higher processing systems (those present in thought, reasoning and consciousness). The unconscious of the neurosciences coincides with that of which the subject is unaware and not with the repressed. Being merely the emotional unconscious, it is far removed from the Freudian dynamic unconscious, the fruit of the conflict between the drives and civilization, between our animal heritage and our assumption of social responsibilities. This fact, which has for some time been very important in the context of clinical analysis, indicates that, in both our language and our practice, the terms *unconscious* and *unaware,* although referring to different realities and functions, are used as synonyms. How many emotions, after all, are conveyed in the transference and, in particular, in the countertransference by communications of which the protagonists are unaware?

It has long been known that significant and constantly active communication takes place between the analyst's unconscious and that of the patient, and that the patient may, although unaware of it, perceive certain non-verbal communications or unconscious mental manifestations of the analyst, of which the analyst is not conscious, which are recorded and appear in dreams in the next session. This unaware perception bears witness to the ability to grasp correctly one's own and the others' mental states through the emotional unconscious – an unconscious that has eyes and can see. It is surely this kind of unconscious perception, when not detected and brought into awareness by an appropriate interpretation (or even, on occasion, actually distorted by the analyst) that underlies the psychoanalytic impasse.[2] There is therefore an unaware function of emotional awareness, which must be made conscious in the affective and intellectual relationship between analyst and analysand if personal development and progress in the analysis are to become possible. This progression, which is essential in any analysis, is in my view particularly important for patients who lacked a suitable emotional container in their primary objects and are therefore unable to make appropriate use of their own emotional unconscious.

Theory of technique (some references)

Contemporary psychoanalysis uses the 'unaware' component of our mode of being – the cognitive, emotional and relational aspect – rather than the drive-related and sexual component emphasized, albeit not unequivocally, by Freud (1912, 1915). Psychoanalysis thus seems to have increasingly distanced itself from the original energy- and drive-based conception of the unconscious. With the developing theoretical understanding of the importance of the analytic relationship as a transformative function, analytic technique, too, has gradually changed.

I should now like to outline the main characteristics of the analytic techniques derived from the various conceptions of the unconscious. The three technical parameters enumerated below basically correspond to the evolution of the concept of the unconscious during the course of the development of analytic thought. It should be noted that the different conceptions of the unconscious support different models of mental disturbance and different therapeutic strategies.

- Freud's dynamic unconscious entails a technique in which the analyst interprets repressed contents. This technique stems mainly from the discoveries about dream dynamics and presupposes the existence of an unconscious conflict underlying the symptom. The manifest content becomes understandable through the unveiling of the latent content. Interpretation means precisely the uncovering of the underlying content: analysis of the transference, which refers back to the repressed of the past, is therefore of central importance. Freudian technique comprises mainly interpretative interventions intended to make the unconscious conscious and to reduce the severity of the superego by the transformation of archaic unconscious fantasies.
- Klein's introduction of the concept of splitting, alongside that of repression, gives rise to a modification of technique, which now concentrates on recovery of the split-off and projected parts of the personality. The analyst serves as the recipient of the projections and split-off parts, so that in this type of technique the here and now is more important than reconstruction of the past. Through systematic analysis of the transference, classical Kleinian analysis sets out to help the patient to recover an image of the internal world in which libidinal aspects hold sway over their destructive counterparts. The libidinal aspects can emerge only when the split-off parts of the self, which are unwanted owing to the unconscious destruction and envy they contain, have been experienced and recovered and reparative processes have been initiated.
- The emotional unconscious implies that a high proportion of emotional communication is unconscious and that perceptions of the emotional reality of the analytic couple are mediated by non-verbal communication. The notion of projective identification for the purposes of communication is paramount in this context. The capacity for construction and restitution of the container by the recipient of the analysand's unconscious communication, of which the analysand is

unaware, is of fundamental importance. Particular significance attaches to the analyst's countertransference and emotions, the level of symbolic and emotional communication and the type and quality of the dreams. Much of the theoretical discourse on the analytic relationship (Mitchell, Greenberg and Ogden) and on the analytic dialogue (in Italy, Nissim and, for certain other aspects, Ferro) results from the implicit assumption of the existence of an emotional unconscious that communicates, or of two unconsciouses speaking to each other on a level beyond the participants' manifest awareness.

Even if every analyst has a model of his own that may be reflected to a greater or lesser extent in the three parameters outlined above, the various techniques ought actually not to conflict with each other. A good analysis should be capable of exploring all the simultaneously operating aspects of the unconscious. I contend that we must therefore always identify the main area of the unconscious specifically implicated by the disturbance and the type of analytic communication. We must know which unconscious to address.

Which unconscious is relevant to psychosis?

Bion's view of the unconscious as an entity embodying the function of metabolizing thoughts and emotions (the emotional unconscious) oddly and unexpectedly anticipates the neuroscientific theory of the unconscious processing of emotions.[3] Like Bion, the neurosciences tell us that the emotions are not only unconscious but must be transformed in order to become conscious. That is to say, in Bion's terms, preverbal and presymbolic unconscious material must be continually subjected to dream work (the contact barrier, beta elements and alpha function) that operates outside consciousness. How indebted we still are to Bion for his visionary and revolutionary intuitions! For Bion, the unconscious is a function of mind, an unaware memory that processes experience, characterized not by repression but by communicative semi-permeability. The conscious content is the fruit of a process of which we are never conscious; we are conscious only of its result.

For the sake of simplicity, I have attempted to distinguish two unconscious systems, the dynamic and the emotional.[4] The first is the repressed unconscious discovered and described by Freud, whereas the second is the unconscious intuited by Bion and confirmed by the neurosciences, which relates to that of which we are unaware. How are we to place these two models of the unconscious and what is the relationship between them? Must the Freudian model be deemed obsolete? If different models explore different aspects of the psyche and different possible fields of human pathology, it may be postulated that Bion and the neurosciences are concerned with what 'lies below', whose functioning does not enter consciousness because it is *unaware consciousness*. We must accept that there are structures and functions of our minds of which we are unaware, whose constitutive components are unknowable, but which make emotional life possible.[5] So if the emotional unconscious exists side by side with its dynamic counterpart, Freud tells us what happens when the system 'below', which makes psychic life possible, is operational: only then can a personal unconscious permeated with conflict or relational wishes come into being. The emotional unconscious, in this view, is the container of the dynamic unconscious.[6] The latter, constituted as a psychic system in which various agencies (the ego, id and superego) influence each other, is engaged in a continuous dynamic relationship with the former. Unlike the emotional unconscious, which serves to provide knowledge but is not knowable, the dynamic unconscious can be brought to the light of day. The emotional unconscious is fuelled by affective life and early infantile relational experiences; it constantly constructs the sense of personal identity, determines the subject's relationship with the world, generates the capacity to perceive and deal with emotions, makes relations with others possible, and defines the unaware consciousness of existence (of the self).[7] The components of this unaware consciousness of self are damaged in the course of psychosis. Whereas neurosis is the result of inharmonious functioning of the dynamic unconscious, psychosis stems from an alteration of the emotional unconscious – that is, of the mental apparatus that can symbolize emotions, use the function of thought and introject perceptions.[8] During the course of the psychotic process the emotional unconscious undergoes a series of transformations, initially gradual and later radical and violent, whereby it entirely forfeits its function of intrapsychic and relational communication. As the basis of the potential space of the self and an entity necessary to our unaware perception of psychic identity, how does the emotional unconscious come into being? What happens when the conditions for its formation are altered or inappropriate at the beginning of life? Why does psychological and emotional life collapse into psychosis at a certain juncture?

Even a partial answer to these questions would take us further in understanding the nature of the psychotic state, the conditions that pave the way for it and its consequences. As we know, in the normal developmental process, the child becomes increasingly aware of the lack of something that is unknown but necessary for its peace of mind; in other words, the child senses that there must be a mind outside itself, which it does not possess and that is capable of receiving it. In a chapter headed 'the tropisms', Bion (1992) writes that the development of personality depends on the existence of an object similar to the breast into which the tropisms (projective identifications) can be projected. If this object does not exist disaster ensues for the personality, which ultimately becomes structured in terms of loss of contact with reality, apathy or mania. The sense of self stems from the successful restitution, by an object endowed with sensitivity and emotional receptivity, of projections in search of meaning. This aspect of the experience of the child's relationship with the primary object accounts for the environmental element in the formation of the psychotic part of the personality: in this case, the child does not learn to internalize a 'breast mother' who provides psychic containment and uses emotions in order to understand. A vulnerability to psychosis exists when the emotional unconscious has been blinded since early infancy. I agree with Fonagy and Target (1996) when they assume that patients with severe personality disorders inhibit a particular phase of the normal developmental mentalization – their reflective function – and fail in reaching the capacity to symbolize and understand the other's mental functioning. Nevertheless the true psychotic process includes other and still unknown destructive mechanisms, which rely on the omnipotence of the perceptions. Failure to introject an object that understands emotions distorts growth and impedes the development of a function fundamental to the constitution of our 'innate' sense of existence. The result is the formation of an explosive mind lacking emotional resonance, on to which psychotic defences are subsequently grafted. The crucial point turns out to be the constant deterioration of the apparatus concerned (the emotional unconscious), damaged as it is from the beginning, through the agency of a system (the psychotic defence) that prevents the subject once and for all from coming into contact with the perceptual aspect of the self. In psychosis, the unconscious is blinded. The destructive onslaught is not direct. The perceptual-altering system includes omnipotent and illusional mental transformations: maniacal, drug-addicted states of the mind or masturbatory withdrawal, which underlie a mental catastrophe (the psychotic breakdown) and which are subsequently experienced as highly guilt-inducing.[9] The self is altered, disorganized and destroyed by an anti-emotional pathological organization that devalues, condemns and kills the subject's sense of pain and unpleasure, alters emotional truth and continuously transforms and distorts the subject's mental state. Psychosis may be seen as a destructive way of dealing with mental pain, a *psychic strategy directed towards self-annihilation* (De Masi, 1996), which leads imperceptibly to the crossing of a certain threshold of tolerance and psychic containment beyond which personal identity is destroyed once and for all and perceptual chaos ensues. This self-destruction, the origins of which lie in the subject's primitive object relations, becomes the tragedy enacted in the psychotic state, when the patient no longer possesses the unity and potential space of existence whereby he can feel alive, whole and separate from others. The psychotic patient must deal with his own psychic death, the unbearable pain of the destruction that has taken place, confusion with the rest of the world, which rushes in on him through hallucinations and delusions and the enforced, breathless search for his own self in others. A corollary of the loss of the functions of the emotional unconscious is that the patient is completely deprived of the capacity for self-observation and awareness of his own mental and emotional processes. One of the major obstacles to progress in analytic therapy is the extremely high level of unawareness in the psychotic process, due to the impossibility of making practical use of the unconscious emotional function. The patient is conscious but quite unaware of what is happening to him.[10]

I shall now present and comment on two case histories in order to illustrate my views.

Even a 'normal' patient may mistake the time of a session, try to understand the reason for his error and possibly feel sorry. Luca, however, was not 'normal'; at least, he did not appear so when, after spending a fruitless 20 minutes or so in the waiting room (having arrived 20 minutes early for his session), he insisted, immediately upon lying down on the couch, that he had got the time right and that it was I who was late. Once I had succeeded in clearing up the mistake, I asked him what his thoughts had been during his wait. A 'normal' patient might perhaps have said that, while waiting, he had imagined that the analyst had come under the spell of his predecessor and lost track of the time, or perhaps that he had been so caught up in the other's need that he had not been able to end the session sooner. But Luca told me that, on seeing a well-dressed man leaving, he had realized that I had carried on over time so as to talk to an executive of the firm for which he (Luca) had worked abroad (he had guessed his identity from the man's smart attire). Since he (Luca) had left and not been in touch with the firm since, the firm obviously wanted to know where he had been hiding and had sent someone along to my consulting room to find out. Questions about Luca having had to wait outside had had no time or place to form in Luca's mind. The certainties that characterized his stance stemmed from his recent past, which was characterized by a delusion that had transformed his perception of the reality around him. Although Luca was unaware of it, his false perceptions bore out his anxieties. When I now tried, in the session, to examine with him the sequence of thoughts that had passed through his mind during his time waiting for his session to begin, Luca said he had realized subsequently that a 'little worm' had slipped into his brain while he was waiting and had suggested to him something that he had not hesitated to see as reality. This 'little worm' seemed to lie at the root of his tendency to relapse into a psychotic state.

Luca is a 26-year-old graduate engineer. He had spent the previous two years abroad completing his training, having won scholarships as a brilliant and highly promising worker in his field. After graduation he had decided to go abroad to study and work, not only for professional reasons but also for the sake of his 'maturation'. He had wanted to separate from his family – in particular, from what he called the 'maternal river bed', a complex of affective relations that he had experienced as immature and constricting. According to my reconstruction during the course of the treatment, Luca, the eldest child of a mother who was good but who lacked emotional resonance, and a father who had always urged him to assert himself aggressively, had been unable to see himself as having the position and status of a child. Following the birth of his sister and a number of little cousins, he had felt compelled to uphold his prestige as the eldest by force. In order to stand out he had had to impose his will on the younger children and assert himself to his parents through his intellectual performance. He had kept himself going in adolescence with strongly idealized friendships. Working successfully as an employee of a multinational corporation in a foreign country, Luca gradually became convinced that he could quickly become its leader. Once he had risen to the level of worldwide president, he would implement his plan to rid the world of all its ills, such as poverty, racism and war (by association, this was reminiscent of the role he had played at home since early childhood in pacifying his constantly quarrelling parents). To confirm the reality of his own power, he had also needed to be able to conquer women. One day, however, he had bumped into an Arab colleague, who stole his girl. He had tried to overcome the difficulty by attempting to persuade his rival to stand aside, but to no avail. Luca's impotent rage assumed colossal proportions. Unable to release or process his rage he came to live in ever increasing fear of possible secret reprisals from his rival and colleague (who had meanwhile disappeared) or compatriots who were in league with him. This episode had ushered in a progressive delusional state in which he had seen people he did not know as possible Islamic persecutors who were out to kill him. The patient had been afraid that he might be poisoned in all kinds of ways, including by poison gas.

When the analysis began (his parents having fetched him from abroad and arranged for him to be treated with drugs) Luca was no longer suffering from delusions and felt reassured by his return home. In the psychotic episode, it seemed, his mind had been progressively colonized by an anti-emotional, arrogant system that had first made him omnipotent and then caused him to feel threatened and helpless. In some of my initial interventions I stressed the effort to transform his personal identity, which he had consciously undertaken very much earlier, and pointed out the analogy between the physical fear for his endangered life and the anxiety about his own psychic self, which seemed to have been laid bare and worn down by an anti-human system of extreme arrogance. However, the problem as presented in the analysis was complex and could not readily be tackled by reconstructive interpretations. Although Luca had now resumed work, he nevertheless lived in a potentially 'other' reality – or rather, there were two adjacent realities, one of which could unexpectedly spill over into the other. Luca was still sometimes afraid of being poisoned in the bar where he went for his lunch break. His two worlds co-existed, as if belonging to different minds, and the two perceptions, normal and psychotic, alternated. He could switch his mind into either the normal or the delusional mode. If an acquaintance told him that he 'knew' the location of his house in the country (because he lived nearby), Luca could feel spied on and discovered by the 'organization' that was persecuting him: the acquaintance might after all be a spy. If I spoke about him in his analysis, linking up with things he had told me about his past or merely using my intuition, I realized that I became an object of suspicion for him. He felt that I knew much more than he imagined. I was endowed with telepathic powers and therefore belonged to the organization that was spying on him, keeping him under surveillance and wanting to eliminate him. As the analytic work progressed, there were more and more psychosis-free intervals that enabled him to gain a better understanding of the power exerted over him by the psychotic state. In the past he had been convinced of his great need to conquer and to 'possess' (he now said this almost with a sense of shame). The meeting with his Arab colleague had been catastrophic because it had shattered the dominant and omnipotent part of himself that always had to come out on top. He now understood that the alteration of his state of mind had served to construct a grandiose world when he was faced with an impoverished self that he was afraid did not even exist. In place of a self that had not formed, Luca had constructed megalomanic defences that had altered his psychic truth and that preached the freedom of arrogance.

Now he felt threatened by the very system he had created. Luca's fear was that the 'organization' might penetrate everywhere and not allow him to live when he tried to get out of it. Whenever he succeeded, in the analysis, in gaining some insight and felt able to delimit and understand the psychotic world, he noticed that this world became more threatening. When he was apart from his analyst, the psychotic organization would become capable of dominating him. However, areas of freedom and thought began to open up even for him: he realized that, in his maniacal race for success, he had taken no account of himself and he was now aware that he had no sense of personal identity, did not know what real qualities he had, what objects he loved or how he could develop. He was always concerned about what others thought of him, but not about what he thought of others – what his own emotions were in personal relationships. Luca's gradual emergence from psychosis enabled him to confront the identity problems that had preceded and determined his illness. This new awareness came about in a relatively benign situation, since his breakdown had not involved substantial psychic mutilation.

My reason for describing this patient is to show how the psychotic transformation is rooted in infancy, takes place in silence and develops long in advance of clinical manifestations (hallucinations and delusions) that make up the psychotic episode proper. Luca's psychosis began with a gradual transformation of his self-perception; whereas the early stages of the alteration were tranquil in character, the process of disintegration of his perceptions later became terrifying. This example helps us to understand the qualitative difference between psychotic and neurotic mental functioning. The latter remains anchored in the properties of the dynamic unconscious, which admittedly undergoes quantitative alterations (for example, excessive use of repression, or a dynamically unbalanced relationship between the various psychic agencies), but these are never stable, structured and progressive in such a way as to destroy perception. Psychosis alters the unaware perception underlying the construction of psychic truth. Hence the aim of 'making the unconscious conscious' remains appropriate for a neurotic patient who, while repressing the truth, preserves it unconsciously and does not destroy it. The destruction of meaning in the psychotic state stems from an attack – not experienced as such – on the functions of learning from emotional experience and generates an ever closer dependence on an omnipotent system that proves to be a parasitic production of the mind (my patient's 'little worm'). Meltzer has creatively developed some of Bion's ideas on the relations between psychosis and thought and transposed them to the clinical level, investigating how dreams succeed in generating symbolic forms appropriate for the representation of emotional experience and hence of truth. In his exploration of dreaming as a function of which the subject is unaware and that confers emotional meaning on experience, he has shown how this process sometimes succeeds, thereby enriching thought, whereas it fails in the psychotic state (Meltzer, 1984). The psychopathology of the process of dreaming coincides with the distortion of thought – that is to say, with the formation of hallucinations or delusions. Lies, like hallucinations and delusions, are a distorted representation of emotional experience and correspond to mental self-poisoning.

The second case history, which is similar to my first example, shows how the patient is unaware of his psychotic functioning and how important it is to direct the analytic work towards bringing about an awareness of the meaning of the psychotic organization, which tends to engulf the self and destroy the sense of reality. Andrea, a young man of 24, was the only son of separated parents and had always lived with his mother. Although he had been a lively, seemingly sociable boy, I knew that he had had difficulties in the past, having constantly been unable to adapt to the regular rhythms, schedules and tasks of school life. A tendency to withdraw and to minimize the difficulties and demands of life, as if he were living in an infantile dream world, had often caused him to fail. Having had a passion for rock music since his teens, he had joined with some friends to form a band, which had begun to enjoy a degree of success among young people before his psychotic explosion. Andrea participated spasmodically in his group's activities and dreamed of becoming a rock star (this for him represented a kind of change of status: becoming a celebrity meant being bathed in success, admiration and power). However, he seemed unable to understand that success in the musical world was difficult, conditional upon improvement of one's skills and talent and the ability to maintain empathic relations with others. He often interpreted conflicts as deliberate attempts by others to exclude or attack him, cut him out and make him feel worthless. Andrea began to exhibit clear-cut psychotic symptoms while in the midst of his musical activities and whilst in a difficult relationship with a girl – his first real love relationship. The relationship was stormy partly because of his partner's character, and it consumed his energy to such an extent that he was afraid of being totally absorbed by it and losing himself. In reaction to this feeling, he sought other relationships and went with two prostitutes. After confessing this to his girlfriend he felt that he had committed a catastrophic act, news of which had now entered the public domain, and he felt constantly reproached and accused by people.

In this delusional atmosphere Andrea sought psychological help, and at first this brought some relief. He continued to take part in the band, although he found it increasingly difficult, and eventually the group excluded him and went on tour without him. The particular figure of Peter, a rock musician he admired, began to assume a prominent position in the sessions. Andrea spoke of this British musician as if he were an acquaintance, a brother or imaginary twin who wanted nothing but to link up with him. From then on, the figure of Peter took a delusional hold on Andrea's mind. The patient 'knew' that Peter was in Milan; he would meet him in the street and give a sign of recognition. Andrea seemed anxious and disoriented, and sometimes positively afraid. It was not easy to enquire about his state as his replies were evasive. He often skipped sessions, telephoning from home and giving me the impression that he was in a state of great persecutory anxiety. The analytic communication was very fragmented and it seemed to me that the patient was unable to talk about what was happening and did not trust me as a reliable interlocutor. Members of his family reported that Andrea would leave the house in the middle of the night or go wandering in the suburbs where he would get lost. Systematic psychiatric intervention became necessary and anti-psychotic therapy had to be resumed. The holidays were approaching, but I knew that his father was not far away and that Andrea was receiving medical attention, and so I was able to leave the patient in a relatively safe situation. When the analysis resumed after the holidays, it became possible to 'work' on the delusion without the emergency of the acute psychotic state thanks to the pharmacological intervention. The image of Peter remained dominant in the sessions. Andrea told me about his music, about his certainty that he would be working with Peter and how he would pursue his music into depths to which even Peter had hesitated to delve. He described idyllic moments during the holidays of union and communication with Peter: he was always there for him. A few weeks later, he told me he had decided to go to Florence for an important international music festival. I then asked him whether he would be meeting Peter. He said no. I added that it seemed easier to meet Peter when he was fused with him (he had 'seen' him a week earlier in the window of a block across the road) than when he was separate from him. Andrea said he really did see Peter, he saw him from a distance but then Peter would run away. I answered that it was when he felt he did not exist that he saw Peter, an imaginary twin, who protected him and promised to save him, just as a mirage was generated by the need to survive, but then dissolved if one approached it. He replied that Peter was there but ran away because he did not wish to trivialize the meeting. Their meeting would be extraordinary and would transform his life. I remarked that Peter was like a messiah who had to make him completely happy and held out the promise of a complete transformation of his existence – something different from and far above the analytic work he was doing with me. The patient confirmed this and went on: 'Just imagine when he comes to collect me: all the papers in England will be full of me...Yes, it's true!' I continued to press him, asking why, if this were so, he gave himself things to do, tried to get involved, came to analysis and was even thinking of getting a job. 'Because, when Peter comes', the patient replied, 'I shall follow him, and I think I would then feel guilty at the life I have left behind here.' I pointed out to the patient that he 'knew' that the meeting with Peter was tantamount to becoming someone else and losing himself. In the exchange, he would lose the real Andrea and was afraid of losing him forever. Andrea answered: 'My idea is that I shall be able to become Peter and he me.' It was now clear how the delusional transformation killed the self and how, concealed behind the wish to turn into something grandiose and false by entering into a delusional world, lay the impulse to cease existing or to die psychically, obliterating his own failing self. I noted that the patient on this occasion was listening to me very attentively. In fact, by this stage of the therapy, Andrea had managed to distance himself from Peter to some extent; he could be snatched out of his world, or also not, as in this session. The function assumed by Peter in Andrea's mind was very complex. Peter had become not only his 'protector' but also his 'dominator'. He would often tell him all the things he had to do and give him orders; he would suggest, for example, that if he really wanted to meet him in order to gain access to the musical Eden (lots of money, power and girls), he would have to obey him. For instance, he would have to have sexual intercourse with a girl who was standing in front of him in the presence of her boyfriend. Whenever Andrea attempted to extricate himself from Peter's power and expel him from his mind, Peter threatened to kill him. The period of persecutory anxiety was bound up with this aspect of the relationship with Peter: it was Peter who threatened him with death and that was why he was afraid for his life. At a certain point in his development, the psychotic representation moved into the world of intimidation and the protective figure was transformed into a dictator of the mind. Andrea recognized that Peter's world was a trap, an egg, a prison from the recesses of which he could communicate only by silent and secret means in order to stay alive. For the time being these channels of communication remained open and were more evident in the analytic relationship.

It is, in my view, very important in analytic therapy to reach a stage in which the neurotic part can 'see' the psychotic construction without taking fright and fleeing, as seemed possible for Andrea at this time. This often seems like an impossible task: a condition for tackling it is possession of the normal 'unaware' functioning of the emotions. In this case, as the defences and psychotic constructions, as delusional alterations of the self, could proliferate only by blinding the emotional unconscious and destroying its emotional-perceptual function, we found ourselves in a paradoxical situation. Analytic work here seemed impracticable because the patient had completely lost the capacity for self-observation of his own mental processes and was unaware of what was happening to him. With psychotic patients, we have to encourage the use and reintegration of the mechanisms of neurotic functioning, such as introjection, repression and learning from emotional experience, which underlie the functioning of unconscious emotional life and the consciousness of existing. The delusional construction strikes at and obliterates this function.

I have presented this case history to show that there is no possibility of analysing the patient outside the delusional system: one can only try to analyse the parts that have remained outside, while seeking not to attract them, and thereby helping them to 'see'. This is possible only at certain moments in the analysis. The psychotic solution exerts a powerful attraction, and if it has engulfed and obliterated the neurotic part, it is understandable that the patient must – as it is the only solution remaining to him and he is afraid of its destruction – defend it tenaciously, and that he distrusts the analyst. If a return is to be possible, the path covered must be gone back over and the thread of the emotional unconscious taken up again so as to 'undo' the psychosis. For example, Peter (the second clinical case) is a new character speaking to Andrea, a vision promising sex, money and success. I think this character doesn't replace the father or the analyst, nor can be explained with symbolic or transferential meanings. It is a 'vision', as happens to people who experience religious miracles. 'The vision', in which he retreats when the reality becomes unbearable, could be called a dream, but it doesn't appear when he sleeps. For Andrea, Peter is a 'vision' built out of his awareness, an idol to be venerated, which pretends submission. Psychodynamically it can be considered an anti-emotional split-off part of Self, which muddles him by promising him Heaven if he becomes cynical (that is, if he has sex with the girl who is standing in front of him

in the presence of her boyfriend). It is possible that it results from a
dread of dependence, including dependence on the analyst, or that it
represents a defensive construction with respect to father's
abandonment; at any rate, we are faced with a psychotic construction
that appears when the oniric work and the emotional awareness of the
awakening state disappear. As a consequence, in the analytical
relationship the intuitive capacity of the analyst can't be understood by
the patient and crashes into the psychotic thinking. I and my patient are
not speaking at the same level; we have two different psychic states that
don't meet. We are, reciprocally, strangers. In such cases analytical work
doesn't mean intuitively finding a causal link and formulating a
meaningful interpretation (for example: 'you are building an imaginary
twin to deny the perception of separation'): it must instead help the
patient to understand the transformations of the psychic experience and
the alterations to his perceptual system.

It is because of the attraction of the psychotic mode of functioning that
the patient may easily lose insight during the course of therapy even if he
seemingly becomes able to introject and integrate. Years of precious
analytic work sometimes melts away like snow in sunshine. The patient
may resume his psychotic functioning and a relapse may wholly abolish
important parts of the analytic work. Owing to the lack of a mental place
for depositing, processing and utilizing memories and hence of one of
the basic conditions for the synthesis and integration of thoughts and
emotions, particular modalities apply to the attempt at recovery from the
psychotic state.[11] After the breakdown, the patient tends to re-establish
the previous equilibrium, putting together shattered parts of the personality. It is a kind of glue-ing operation, followed by successive relapses.
The psychotic repair (reconstruction) takes the form of gluing together
parts of the personality by omnipotent and violent means (Steiner, 1991),
and, irrespective of the patient's personal history and the reasons for the
crisis, is therefore doomed to failure. For this reason one of the main
functions of the analysis is to support the patient in the quest for a more
appropriate means of healing.[12] The alteration of the emotional unconscious in the psychotic state gives rise to qualitative alterations in the
dynamic unconscious; for example, it produces a psychotic superego that
seemingly lacks any kinship with its neurotic counterpart. The superego
of the psychotic state is full of terrorizing objects and cannot be
compared to the neurotic superego (De Masi, 1997), which stems from
the introjection of parental figures, albeit with degrees of distortion. Like
a kind of catastrophic magma that alters the land and undermines the
building constructed on it, the psychotic state impacts on the emotional

unconscious and at the same time devastates the Freudian unconscious. The destruction of the emotional unconscious, which is accompanied by nameless dread, has lasting repercussions on the capacity not only to think but also to dream. The dreams of psychotic patients contain not thoughts but facts. These dreams have no chains of association (as described in Freud's theory) to other thoughts or concealed emotions but remain things; they lack associations and development. They cannot therefore be interpreted using their latent meaning and symbolic associations: however, when communicated in analysis they nevertheless play a part in the process of reconstruction.[13]

Conclusions

I have attempted to show that psychoanalytic theory is not identical with the principle of the dynamic unconscious but includes the entire area outside the subject's awareness. The psychoanalytic unconscious may be said to include the presence and co-existence of more than one unconscious: the dynamic unconscious and the emotional unconscious, defensive unconscious functions that alter self-perceptions and vital emotional functions of the self divorced from the level of awareness.[14] I have distinguished the dynamic from the emotional unconscious. Since the 'system above' (the dynamic unconscious) does not coincide with the 'system below' (the emotional unconscious), psychoanalytic treatment of the psychotic state cannot use the dynamic theory derived from therapeutic experience with neurotic patients, however seriously ill. The usual interpretative attitude is not only impractical but is also liable to confuse the patient. Once the breakdown has occurred, analytic therapy of the psychotic state consists essentially in an attempt at non-omnipotent reconstruction, with the aim of restoring the functioning of the emotional unconscious, so as to give the patient back the use of his own awareness, thereby helping him to reconstitute his self-perception, personal identity and the functions that support it. This process of reconstruction, involving renewed confrontation with the reasons for or methods of destruction of the self, entails enormous pain and potential catastrophe: it is a challenge to the darkness from which we ourselves still have much to learn. Analytic treatment of such patients presupposes painstaking investigation of the primal processes (the child's early relations with its objects) which alter 'unaware' consciousness and the potential space of the self and which, in combination with other subsequent defences that abolish awareness, give rise to mental processes of self-destruction, the effects of which are often not easily reversible. We must concentrate on these as yet badly understood special mental states, which pave the way for psychotic breakdown, as well as the fairly typical processes governing the balance between the consequences of the destruction of the emotional and cognitive functions and the attempt at reconstruction that follows the catastrophe. I hope I have succeeded in conveying some of my convictions on the subject of psychosis, which, of course, call for further verification and elaboration. I myself believe that the broadening of clinical and theoretical research in this field can give rise to genuine development within our discipline and help save psychoanalytic work in the future from a risk of turning in on itself.

Notes

[1] Freud points out in *The Ego and the Id* (1923) that, whereas all that is repressed is unconscious, not all the unconscious coincides with the repressed. A part of the ego, too, is unconscious – not preconscious but actually unconscious without being repressed. Freud in my view thus anticipates some of the modern conceptions of 'unaware' components of emotional perceptions and of the unconscious roots of the self. Although he stresses (Freud, 1912, 1915) the highly evolved unconscious functions involved in emotional communication, Freud did not consistently pursue these intuitions, which were not taken up for a long time by anyone else either. More emphasis in analytic theory has been placed on the repressed unconscious, bound up with our animal heritage, as described in *Civilization and its Discontents* (Freud, 1930) according to which, human unhappiness is a function of the irresoluble conflict between nature and culture.

The free-association method used by the analyst to formulate a psychoanalytical interpretation demonstrates that the intuition of meaningful ties and the origin of creative thoughts (such is a psychoanalytical interpretation) stem from unconscious thought. As a matter of fact the psychoanalytical interpretation is a thought that originates spontaneously out of the awareness and looks like a veritable intuition. Such intuition needs a long time to be born.

The Freudian advice to the psychoanalyst to be a blank screen or the Bionian warning to be without memory or desire means that the analytical interpretation stems from the unconscious; such interpretation occurs when all the mnestic images and the conscious desires have gone away. Freud understood that a new idea might appear if there is a free-floating state of mind. In fact Freud has been, with scientists and mathematicians like Poincaré and Hadamard, a forerunner of contemporary intuitions on the unconscious cognitive processes.

[2] One of the earliest reported examples of the analytic impasse is Freud's Dora case. Dominated as he was by the idea of understanding the material in terms of seeking out the repressed, Freud interprets the second dream, which accompanied Dora's decision to break off the analysis, in terms of the dynamic unconscious – uncovering the latent content – rather than as an unconscious communication. In describing the dream,

Dora tells how she saw a deserted square with a monument in it, how she returned home to find that her father had died, and how she did not attend the funeral but took refuge in her room. Freud interprets Dora's complexes and her love for Herr K, but takes no account of the relational and communicative meaning of the affective desert in which Dora found herself, of the monument to the important man that Freud was constructing for himself, and of the challenging indifference with which the patient characterized the breaking off of her analysis. Dora was using the dream to communicate what she was observing and doing, but hoped that Freud would be able to recognize and transform these elements. Freud himself stresses the importance of the emotional unconscious as something capable of directing the analyst's listening: the analyst, he writes, 'must turn his own unconscious like a receptive organ towards the transmitting unconscious of the patient' (Freud, 1912, p. 115).

3. The neurosciences describe the conscious and unconscious aspects as serial and parallel functions. Consciousness seems to operate serially, one step at a time, whereas the unconscious mind is made up of a large number of different systems working in parallel. The serial processors create representations by manipulation of symbols, the only entities of which we are conscious. At a lower level, processing takes place subsymbolically with codes that cannot be deciphered by consciousness.

4. This distinction throws light on the vexed question of wishful dreams and traumatic dreams. The former are the product of repressed wishes in the dynamic unconscious, while the latter communicate a suffering not yet worked through and operate by way of the emotional unconscious.

5. We thus require a threefold distinction, namely between unconscious, unaware and unknowable. We shall never be able to know the essence of a beta or alpha element or a pre-symbolic emotional element. The elements and functions whereby the emotional unconscious operates are unknowable.

An important contribution to this subject was made by Sandler and Sandler (1987) who maintain that there are unconscious functions, objects or representations that we can conceive but not perceive. One of these is the 'past unconscious', containing the vicissitudes of the infantile self, which has a history and an organization that crystallises in the first years of life but is not accessible to the conscious mind and about which only hypotheses are possible.

6. Freud understood that psychosis involved a different level of disturbance of the unconscious. He wrote to Abraham on 21 December 1914: 'I recently discovered a characteristic of both systems, the conscious (cs) and the unconscious (ucs), which makes both almost intelligible and, I think, provides a simple solution of the problem of the relationship of dementia praecox to reality. All the cathexes of things form the system ucs, while the system cs corresponds to the linking of these unconscious representations with the word representations by way of which they may achieve entry into consciousness. Repression in the transference neuroses consists in the withdrawal of libido from the system cs, that is, in the dissociation of the thing and word representations, while repression in the narcissistic neuroses consists in the withdrawal of libido from the unconscious thing representations which is of course a far deeper disturbance' (Freud, 1965, p. 206).

7. 'Higher-order consciousness depends on building a self through affective intersubjective exchanges' (Edelman, 1992, p. 150). 'Tragedy becomes possible – the loss of

the self by death or mental disorder, the remembrance of unassuageable pain . . . Ironically, the self is the last thing to be understood by its possessor, even after the possession of a theory of consciousness' (p. 136). Despite Freud's assertion that part of the ego is unconscious, the ego is the organ with responsibility for consciousness because it stands in relation to the preconscious–conscious system. The concept of the self, which is alien to Freud's theorizing, was put forward with a wide semantic aura by Winnicott and Kohut. Here it is presented without any theoretical reference to the two authors mentioned, to indicate the 'unaware' (unconscious) roots of everyone's personal identity and individual meaning. Whereas the function of consciousness is proper to the ego, awareness of the self is a function of the self.

An important issue is the relationship between the unconscious functions that underlie the associative thought (the cognitive unconscious) and the emotional unconscious, aimed at processing emotions. I think there is no separation but integration between these two functions; actually, I think of an unconscious that unites emotions and perceptions.

The cognitive unconscious is also knowledge of emotions: the perception of the inner and outer reality depends on the state of the emotional field. The psychotic state unfolds the alterations that blind the emotional unconscious, paralyse and warp its self-reflexive and cognitive function.

I assume that the destruction of the emotional apparatus (emotional unconscious) is responsible for the alterations of thought and perceptions (cognitive unconscious) in the psychotic state.

8. A possible example of the failure to distinguish between the unconscious levels is Freud's analysis and interpretation of the illness of Senatspräsident Schreber. Schreber's psychosis begins with a state of sexualization, based on a delusional wish to be a woman in the act of intercourse and the subsequent conviction of being penetrated by rays of God in an ecstatic state. Persecutory elements enter into the relationship with God and with Flechsig, the psychiatrist in charge of his case. Using the model of the dynamic unconscious (unwanted content, repression and return of the repressed), Freud explains Schreber's delusional state as an expression of the relationship with the father (God) and with the unconscious homosexual component. Psychosis, like neurosis, is interpreted in accordance with the theory of dreams and the revealing of unconscious contents. Note, too, how Freud equates Schreber's trans-sexual delusion (he was sometimes caught in women's clothes) with unconscious homosexuality.

9. It is important to note that psychotic defences involve altered states that destroy awareness, so that it is difficult to subject them to integration. There are therefore no definite answers to the question of what is actually transformed during a psychoanalytic therapy of a psychosis and what is destined to remain inaccessible in the 'deep layers of the unconscious' (Klein, 1958) as a potential source of madness. Paul Williams, a British analyst awarded the Rosenfeld prize for a contribution on a borderline case (1998), also mentions the difficulty of predicting how far a truly psychotic terrain can be reclaimed by analysis, however deep and systematic (see this volume).

10. If thinking is to be possible, an apparatus to 'contain' thoughts must be developed. In the absence of this apparatus, there may be consciousness but there will be no awareness. In the psychotic disturbance, it is impossible for the subject to be aware of

what appears in consciousness (cf. the 'film projected by the mind on to the screen of the unconscious' described by the patient mentioned at the beginning of this chapter). The normal intuitional function (the intuitive thought which first hypothesizes and later tries to understand the reality) is blinded with the psychotic 'revelation'.

In the psychotic state the 'voice' assumes a fundamental role. In fact the psychotic thinking is actually a sensorial thinking that 'sees' and 'feels'. The psychotic revelation is like a movie (in which the patient, unbeknown to him, is starring) shown in the patient's mind.

[11.] Psychotic functioning extends its dominion to the field of memory. Freud has already shown how the emotional experience of the present modifies the past, which is continuously remodelled. In the psychotic state, the alteration of perception can continuously modify the past, which is reinvented, recreated and recatalogued as a new, ever-changing reality. What is lost at the same time is the plasticity of memory whereby the intuition of the present enriches and integrates the experience of the past. This applies particularly to the working through of the psychotic episode, which resists any remodelling.

[12.] Genuine repair is impossible because the dream work is inaccessible. In the treatment of borderline patients, it is therefore particularly important, as Resnik also points out (see Bateman, 1996), to pay close attention to dreams, which often constitute an attempt to reconstruct the emotional unconscious. However, other possible meanings of psychotic 'dreams' must also be distinguished.

[13.] Psychotic dreams, too, have meanings. Sometimes they may constitute an attempt to make delusional contents assimilable – to dream the psychosis – in order to re-enact it in the potential space of the analytic relationship. On other occasions, dreams may describe primitive mechanisms for dealing with persecutory reality: a patient emerging from a delusional state of guilt may dream of destroying a dangerous enemy ship. Alternatively, dream may herald the entry into the psychotic state (as in the case of Schreber). Grotstein's contribution on the relations between dreams and psychosis (1981) is also illuminating. In this author's view, a normal dream includes an unseen observer observing the plot, verifying and confirming its truths and messages. The function of the dream is to evacuate psychic stimuli in narrative-theatrical form and to communicate the evacuation to an audience that receives the dramatic communication. The dream, for Grotstein, is also a dramatic form of therapy, because it takes place within a relationship that confers meaning. The function of dreaming usually activates a dreamer who dreams the dream and an unseen spectator who can observe, listen to, understand and record the message. The dreamer who listens to and understands the dream has the function of a container-mirror-spectator; this function is altered in psychosis and ultimately confuses instead of clarifying. In addition, during the course of the psychotic process, the dreamer who dreams the dream does not find a narrative solution acceptable to the dreamer who understands the dream, and the narration is achieved by altering the structure and coherence of the mind. A new psychotic order, to which both must submit, is established.

[14.] Many authors, without referring to the emotional unconscious, have explored the unconscious functions necessary for psychic development that have been mortified by the relational trauma. Ferenczi was one of the first to stress the importance of the intrusion of the adult into the private space of the child, whereas Winnicott theorized about the potential space of the self and the 'true self' that has remained hidden. This individual nucleus of human experience, the self, is an important element in the theories of various authors from Kohut to Bollas, the self psychologists, the relational analysts and the intersubjectivists.

References

Baranger M (1993). The mind of the analyst: from listening to interpretation. Int. J. Psychoanal 74: 15–24.

Bateman A (1996) Psychic reality in borderline conditions (Panel Report). Int. J. Psychoanal 77: 43–7.

Bion W (1965) Transformations: Change from Learning to Growth. London: Heinemann.

Bion W (1967) Second Thoughts. London: Heinemann.

Bion W (1992) Cogitations. London: Karnac.

De Masi F (1992) On Transference Psychosis: Clinical Perspectives In Work With Borderline Patients. In L Nissim Momigliano, A Robutti (eds) Shared Experience. London: Karnac, pp. 167–88.

De Masi F (1996) Strategie Psichiche Verso L'autoannientamento. Riv. Ital. Psicoanal 44: 549–66.

De Masi F (1997). Intimidation at the helm: superego and hallucinations in the analytic treatment of a psychosis. Int. J. Psychoanal 78: 561–76.

Edelman GM (1992) Bright Air, Brilliant Fire. On the Matter of the Mind. London: Allen Lane.

Eigen M (1986) The Psychotic Core. Northvale NJ: Aronson.

Fonagy P, Target M (1996) Playing with reality: I. Theory of mind and the normal development of psychic reality. Int. J. of Psychoanal 77: 217–33.

Freud S (1912) Recommendations to physicians practising psycho-analysis. London: Hogarth.

Freud S (1915) The Unconscious. London: Hogarth.

Freud S (1923) The Ego and the Id. London: Hogarth.

Freud S (1924) A Short Account of Psycho-Analysis. London: Hogarth.

Freud S (1930) Civilization and its Discontents. London: Hogarth.

Freud S (1940a) An Outline of Psycho-Analysis. London: Hogarth.

Freud S (1940b) Splitting of the Ego in the Process of Defense. London: Hogarth.

Freud S (1965) A Psycho-Analytic Dialogue: The Letters of Sigmund Freud and Karl Abraham 1907–1926, Ed. HC Abraham, EL Freud, Trans. B Marsh and HC Abraham. London: Hogarth.

Grotstein J (1981) Who is the Dreamer who Dreams the Dream and Who is the Dreamer who Understands It? In Grotstein J (1981) Do I Dare Disturb The Universe? London: Karnac, pp. 358–416.

Henry M (1985) Généalogie de la Psychanalyse. Paris: Presses Univ France.

Isaacs S (1952) The nature and function of phantasy. In J Riviere (ed.) Developments in Psycho-Analysis. London: Hogarth, pp. 67–121.

Kihlstrom JE (1987) The cognitive unconscious. Science 237: 1445–52.

Klein M (1958) On the development of mental functioning. In Envy and Gratitude and other Works 1946-1963. London: Hogarth, 1975.

LeDoux J (1996) The Emotional Brain. The Mysterious Underpinnings of Emotional Life. London: Weidenfeld & Nicolson.

Meltzer D (1984) Dream Life. Perthshire: Clunie For Roland Harris Trust Library.

Pally R (1997) Memory: Brain Systems that Link Past, Present and Future. Int. J. Psychoanal 78: 1223–34.

Sandler J, Sandler A-M (1987) The past unconscious, the present unconscious and the vicissitudes of guilt. Int J Psychoanal 68: 331–41.

Steiner J (1991) A psychotic organization of the personality. Int. J. Psychoanal 72: 201–7.

Williams P (1998) Psychotic developments in a sexually abused borderline patient. Psychoanal. Dialogues 8: 459–93.

CHAPTER 6

The 'living dead' - survivors of torture and psychosis[1]

ANDRZEJ WERBART AND MARIKA LINDBOM-JAKOBSON

We begin with a quotation from the Spanish author Jorge Semprun (1984, p. 95), survivor of Buchenwald:

> Let me be quite clear about it. It was not the Gare de Lyon, the crowd, the swirling of that sudden spring storm: it was not, in short, the world around me that seemed unreal. It was I who seemed unreal. It was my memory that held me in the unreality of a dream. Life was not a dream, oh no! It was I who was. What's more it was the dream of someone who appeared to have been dead for a long time . . . That serene, quite desperate certainty of being no more than a dream of a young man who died long ago.

Regardless of apparent differences, certain features can be recognized in patients who have suffered repeated psychotic breakdowns and those who have suffered the sequelae of torture. In this paper, we discuss what it means for a psychotherapist to meet torture survivors and psychotic patients who experience themselves as the 'living dead'. The clinical material presented focuses on aspects of regression to, and activation of, a universe of archaic, pre-oedipal object relations, which illustrates similarities and differences between the two groups of patients who have suffered massive external or internal traumata.

The experiential universe of torture and psychosis

'Living dead'

Some survivors of torture and schizophrenic patients describe their feeling of unreality as 'living dead'. This can be the case with other patient groups:

---

[1] This chapter is a revised version of a paper previously published in 1993 in Psychoanalytic Psychotherapy 7:163–79.

for example, melancholics. However, not all torture survivors or schizophrenic patients report this experience. One torture survivor said: 'I am
different than I was before the mock-executions. I don't feel so much for
the things I used to like. I feel as if I am sliding further and further away
from life. I am pulled towards something dark. It is as if I were dead,
though I am alive.' At the same time, survival for this patient also seemed to
represent a narcissistic triumph in having overcome death. A schizophrenic
patient, referring to a violent suicide attempt during a paranoid psychotic
episode, said: 'It is difficult for me to tell my family that I killed myself five
years ago.' In cases of extreme man-made traumata the experience of being
'living dead' can be seen to be located in time and linked to acute, external
events. Most schizophrenic patients, at least according to our observations,
also give a specific date of onset of their particular experience, even if no
concrete external cause or event can be identified.

The writer Elie Wiesel (1961), a Holocaust survivor, describes his
experience thus: 'It took me a long time in the beginning to get used to
the idea that I was alive. I thought that I was dead . . . I thought that I was a
dead man who in his dream imagined that he was alive . . . I was only the
skin that the serpent left behind – which it never owned.' Jorge Semprun
(1963) writes: 'I feel like telling you, doctor, that the unbelievable thing is
that I find myself within the skin of a living creature.' Both formulate
themselves in terms of a 'second-skin' formation (cf. Bick, 1968). In both
quotations, aside from the experience of being 'living dead', we see
expressions of survivor guilt and shame, identification with dead victims,
and the temptation to die to escape a plague of memories.

Mary-Ann, a schizophrenic woman in her thirties, began psychoanalytically oriented therapy. She said she was waiting for 'the life
hereafter', for someone to collect her to bring her to the 'other world' on
the other side. There she would come alive again. Angels, people of God,
would deliver her from evil. Sometimes she felt she was in a black tunnel.
Outside the tunnel God waited with his long beard, like a benign
therapist. God would say 'Welcome Mary-Ann' and hug her. There were
times when God changed into a cruel and horrifying figure. The therapist
was felt alternately to hold out the promise of a new life or to pose a threat
of hellish persecution. Mary-Ann lived with a feeling of approaching,
inescapable cataclysm. A specific infantile prototype of this catastrophe
will be discussed below.

The end of the world

The experience of psychic catastrophe and death is for schizophrenic
patients not only something that has already occurred but is a repetitive
event and it may happen at any point in the future. Mary-Ann experienced

pressure in her head, which felt like a bomb that might explode. She feared she would lose her head. 'I have only one hour left to live' she would insist. She had nightmares that she was falling into a well or 'black hole'. She imagined the end of the world as a gigantic earthquake. At the beginning of therapy she felt there was no future in the real world. A therapy session the following week was not something to rely upon because the world might come to an end before then. Some years later Mary-Ann took to listening to the five-day weather forecast to be reassured that the world would last a further five days. Slowly she came to experience sessions as an indication that the end of the world had been postponed. After a few more years she began to trust that there would be a world after the summer break, although it was uncertain whether there would be any further summers.

In both groups – schizophrenic and the tortured – we meet individuals who may retrospectively refer to their experiences as though they are survivors of the 'end of the world'. For schizophrenic patients this is an internal experience that subsequently becomes a feeling of external catastrophe in retrospect (*nachträglich*). People who have been forcibly submitted to torture experience the end of the world as an actual, external event.

John, a 27-year-old schizophrenic with paranoid and catatonic episodes, said during his first interview that it was Wednesday the 175th. He had survived 175 weeks since his first psychotic breakdown and suicide attempt, and his chronology began, for him, with these events. Since then he had felt that he belonged to the 'living dead'. However, the world had come to an end earlier when he was 15 when he had found out that he had had an older brother, also called John, who had died a few weeks after delivery, less then a year before he had been born. At that point John committed a series of criminal acts, including arson. He evaded discovery. But even this catastrophe had its predecessors, it transpired. John's life had really ended at the age of four when the family moved to a large town on the mainland, far from the tranquillity of a small island John had loved, and his world had collapsed. Seizing on a date 175 weeks before the interview had precursors in traumatic experiences at the ages of 15 and 4, although they held no contemporary affective charge. However, he experienced himself as alternatively being 'living dead' or else a murderer (John's identification with his dead brother had led to criminal and suicidal acts).

Enforced regression and psychic torture

For survivors of torture the experience seems to be that everything previously known to them ceases to exist – the world as they knew it comes to an end. The systematized violence of torture aims to destroy the prisoner's self-governing capacities: forced into a regressive emotional state he is guided by primitive needs, fantasies, and fears. The prisoner must submit totally: obedience is secured through threats and violence and through power over life. The prisoner is deprived even of the right to control his most basic needs such as hygiene and bodily functions. This deprivation of control and the violent losses involved create a regression to pre-verbal stages of development. Helplessness and vulnerability as a result of enforced regression through torture swell the threat to the ego. The victim may take refuge in a universe of archaic object relations and primitive defence mechanisms such as splitting, incorporation of persecutory objects and identification with the aggressor.

Schizophrenic patients can report their psychotic episodes as 'pure torture'. Mary-Ann had hallucinatory experiences in which she heard battered children screaming, patients in the mental hospital being treated sadistically, cannibals, people with stomachs cut open bleeding to death on operating tables around the world. She herself was whipped, stripped of her skin and cut up; she urinated and wept blood.

Some theoretical aspects

Why is psychotherapy so difficult with schizophrenic patients and torture survivors? Why do their experiences seem impossible to integrate into their personalities, as if we were dealing with irreversible psychic change? Honig (1988) argues that the obstacles are caused by structural personality changes that have the effect of reinforcing themselves. If this is so, how? Both schizophrenic and highly traumatized patients report that they no longer recognize themselves as they were before 'the catastrophe'. They are 'living dead' in a collapsed world where the catastrophe 'happens over and over again'. What inner processes are concealed by these analogous accounts?

The archaic universe

The impression of irreversible changes is a consequence of persistent regression to the psychotic core of the personality (Frosch, 1983). There arises an actualization of archaic forms of relating to distorted and destructive early introjects of parental figures. Torture traumatizes catastrophically by invading and flooding the ego whilst it is in a state of enforced regression. It brings about a parody of 'therapeutic' influence in reverse for its victim. The torturer uses science in a perverted manner to create an enforced transference relationship through which is generated a staged psychotic fantasy induced by violent force – a nightmare realized.

Grubrich-Simitis (1981) inverts Freud's stated therapeutic aim (Freud, 1933) when she formulates the torturer's maxim: 'Where ego was there id shall be.' This paraphrase is even more striking in a literal translation of the German terms *Ich* and *Es:* 'Where I was there it shall be.' Torture evokes a dependency relationship towards primary objects from place of early developmental phases, especially oral and the anal. The torturer takes the role of a persecuting primary object and the relationship is characterized by an aggressive cathexis mixed with distorted forms of libidinal binding, with far-reaching consequences for the victim's ego ideal and superego. The inner space of the prisoner's representational world (Green, 1983) is invaded from without, and the torture situation becomes a stage where the prisoner is forced to perform and act out his archaic inner conflicts.

We should like to illustrate this through the example of a young man who had become unable to enjoy life. He said he had been prepared for the hardships of the torture he had had to face, and he reported that he had withstood it for about three days. He was pressurized to report on his mother, amongst other things, and he experienced a sudden strong wish to do so, knowing that if he did, his mother would be executed. With much effort he resisted this impulse, but in psychotherapy he became preoccupied with this crucial event. The patient was the second son of a father who was young and somewhat irresponsible. The mother was the de facto head of the family and overprotected the patient who was a thin, sickly child. He experienced powerful rivalry towards his older brother and had a yearning to be a man among the men, but felt constrained by his need to resort to mother's care. In early adult life he had had some homosexual experiences and worries about his sexual identity surfaced in therapy. During torture he regressed to a state of early merging with the oral (pre-oedipal) mother, and his murderous impulses toward her were revived. Getting rid of her by execution removed the threat of female identification. Unresolved conflicts in this area, with accompanying feelings of guilt, became (retrospectively) the essential trauma that had brought him into psychotherapy. He had resumed life after the torture identified to a considerable extent with a mother whom he had killed, and consequently he had had to deny himself any benefit or pleasure in being alive.

One common intrapsychic constellation after psychotic breakdown and torture is an ongoing rupture of 'basic trust' alongside the regression to a 'psychotic core'. Regressive forms of libidinal and hostile binding towards persecutory primary objects are re-established. Actualization and projection of the patient's sadism and destructiveness are central features of the regression and this is the decisive factor for re-emergence of distorted and hostile imagoes in the transference. At the same time, these infantile roots seem to be largely absent in the patient's conscious perception of the therapist. Behind the experience of breakdown and chaos in both categories, a structure of oral or pre-oedipal relationship to primary objects is evident (Kolev, 1991; 1997), and this actualizes tendencies towards merging. Longings toward basic unity are aroused (Little, 1960) and an attempt to establish a state of complete identity occurs, be it with the torturer, a new partner, a leader or an analyst. The tendency to fuse seems to be at the root of compulsive repetitions and to a persistent attachment to destructive and aggressive patterns of relating. For example, Mary-Ann, cited earlier, experienced her mother as invasive and controlling. She never left her in peace, she complained, visiting her house and throwing out old newspapers and junk that Mary-Ann had collected. Still, Mary-Ann could not let go of her mother. For years she had borrowed the same amount of money from her each month, which she paid back at the beginning of the next. She managed to attend therapy on her own for some time, but eventually had to have her mother bring her. An example of her need to preserve a sense of self in relation to an invading and controlling mother occurred in the transference when she kept secret from the therapist, for 18 months, that she had established a relationship with a man.

Differences

Similarities between regression in schizophrenic patients and in torture survivors have been emphasized: however, there are also important differences. In *psychosis* regression is generated from within, but in *torture survivors* it is triggered by external trauma. Torture is located in actual time and space and is experienced as a massive, concrete, painful event, even if it also unavoidably activates earlier traumata. In schizophrenia, even if therapist and patient know about repeated traumatic events in the patient's earlier life, these are usually neither recognized as such by the patient nor are they accompanied by concomitant painful emotions. One of the central aspects of psychosis is the patient's own destructive attacks on meaning (Ogden, 1982) and on linking (Bion, 1957; 1959). Evil, unreliable objects often dominate the inner world of psychosis, whereas in torture survivors 'islands of archaic structures' are apparent where the recent trauma has hooked up with earlier traumata and unresolved conflicts. Torture generates experiences that the patient finds impossible to integrate into a world of meaning, which is one reason why torture and concentration-camp survivors often say that no one, include therapists, can possibly understand what they have gone through. In psychosis, it is an archaic introject of the parent with which the patient is identified: in the torture survivor it is a pathogenic identification with the torturer that actualizes undigested fragments of archaic parental introjects. In schizophrenia the picture is often dominated by a deficit in libidinal cathexis – destructive and aggressive aspects dominate in relation to primary objects. In torture we deal with secondary libidinization of an aggressively cathected dependency relation, in the service of survival in a universe of evil. Ikonen and Rechardt (1993) pointed out that torture survivors have also been caught in a net of shame at their inability to induce empathy and care in those upon whom they have been dependent. The shared symptom of a tendency towards social isolation in both schizophrenic patients and in torture survivors also seems to spring from different sources. In torture survivors expressions of, and defences against, sadomasochistic object relating imprint relationships, including that with the psychotherapist. By contrast, schizophrenic patients attempt to avoid and destroy any and every form of relating.

Trauma as a link between psychosis and torture

The concept of trauma may be seen as a theoretical link that connects psychosis and torture. In *torture* we point to the actual external trauma and its consequences. A *psychotic breakdown,* like a nightmare, can function as a new traumatizing event. From his earliest to his last works Freud returns to the description of trauma as a break in the protective shield, a 'wound', a 'hole', an 'internal bleeding' in the psychical sphere (1895a; 1917), and as damage inflicted on the ego (1940). In economic terms this involves collapse of the protective shield when extreme quantities of energy break through. The experience of trauma presupposes a certain level of ego development: 'the very first traumas escape the ego altogether' (1895b, p. 359). Freud (1939) describes the 'positive' fixations to the trauma as a compulsion to repeat, and the 'negative' as defensive reactions and avoidances. Anzieu (1989) regards the protective shield as a 'psychic skin'. In psychosis and torture this psychic skin is perforated from within and without respectively. Our patient Mary-Ann illustrates this: in the beginning and during repeated crises in the therapy, she sat wearing her overcoat and held tightly on to her handbag and to some plastic bags. She felt cold and wore several layers of dishevelled clothing. When she felt more coherent she came more neatly dressed and rather carefully made up. Repeated experiences of rupture in her 'psychic skin', which included hallucinations of torture, occurred in relation to breaks in therapy. 'We are Siamese twins, our backs glued together and we are ripped apart', she would say to her therapist. Or she would say that she was bleeding to death from a wound that ran down the right side of her body where she was attached to the left side of the therapist. In the transference, breaks in therapy meant that Mary-Ann's and her mother's shared skin burst.

The broken protective shield; the dead nucleus

An intrapsychic consequence of torture is that the earliest infantile intro-jections of protective parental figures are replaced by actually evil dependency objects that annihilate basic trust. For schizophrenic patients the first infantile introjections of protective parental figures are not access-ible, rendering the individual's 'basic trust' deficient for one reason or other. Salonen (1989) calls this a break in the protective shield of primary identifications. A 'dead nucleus' may arise as a defensive structure that contains lost aspects of the self and objects, linked to primary identifica-tions with protective parental figures. To be 'living dead' is the ensuing subjective experience of surviving these losses. The 'dead nucleus' hides devastating and overwhelming affects of helplessness, despair, rage, and hate. In this way, survivors of torture and schizophrenic individuals defend against, and keep clandestinely alive, unbearable affects and aspects of self and objects. Sidney Klein (1980) and Tustin (1986; 1990) describe this process in terms of autistic defences. Hopper (1991) and Rosenfeld (1990; 1992) refer to encapsulation. Abraham and Torok (1986; 1994; Torok, 1968) introduce the idea of endocryptic identification – the creation of a cocoon in the self, containing the cadaver of lost objects and aspects of the self. Paradoxically this 'dead nucleus' contains those parts of the psyche that are most alive following trauma or psychotic breakdown.

Every change can bring fresh catastrophe for schizophrenic patients. Mary-Ann reacted with panic-stricken anxiety to the slightest alteration in the consulting-room configuration during the early years of her therapy. New covers in the bookshelves, a flower disappearing, a picture replaced; these events elicited micro-episodes of psychosis. The experience of being 'living dead' is linked to the effort to survive the catastrophe of breakdown of the world of meaning and loss of protective parental figures. For schizo-phrenic patients it is felt as an ongoing, limitless experience; for torture survivors it is limited to sectors of relating such as intimate relations with loved ones and authority figures. The patient's repetitive return to enact trauma is an attempt at self-healing by recapturing lost aspects of the self linked to protective primary objects, thereby rebuilding the world of meaning. Freud's (1911) classic analysis of Schreber's paranoid system illustrated how delusions are an attempt to restore the world after the 'catastrophe' has occurred. Salonen (1989) describes the repetition compulsion as 'a cyclical phenomenon related to psychical trauma, creating the conditions necessary for the recovery of the primary object'. In order to survive catastrophe and restore the world of meaning, the individual tries to eject, close off, block or encapsulate unbearable psychic pain, rage and unmanageable inner conflicts. When powerful affects are provoked these defensive operations produce what patients often describe as a 'black hole' (Grotstein, 1990; 1991) or a 'fog' experience. Schizophrenic patients tend to launch themselves into psychotic episodes as a result of their attacks on meaning. Survivors of torture fade into autistic states when the restitution of meaning is unsuccessful. Defensive aspects of patients' prior attempts at self-healing can prove to be severe obstacles to the therapeutic process as earlier traumata are actualized and re-enacted in the therapeutic relationship in a rigid and unchangeable manner.

Encapsulation and ejection of psychic pain following torture can be expressed as chronic physical pain or as hysterical symptoms such as partial paralysis, numbness and passivity. Highly traumatized people can break down rapidly under new stresses when their efforts to achieve isolation, denial and encapsulation fail. A patient in therapy said: 'Would you really want me to speak about my experiences? That would be to be sent into the darkness; I might get mad and never come back.' Another patient said: 'I cannot think: there is a fog in my head.' The schizophrenic patient attempts to encapsulate (usually without success) his devastating rage against his primary objects, which threatens his survival. Mary-Ann said she had something black and empty inside her, a tunnel that traversed her entire body – a tube instead of intestines through which blood was running. She had recurrent dreams of falling into a well or a black hole. If she became angry with the therapist it signified to her the end of the world. In fact the catastrophe had already occurred: when Mary-Ann was 20 she gave birth to a daughter and was transferred promptly from the maternity hospital to the psychiatric ward. The delivery awakened a primitive rage against her mother who had given birth to her younger sister. Becoming a mother meant Mary-Ann became acutely psychotic.

Precursors and prospective effects

Therapeutic experience with torture survivors teaches us that torture evokes earlier unintegrated traumata that have not necessarily had visible consequences in the patient's previous life. Even the psychotic episodes of schizophrenic patients have their infantile precursors. Most patients have notions of forerunners to their current problems and difficulties. One or more core episodes delineated in time and space occur in their narratives and are seen as 'causal' manifestations of later difficulties. These 'explanatory events' often have the psychic quality of screen memories – they may be apparently insignificant scenes representing a compromise between banal memory traces, repressed content, and retroactively projected fantasies. The events constitute a 'navel' of repetition and distil the essence of the patient's conflicts and failures, past and present, which have been distorted unconsciously by condensation, displacement and secondary revision. There were several such traumatic episodes to Mary-Ann's background: the predecessor to her schizophrenic catastrophe was probably an infantile psychosis that was never noticed or that never received attention. When she was three or four years old, shortly after the birth of her younger sister, she panicked when she realized that she would one day die. In her narrative this was her first experience of the 'end of the world'. Her inability to tolerate her hostile feelings towards the mother and new-born sister were transformed into a fear of a death sentence. She hid for a week under a table that was covered with a tablecloth that came down to the floor, persuading her mother to accept this arrangement. She took her food, used her potty and kept her pillow under the table. Eventually mother said: 'If you don't stop this thinking [about death] you can stay under the table for the rest of your life.' Mary-Ann stopped thinking. During schooling and later during repeated stays at a psychiatric clinic she was viewed as mentally retarded, and she received her first psychiatric diagnosis after giving birth to her daughter. She was described as suffering a 'debility' and not a 'delivery (puerperal) psychosis'.

Actual trauma, whether torture or a psychotic episode, possesses not only precursors but also prospective influences. Torture survivors and schizophrenic patients react with chronic vulnerability to new and potentially traumatic experiences in their lives because of the ongoing influence of the traumatizing effects of previous experiences. Separations from significant others are typical situations in which patients in both categories are at greater risk of suicidal acts or mental collapse. The archaic aspects of the self and the aggressively cathected, persecutory primary objects re-established in torture situations and in psychotic episodes henceforth function as a 'magnetic pool' for prior *and future* painful affects and unresolved conflicts. This can lead to a more-or-less stable reorganization of the ego and changes in the patient's instinctual balance observable in clinical practice as passivity, destructiveness, hate or rage and as secondary libidinization of perverted forms of relating in real life, as well as in the transference. The prospective effects of torture and psychosis may leave the therapist with the impression that he or she is dealing with irreversible intrapsychic change.

Common difficulties in psychotherapy

Restoration of meaning

The serious difficulties suffered by both types of patient present themselves in the therapeutic relationship as enactments, as well as in the transference and countertransference. Passive resistance, avoidance of forming an attachment to the therapist, crisis in the relationship when attachment is being established, longings for a state of fusion with the therapist (and defences against it), absence of recognition of negative feelings, criticism, discontent and sudden outbursts of aggression are all commonplace. Therapeutic work in both cases aims to give the traumatic and psychotic experiences psychological meaning; to help the patient reinterpret what he lived through in terms of inner conflicts; and to help him discover components of his own contribution to the repetitive enactment of trauma in ongoing life situations. It is also our task as analysts to make contact with the encapsulated imagoes of protective parental figures in the patient in order to interrupt the endless repetition and enactment of traumata. A crucial psychic change is the development of the patient's ability to verbalize experiences rather than avoid affects through primitive defences. As Semprun (1984, p. 39) put it so well:

> Yet it is not so simple. Has one really experienced something that one is unable to describe, something whose minimum truth one is unable to reconstruct in a meaningful way – and so make communicable? Doesn't living, in the full sense of the term, mean transforming one's personal experience into consciousness - that is to say, into memorized experience that is capable at the same time of integration into the future? But can one assume any experience without more or less mastering its language? The history – the stories, the narratives, the memories, and the eye-witness accounts in which it survives – lives on. The text, the very texture, the tissue of life.

The emotional climate of therapy

The therapeutic relationship offers the patient an illusion (in Winnicott's sense) that everything he or she has lived through and experienced can be felt, remembered, and shared with another human being. However, to have a witness is not enough, even if it is a prerequisite for the emergence of hope. The emotional states of the patient, experienced as unbearable, are often only initially identified through the therapist's countertransference feelings. The torture survivor in therapy needs gradually to come to see that what happened is not only an external catastrophe that has struck him. He needs to discover which earlier intrapsychic conflicts have gathered together as a focal point of the catastrophe. Therapy is then an attempt to approach this painful focal point that resonates with earlier and future conflicts and stresses. With the schizophrenic patient we need to create a feeling of temporality and an experience of a common history out of a state of timelessness and the eternal return of the same. Our task is to establish a relationship that cannot be destroyed and one in which the therapist establishes himself as a less devastating, more integrated primary object. In both cases, therapy can create space for experiences that threaten both the patient's and the therapist's ego with regression, distortion, and disintegration as distorted relations to primary objects are actualized and staged in the analytic relationship. The therapeutic relationship is ideally a sheltered place for the working-through of traumatizing experiences, but it can also become a new traumatizing event itself. The therapist may come to be perceived as a new torturer or new version of the persecuting primary object. As a result the torture survivor may fail to show up, or drop out of treatment. The schizophrenic patient may leave or have a new psychotic breakdown. In the therapist, both patient categories can evoke feelings of therapeutic impotence; a sense of impossibility of the task, hate towards the patient, extreme fatigue and so on. The work elicits in the therapist defensive measures against regression and identification with the patient's predicament. In everyday life we suppress our knowledge of the horrors of the world. When we are exposed to these experiences, they awaken fears in us that our own ego will be destroyed, distorted, perverted, or marked for life. Characteristic symptoms in torture survivors include sadomasochistic relating, problems controlling aggressive impulses, passivity, and feelings of being persecuted. These are awakened from repression during torture and as a result a feature of working with a torture survivor is the experience of being tortured by the therapist and/or of torturing the therapist. The therapist may experience similar, corresponding phenomena, when confronted by a world of psychotic fantasies staged in the patient's actual experiences.

In psychotherapy with schizophrenic patients we see patients evacuate and project their destructiveness, depression, or hope, but we also experience how our own painful and unwelcome emotions become actualized in the therapeutic relationship, as illustrated in the following clinical vignette.

Ivan, a schizophrenic patient just over 30 years old, had spent 12 years in a mental hospital before embarking upon a six-year psychotherapy. He wanted to know whether his therapist understood his language – supposedly Chinese. At the same time, he did not know in which direction home was; he had difficulty in orienting himself in life, and he was unsure of his identity. In order to save and restore a world of meaning after his catastrophe he developed a 'secret geography'. His fixed point of orientation was the Bering Strait. His inner drama took place between the rivers Mississippi and Missouri in the United States, in the battle for the city of Omaha between Indians and settlers. In his representational world he had placed himself between his two sisters and had fought for possession of his mother. When his therapist had to move her office Ivan dropped out of therapy. A few years later, another therapist began working with him. He was once again an inpatient at a psychiatric ward for 'specially demanding patients'. He had almost entirely stopped speaking. His earlier reconstruction of relations to primary objects represented by his 'secret geography' has been replaced by destruction of all meaning and links (Bion, 1957, 1959). He ripped up any printed paper he came across and destroyed signposts and name labels in his clothes and shoes. Attempts to communicate with him ended in outbursts of physical violence. A year later, however, he had changed considerably. He had become calm, smiling and compliant, answering promptly when addressed. According to staff he was functioning much better, evoking in them the impression that he was a wise man. They responded with a wishful fantasy of having saved him from himself. This was not the reaction of the three persons closest to him, among them his new therapist. They experienced instead a form of deep grief, as though Ivan was already dead.

Obstacles to change

How can the risk of a repetition of trauma as an outcome of therapy be counteracted? This is best answered through clinical material that illustrates the working through of severely traumatic experiences. In a session during the fourth year of therapy, for example, Mary-Ann told the therapist that she would like to remain in bed to avoid ageing. She also said that there was a person in the room next door to the office. It was her therapist, who she said was laughing scornfully at her. He was not by her side, but siding with her enemies; he hated her and was like 'them' at the mental hospital. She was angry with the therapist because of this. She could hurt him there 'in that other room next door'. Then she became afraid. The more Mary-Ann told her therapist about these experiences the more upset and agitated she became. The therapist began to wonder whether she would be able to control her rage. He said to Mary-Ann that in the room where they were she could talk freely about her anger towards the therapist 'in the next room'. Mary-Ann was quick to respond to this and said she panicked when she had to think of them both in the room next door. If she were to talk about her rage against the therapist next door he would move into their room and into her own therapist's body. It would create chaos and catastrophe. This catastrophe denoted specific intrapsychic meanings:

- splitting of the mother imago into a hated, threatening, and idealized, good mother could no longer be sustained;
- the father who would save the patient from the hated and threatening mother would himself become a sadistic figure;
- the parents were united in sadistic, destructive intercourse.

Eventually, Mary-Ann's anxiety and fear of becoming well constituted a recurring theme. Despite having been able to manage without hospitalization for quite a long time, she decided at a certain point to be admitted. During a session at this time she declared that she had lost 'the evil [psychotic] world' and felt terribly lonely. She would rather die, be run over by a car, and in this way break off the therapy, than to have to deal with this painful reality of having lost her psychosis. Regarding a holiday break she said: 'I am stuck with my mother as if we had the same body. It is horrible.' It seemed to her an impossible task to start her life again, as so much had already been lost. A final crisis arrived some years later when Mary-Ann had become caught up in a triangular situation involving her therapist and her mother around the time of her birthday. Following a summer break, Mary-Ann decided to interrupt therapy (now of eight years' duration). She no longer wanted her mother to accompany her to the therapist's consulting room, but could not manage to travel alone. At this moment the therapist experienced Mary-Ann as impossible. Whatever he said or did was of no help to her, perhaps in the same way as when she was little and hid under the table until her mother told her to stop thinking. She seemed no longer to be prepared to cling to the pre-oedipal mother, whilst at the same time it appeared that she could not get three people together into a triangular situation in order to establish a proper sense of differentiation. In each of these traumatic, and to Mary-Ann potentially catastrophic situations, her therapist was obliged to tolerate feelings of trauma, impotence, uncertainty and hopelessness. It is the capacity for endurance of extreme emotional crises that helps to avoid the re-enactment of previously traumatic events in the therapeutic setting.

Conclusion

The starting point of this chapter concerned similarities in experiences amongst survivors of torture and psychotic patients, their experience of being 'living dead' and 'end of the world' catastrophes. We understand these similarities in terms of regression to psychotic nuclei and revival of archaic relations to primary objects. The differences in regression in schizophrenic patients and torture survivors concern internal as opposed to external triggers, respectively. We have tried to use the torture situation to understand schizophrenia, and psychotic experiences to understand the *sequelae* of torture. We wish to stress that we are discussing neither the etiology of schizophrenia nor the meaning of early or cumulative trauma for the development of schizophrenia. We believe that working with schizophrenic patients and survivors of torture can teach us about common difficulties in the therapeutic task and increase our understanding of the inner worlds of both categories of patient. Studying extreme cases such as these may prove to be of help in gaining further knowledge of archaic

levels of human functioning. In order to be able to do so, we need to learn
to listen more carefully to the patients' descriptions, metaphors and
attempts at explanation. In stories told by our patients there is always a
'kernel of truth' that our psychoanalytic theoretical models can help us to
uncover, provided we take the patient's own formulations as a starting
point for our understanding. In this light, for example, notions such as
'living dead' and 'end of the world', which occur in the narratives of many
patients, need to become better integrated into our theoretical frameworks in order to expand their meaning.

In his description of the schizophrenic individual's experience of his
world, Searles (1967, p. 22) concludes:

> that we therapists make contact with the patient's own tenacious clinging to his
> illness. He clings to it in order to defend himself unconsciously against a too-
> painful and too-disillusioning awareness of his own emotions, and in order to
> act out unconsciously, through his schizophrenic behaviour, his hatred and
> rejection of the outer world. Schizophrenia cannot be understood simply in
> terms of traumata and deprivation, no matter how grievous, inflicted by the
> outer world upon the helpless child. The patient himself, no matter how unwit-
> tingly, has an active part in the development of, and tenacious maintenance of,
> the illness, and only by making contact with this essentially assertive energy in
> him can one help him to become well.

This may prove to be a valid description of the torture survivor's
predicament. The difficulties in treating schizophrenic patients and
survivors of torture are also discussed here as expressions of the patient's
persistent holding on to distorted forms of relating and to projection of
hate and sadism. Why such tenacious holding on? Our first hypothetical
answer addresses the adaptive aspects. The schizophrenic patient holds
on in order to 'survive' in an archaic universe of persecutory, sadistic, and
hated parental imagoes. The torture survivor brings structured order to
the chaos caused by extreme external trauma through his holding on. Our
second hypothesis deals with the regressive aspects. There is a compelling
'power of temptation' that is aroused in states of fragmentation and disintegration that can lead, in schizophrenia for example, to a euphoric sense
of being an 'unlimited psychical self', which is deeply appealing to the
patient. For torture survivors it is the temptation to merge with primary
objects. In both cases, these wishes embody a hope of reparation of inadequate, hated and hostile imagoes of primary objects. The major obstacle to
this work by far, however, remains our lack of knowledge about schizophrenia and the *sequelae* of extreme, man-made trauma. The paucity of
our understanding of what it means to live in an internal or external world
of hate, destructiveness, and terror is the principal obstacle to be
overcome.

References

Abraham N, Torok M (1986) The Wolf Man's Magic Word: a Cryptonymy. Minneapolis: University of Minnesota Press.

Abraham N, Torok M (1994) 'The lost object – me': notes on endocryptic identification. In Abraham N, Torok M (1994) The Shell and the Kernel. Vol. 1. Chicago and London: The University of Chicago Press, pp. 139–56.

Anzieu D (1989) The Skin Ego: A Psychoanalytic Approach to the Self. New Haven and London: Yale University Press.

Bick E (1968) The experience of the skin in early object-relations. International Journal of Psychoanalysis 49: 484–6. Also in Williams MH (ed.) (1987) Collected Papers of Martha Harris and Esther Bick. Strathtay, Perthshire: The Clune Press, pp. 114–18.

Bion WR (1957) Differentiation of the psychotic from the non-psychotic personalities. In Bion WR (1967) Second Thoughts. New York: Jason Aronson, pp. 43–64.

Bion WR (1959) Attacks on linking. International Journal of Psychoanalysis 40: 308–15.

Freud S (1895a) Draft G: Melancholia. In Standard Edition. Vol. 1. London: Hogarth Press, pp. 200–6.

Freud S (1895b) Project for a scientific psychology. In Standard Edition. Vol. 1. London: Hogarth Press, pp. 1–122.

Freud S (1911) Psycho-analytic notes on an autobiographical account of a case of paranoia (dementia paranoides). In Standard Edition Vol. 12. London: Hogarth Press, pp. 1–82.

Freud S (1917) Mourning and melancholia. In Standard Edition. Vol. 14. London: Hogarth Press, pp. 237–60.

Freud S (1933) New introductory lectures on psycho-analysis. In Standard Edition. Vol. 22. London: Hogarth Press, pp. 1–182.

Freud S (1939) Moses and monotheism: three essays. In Standard Edition. Vol. 23. London: Hogarth Press, pp. 1–137.

Freud S (1940) An outline of psycho-analysis. In Standard Edition. Vol. 23. London: Hogarth Press, pp. 139–207.

Frosch J (1983) The Psychotic Process. New York: International Universities Press.

Green A (1983) Narcissisme de vie – Narcissisme de mort. Paris: Editions de Minuit.

Grotstein JS (1990) Nothingness, meaninglessness, chaos, and the 'black hole', I & II. Contemporary Psychoanalysis 26: 257–290; 377–407.

Grotstein JS (1991) Nothingness, meaninglessness, chaos, and the 'black hole', III. Contemporary Psychoanalysis 27: 1–33.

Grubrich-Simitis I (1981) Extreme traumatization as cumulative trauma: psychoanalytic investigations of the effects of concentration camp experiences on survivors and their children. Psychoanalytic Study of the Child 36: 415–50.

Honig AM (1988) Cumulative traumata as contributors to chronicity in schizophrenia. Bulletin of the Menninger Clinic 52: 423–34.

Hopper E (1991) Encapsulation as a defence against the fear of annihilation. International Journal of Psychoanalysis 72: 607–24.

Ikonen P, Rechardt E (1993) The origin of shame and its vicissitudes. Scandinavian Psychoanalytic Review 16: 100–24.

Klein S (1980) Autistic phenomena in neurotic patients. International Journal of Psychoanalysis 61: 395–402.

Kolev N (1991) An unknown dimension of paranoia: the significance of archaic space. Paper presented at the Tenth International Symposium for the Psychotherapy of Schizophrenia, Stockholm, August.

Kolev N (1997) Introduction à l'étude de l'espace archaïque. L'Évolution Psychiatrique 62: 721–42.

Little M (1960) On basic unity. In Little M (1981) Transference Neurosis and Transference Psychosis: toward basic unity. London: Free Association Books and Maresfield Library, pp. 109–25.

Ogden TH (1982) Projective Identification and Psychotherapeutic Technique. New York: Jason Aronson.

Rosenfeld D (1990) Countertransference. Paper given at the Swedish Psychoanalytic Society.

Rosenfeld D (1992) The Psychotic: Aspects of the Personality. London: Karnac Books.

Salonen S (1989) The restitution of primary identification in psychoanalysis. Scandinavian Psychoanalytic Review 12: 102–15.

Searles HF (1967) The schizophrenic individual's experience of his world. In Searles HF (1979) Countertransference and Related Subjects. New York: International Universities Press, pp. 5–27.

Semprun J (1963) Le Grand Voyage. Paris: Editions Gallimard.

Semprun J (1984) What a Beautiful Sunday! London: Abacus.

Torok M (1968) The illness of mourning and the fantasy of the exquisite corpse. In Abraham N, Torok M (1994) The Shell and the Kernel. Vol. 1. Chicago and London: The University of Chicago Press, pp. 107–24.

Tustin F (1986) Autistic Barriers in Neurotic Patients. London: Karnac Books.

Tustin F (1990) The Protective Shell in Children and Adults. London and New York: Karnac Books.

Wiesel E (1961) Le Jour. Paris: Editions du Seuil.

Chapter 7

'The parachute project': first episode psychosis – background and treatment

Johan Cullberg

The stress-vulnerability model – a paradigm for understanding psychosis

According to the stress-vulnerability model certain individuals require a high degree of triggering stress before they react with a psychosis whereas others, who are more vulnerable, require less. Let me briefly summarize some characteristics of an integrated biological-psychodynamic view.

The vulnerability factors can consist of three main types: genetic (including schizotypal personality characteristics), pre- and perinatal respectively (including neuro-cognitive developmental disturbance), and disturbances in childhood environment (including defective internal objects and self-representations). The degree and dominance of these factors vary amongst patients and presumably also represent different clinical pictures even if our current knowledge is not as great as we would like it to be.

Psychosis-triggering factors include non-specific stressors like isolation, lack of sleep, somatic illness and toxic substances (alcohol and drugs). There are also more personality-specific stressors such as life crises, personal loss and bereavement reactions, assaults or violations and 'impossible' or seemingly irresolvable conflicts. An example of the latter is that of a pregnant unmarried woman who loves children but, due to fears about her father's weak heart, does not dare say that she is pregnant by the husband of her neighbour. In her world view she feels convinced that she will kill either her father or the child.

Non-specific stressors often reinforce the personality specific stressors.

Finally, we also have protective factors and three of these are suggested by available research studies:

115

Vulnerability factors, protective factors and stress factors

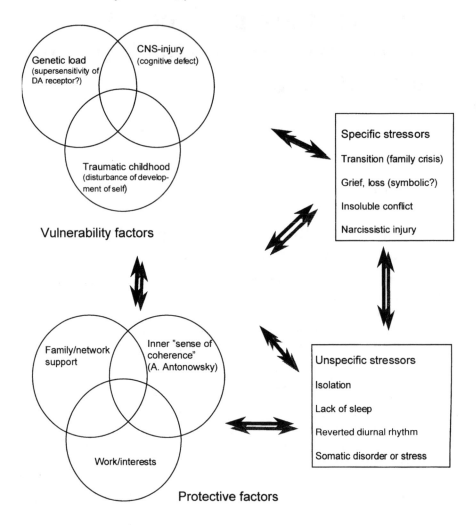

- the network of relations that surrounds us
- access to a meaningful job or occupation
- an inner feeling of coherence.

The latter experience of inner coherence has been demonstrated through research by the Israeli sociologist Aaron Antonowski into the condition of survivors of the Holocaust. In the stress-vulnerability model, the acute psychosis thus may be seen as a crisis reaction in a person who has a specific stress vulnerability of a biological and/or psychological kind. Such

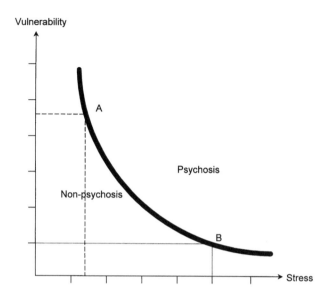

Individual A. High vulnerability. - Small amount of stress triggers psychosis
Individual B. Low vulnerability. - Too much stress triggers psychosis

vulnerability may accompany him or her and remain undetected until it is revealed for the first time during a period of stress, and this usually occurs between the ages of 15 and 30. The *first non-psychotic vulnerability phase* thus passes into a *second psychotic phase*. Finally there is a *third, recovery phase*. Sometimes, however, we observe so-called defective healing, the magnitude and seriousness of which may depend on intrinsic cognitive deficits and psychosocial deficiencies in the patient's surroundings (personal and professional). This tragic development lies at the core of the term 'schizophrenia'.

The acute psychosis as a crisis reaction according to a dynamic crisis model

Such a model makes it possible to understand symptoms that otherwise could be wrongly perceived as primarily pathological. Instead it becomes evident that they are the adaptive strategy of the personality in an otherwise chaotic inner world. As with any ordinary traumatic crisis, you can find a certain 'conformity to rules', which has different phases. In reality these phases may be extended, shortened or sometimes even absent. Let me present a model of such a psychotic crisis, with the different sub-phases outlined in more detail.

Prodromal phase

This may last for a few days up to several years. One can observe withdrawal tendencies, loss of a sense of coherence, feelings of meaning-lessness and finally a premonition of mental breakdown. For some people these prodromal phase symptoms, which may be experienced with much anxiety and depression, may be solved spontaneously, or with profes-sional help. Here the self tries to cope with the problems around the life stresses, which seem overwhelming

Pre-psychosis phase

In the phase of pre-psychosis we find an increase in regressive thinking. Often sexual identity is confused and there can occur extensive projective tendencies with fantasizing about aggressive or integrity-threatening intentions from other people. There are increasing difficulties in separating inner and external worlds and one may discern illusions or unclear hallucinations as well as occasional voices. Affective outbursts may frighten those around the person and there is often an increased inner speed or excitation, which sometimes may approach hypomanic or manic levels. Finally, the continuity of a sense of self is broken when the ego's integrating capacities have reached their limits. Psychotic thinking then dominates the patient's mind. This phase may be successfully treated – however, afterwards it is always difficult to know if the patient's anxiety was a sign of an incipient psychosis or not.

Psychosis – early phase

Now delusions are apparent and are expressions of archaic strategies of the self in the creation of new meanings and coherence in relation to the world. One must understand that for a patient in this situation, the feeling of meaning is more important than a feeling of rationality – this is not a question of intelligence, but merely one of mental survival. When new delusional meaning has appeared, anxiety and depression are reduced. The delusional thinking is confirmed by hallucinations – in this acute phase one might often talk of waking nightmares. Some psychotic patients experience their thoughts and actions as being controlled by others (so-called first-rank symptoms). There is a combination of omnipotence and deep loneliness, as well as a strong resistance towards 'taking in' or accepting anything from the world outside, be it care, medication or trust.

Psychosis – late phase

After a week, a month or more, the patient begins to question the delusions and these in turn become less entrenched. The hallucinations become less imperative and one finds that moments of normality become more frequent. Now depressive thoughts assume greater prominence, through confrontation with reality and through the re-experiencing of stressful life events that preceded the psychosis, as well as other social problems that may have arisen. For some individuals these depressive feelings may prove too painful and they seek protection by once again retreating more deeply into the psychosis. However, this phase affords good opportunities for deepening the co-operation between patient and therapist in an effort to gain a greater understanding of what is, and what is not, happening.

Resolution phase

Here the reality principle once again dominates the patient's psychic life. However, the patient may still experience 'shadows' of the experience of psychosis, especially in the early morning. Self-reliance is damaged and the patient needs a good deal of help in order to regain his self-confidence. There is still a risk of relapse into new prodromal or psychotic symptoms. Patients feel a mixture of pain and shame but also, of course, relief. The overwhelming question is to what extent bridges with society have been burned or retained. Patients now have to live with the memory of the psychosis – hopefully they will not seal over the experience because in so doing they make the prevention of relapses more difficult. The awareness of vulnerability involves the need to investigate the possibility of psychotherapy, the type of psychotherapy to be recommended, and also the extent to which the patient may need continuous neuroleptic medication.

As we can see, this process requires a very careful approach, which varies greatly according to the different phases of the psychosis and to the individual's different needs. This approach is called 'need-adapted psychosis care'.

Need-adapted psychosis care

The Finnish schizophrenia researcher Yrjö Alanen (Alanen, Lehtinen, Räkköläinen, Aaltonen, 1991) coined the term 'need-adapted psychosis care'. This method entails endeavouring to give the patient and his or her relatives the psychosocial and medical care that they most need in every phase of psychosis. Many studies have indicated that this form of treatment yields good effects although the studies still need to improve their methodology and make use of a wider selection of patients.

Pilot project

In order to test out these ideas we carried out a pilot project in an area of central Stockholm with a population of 100,000 inhabitants. All the psychosis care for this area is provided at a health service clinic and the project included all patients being taken ill for the first time with a non-organic psychosis. The concept of need-adapted care was operationalized via six principles that were then applied in practice.

Six principles of 'need-adapted care'

- Early intervention with home-based interventions. A special psychosis team takes full responsibility for every first-episode psychosis patient immediately a patient or relative seeks psychiatric care. If possible, home visits are undertaken during the first phase of contact.
- Crisis and psychotherapeutic approach. The psychotherapy is mainly of a crisis intervention type, and includes the rest of the family during the acute stage. Its aim is to enable each member of the family to formulate his or her main problems, to understand the actual stress and conflict situation, to lessen the dramatic aspects of the psychosis, to motivate the patient for further contact, and to provide realistic hope. Supportive individual or family crisis intervention may later be complemented by systematic psychotherapy according to needs and resources. At that later time the patient is usually not psychotic or less psychotic, and may have an evident need of a deeper understanding of the dynamic background of his or her problems. Alternatively, certain patients may best be served by a cognitive approach that deals with depressive or remaining psychotic symptoms. This entails sessions, which sometimes include family members, at the rate of once or twice a week over a period of up to half a year or more.
- Family orientation. The patient's family (if any) is invited, preferably at once but mostly within one week, for repeated 'family meetings'. Often a 'family map' is constructed during the first meetings. Here every individual in three generations, including grandparents, is identified and written down on the map. This often means that family secrets never spoken of but still known or suspected by members may come to the surface and be put into words. Sometimes the parents' and grandparents' lives may give a greater understanding to the struggles of the patient. It is a recurring experience that the psychotic patient may seem non-psychotic during the family session, and after the session returns to psychotic behaviour. The initial family meetings are later continued with the addition of a supportive, problem-solving and pedagogical component. Some families need extended contact of a supportive or systemic nature.

- Continuity and easy accessibility to the team (which does not always mean individual continuity) is offered, when needed, for five years, the prerequisites being established through the early contact with the patient and his or her family. (After five years most long-term psychoses seem to stabilize and the risk of relapse decreases.)
- Optimal lowest neuroleptic medication. Anxiety and insomnia are primarily relieved with benzodiazepines when psychological support and help from the immediate social environment are not enough. In the case of a first-episode psychosis, neuroleptic medication is usually not given during the first one to two weeks in order to assess the patient's needs and to see whether the psychosis disappears without medication. When psychotic symptoms are prevalent and disturbing, neuroleptic treatment is given. The dose is usually very low at the start (about 0.5 to 1 mg haloperidol equivalent per day) and is very slowly increased. Thus, only rarely is side-effect medication necessary. Lithium and anti-depressants are used when needed.
- Need-adapted overnight care. All patients continue living at home, ideally. When needed, crisis beds are offered in relaxed and personal small-scale surroundings where relatives may also occasionally stay. In cases of dangerous behaviour ordinary psychiatric in-patient facilities are used.

Setting

A special mobile team was formed in 1993 comprising a few members of staff. When at full strength, two years later, the team of five represented both medical and social expertise as well as psychodynamic and cognitive psychotherapeutic competence. In 1994 the outpatient unit was completed with a small flat containing three 'crisis beds'. One member of staff was on duty at night and two during the day. The unit was open round the clock all year round. Every patient accepted by the project had access to a crisis bed any time they were considered to be in need of it. The unit was run as an outpatient facility so this could be done without too many formalities. The centre was situated in a residential area of the city and had a personalized and informal interior. The patients paid a small amount for overnight stays and meals. Later on three more beds were made available in an adjacent flat for long-stay needs. In cases of very disturbing psychotic symptoms or a high suicide risk, the ordinary hospital in-patient resources could be used. In its fifth year the project had a full-time staff of 14, including the overnight crisis bed service. At present about 70 patients continue to be followed-up in different stages of acute psychosis, recovery, and rehabilitation. In the spring of 1998 we had to face the fact that the project was terminated, for 'administrative reasons'. The crisis bed centre was also closed. Thus, the care of new first-episode patients has been integrated into the ordinary psychiatric services. This pilot project proved to be highly successful. The first 32 patients have been followed up over three years. Here we have been able to show that it is possible to care for acutely psychotically ill patients with far fewer restrictions, and with a more personal and psychotherapeutically informed milieu, than are found in the traditional care of psychosis. The use of neuroleptic medication was modest – the mean dosage for those with a prescription was around 2 mg haloperidol equivalent per day. The consumption of in-patient services was considerably reduced. The rate of improvement and outcome seemed better than we were accustomed to in the ordinary care settings. The somewhat increased outpatient costs were balanced by reduced in-patient costs. However, no direct cost-effectiveness analysis has been undertaken. This experience together with studies of the so-called Soteria projects (Cullberg, 1998; Mosher, 1994; and Ciompi, 1992) provided the foundation for the parachute project, which was able to start in January 1996 after two years of preparation.

The parachute project

This is a combined research and development project concerning first episode non-organic psychosis patients. Nineteen clinics in Sweden are involved, with catchment areas covering one sixth of Sweden's population – approximately 1.6 million inhabitants. The participating clinics have committed themselves to endeavour to develop a form of psychosis care that corresponds to the six principles outlined above, and to collect research data on the patients. These data are forwarded to our database in Stockholm. All participating patients have agreed to participate in accord with the decision of the Karolinska Institute's research ethics committee.

The aims of the project are to:

- to contribute to the development of psychosis care (the reason that the project concerns itself only with first episode psychosis patients is purely due to research considerations)
- to determine whether need-adapted care (according to the six principles above) shows an improved outcome compared to that of treatment as usual
- to identify subgroups where it is possible to predict outcome at the baseline level with projective tests, neuropsychological tests, and/or with the help of social and symptom data
- to conduct a cost/benefit study (planned together with The Institution of National Economy at Växjö University).

Methods

The patients agreeing to participate are examined, apart from at baseline, after one month, three months, and after one, three and five years. Apart from diagnostic assessment according to DSM IV (SCID-ratings), symptom assessments and so forth are carried out. Psychological examinations with projective methods are conducted repeatedly in order to determine possible predictive personality factors. These are complemented with various self-assessment instruments. A comprehensive neuro-psychological examination is carried out as soon as the patient's condition permits and again after three years. Further, a computerized axial tomography (CAT) scan or magnetic resonance imaging (MRI) of the brain is carried out on all patients with schizophrenia symptoms. Medical history and social data, as well as the patient's and relatives' levels of satisfaction with the care provided, are recorded.

Comparison groups

For practical reasons a randomized study with control groups selected from the same populations was not possible – committed staff trained in a specialized *modus operandi* cannot shift between two very different approaches. A retrospective comparison group consists of all first episode psychotic patients who fell ill in three catchment areas (which today participate in the parachute project) five years before the start of the project. The inclusion criteria are the same and the drop-out rate low. The patients have been followed up via hospital records as well as register data. A prospective comparison group has been obtained from a university hospital clinic well known for its excellent care of psychosis patients – this clinic is not participating in the parachute project. Data are collected in a similar way with a personal follow-up of the patients. Collection of the data from the comparison groups is not yet complete. We intend to make the comparison of outcomes with clinical and social 'triplets', which will make diagnostic and social differences between the materials less important.

Results and discussion

As the one-year follow-up of data is not yet complete the results are preliminary. A total of 301 patients have been assessed as fulfilling the inclusion criteria. This means 24 per 100,000 of the total population within the relevant age groups. Ninety-two persons have declined to participate in the research – almost 30%. However, we have basic data regarding this group enabling us to see that they do not differ significantly from the rest in terms of these basic variables. The two comparison groups contain 72 versus 64 individuals – their sex, age, and diagnostic distribution are very similar to the experimental group.

Diagnostically the schizophrenia group contains 40% of the population – the numbers here comprise confirmed diagnoses after having had the opportunity to follow the course over one year; 55% were in contact with the parachute project within 48 hours of their first contact with the psychiatric services. It would certainly have been possible to increase this figure if the ordinary psychiatric wards had been more alert in not keeping new patients. It was found that 13% received some kind of systematic psychotherapy during the course. The rest received intensive psychotherapeutically informed supportive treatment during the different stages of the process. In 45% of cases it was possible to make the first family contact within 48 hours. At each follow-up 30%–40% of the patients were receiving neuroleptics. Medication with neuroleptics was given to 82% of the patients at some time during their care. The average dose (for those with a prescription) was the equivalent of approximately 2 mg Haloperidol per day – this means that the patients were seldom bothered by side effects. Regarding inpatient treatment on an ordinary ward, the parachute patients stayed on average 21 days. In addition to that, each patient used 25 days in an adapted 'crisis centre'. (In fact, only about half of the clinics had been able to arrange a special crisis residential home in accordance with the sixth principle.)

Recovery

The GAF score (an expression of general functioning level) is usually under 40 in the case of psychotic symptoms. A score of less than 60 indicates the need for contact with the psychiatric services. The patients attained a good functional status (GAF 63). Similarly, we can see from the symptom assessment with the Brief Psychiatric Rating Scale, that positive symptoms disappeared to a large extent, as did negative ones. At 12 months 25% had positive symptoms to a mild degree and 10% to a medium or strong degree. We do not yet have data from the comparison groups in order to properly assess the implications of these figures. Finally, regarding satisfaction with care, relatives scored 3.6 and the patients 3.5 on a five-point scale, where 5 represents the highest level of satisfaction. This indicates a rather high mean satisfaction, which is unusual with this category of patient.

Conclusions

What preliminary conclusions may be drawn from these experiences? The first is that it is possible to work with this group of patients within a psychodynamic/biological frame of reference in a much less restricted manner using far less medication and still achieve very good results. In order to achieve this, psychosocial support, including psychotherapy, has been incorporated into the treatment according to the 'six principles'. This way of working is probably not more expensive than traditional care. Nothing indicates that this approach is any less effective with relapsing long-term patients. Such a model of working with psychosis can only be achieved if the psychiatric services are reorganized and a psychosis team is formed including those responsible for the crisis home. This way of working provides the patients and their relatives, as well as the treatment staff, with more realistic hope, and I do not think we can overestimate the importance of this for the healing process.

References

Alanen YO, Lehtinen K, Räkköläinen V, Aaltonen J (1991) Need-adapted treatment of new schizophrenic patients: experiences and results of the Turku Project. Acta Psychiatrica Scandinavica 83: 363–72.

Ciompi L, Kupper Z, Aebi E, Dauwalder HP, Hubschmid T, Trütsch K, Rutishauser C (1992) Das Pilotprojekt 'Soteria Bern' zur Behandlung akut Schizophrener. II. Ergebnisse einer vergleichenden prospektiven Verlaufstudie über 2 Jahre. Nervenarzt 64: 440–50.

Cullberg Johan (1998) Integrating intensive psychosocial and low dose medical treatments in a total material of first episode psychotic patients compared to 'treatment as usual'. Paper presented at the Twelfth ISPS Conference, London, 1997.

Mosher LR, Vallone R, Menn A (1995) The treatment of acute psychosis without neuroleptics: six week psychopathology outcome data from the Soteria project. Int J Soc Psychiatr 41: 157–73.

CHAPTER 8

On autism, schizophrenia and paranoia in children: the case of little Jeremy

LUIZ EDUARDO PRADO DE OLIVEIRA

My purpose in this chapter is to emphasize the importance of conversation in psychoanalysis, albeit a conversation of a very special kind. The more difficult our cases are, the more conversation implies the capacity to play, to maintain a dreamlike state of mind, to suspend judgement and to appeal to discrete humour. Psychoanalysis strives to enable us to think about our personal history and how it is intermingled with desire, dreaming and language. What was once unconscious history will become conscious history as a consequence of recollection and reconstruction through the transference. During this process, psychoanalysts are simultaneously engaged in mute conversations with one another, conversations carried on mostly through reading and writing. Psychoanalysis implies transference, countertransference and its own forms of knowledge transmission. Psychoanalysts transmit ways of thinking about life that take into account the possibility of dreaming, the ambiguities of sex and the certainty of death, as well as the fact that signifiers and language dominate us. As we know, ideology can often fill the gap between wisdom and knowledge, on the one hand, and ignorance and distraction on the other. Knowing history – our own, that of our discipline and that of humanity – may protect us from the dangers of ideology.

'Before us'

Andron paranoia (human paranoia) is how our history begins, in an all too human way, with the fear of strangers, of foreigners, of angels, of eerie familiarities, of our intimate enemies. Psychoanalysis has taught us to recognize the threats generated by our innermost being. Paranoia derives from the Greek 'para' which means 'near', 'almost' and 'against' in two senses: next to the other, close together, intimate, but also warring against or fighting against the other. 'Noia' means 'reason', 'understanding', 'comprehension'. Paranoia is thus a composite term used to signify what reason or understanding is up against, in both senses. The first two occasions on which this word appears occur in Æschylus' *The Seven Against Thebes*, and in Euripides' *Orestes*. In Æschylus' play, the chorus tries to describe the link between Oedipus and Jocasta. According to Buckley's translation, 't'was frenzy linked the distracted pair'. Frenzy here is a translation of the Greek word *paranoia*. Mother and son in love, driven by paranoia, went so far as to have sexual intercourse. They could not understand their folly as their reason was impaired. In Euripides' play, the situation is altogether different. The chorus describes Orestes after Clytemnestra's death:

> Oh, 'tis the slight
> Of impious sophistry putteth for right
> The wrong: 'tis the sinner's infatuate folly.

'Folly' is a translation of 'paranoia'. 'Andron paranoia', or human erring – represents our inability to fully comprehend the world whilst pretending to do so all the same. The first two occurrences of paranoia highlight that the word indicates either a son in sexual intercourse with his mother or a son in murderous intercourse with his mother. This establishes a parallel between sexual intercourse and murder, and could imply that our inability to understand may stem from our relationship to our parents. I say parents rather than mother, as we must not overlook Laios and Agamemnon.

Related to these historical considerations of the concept of paranoia is the fact that the concept of autism first appears with the concept of schizophrenia. In his seminal work on dementia præcox (1911), Bleuler writes (my translation): First, 'autism is more or less the same thing Freud called auto-eroticism' (p. 112, n. 80). Second, 'there is a normal autistic thought that does not need to take reality into consideration and its orientation is determined by the affections. Children play with a piece of wood which stands for a baby, then a house' (p. 474). Third, 'we may also find an insufficient distinction between imagination and reality in a lack of attention, in dreams and among children' (p. 474). In fact, autism is fundamentally a schizophrenic symptom, and even more so for later authors, for whom it corresponds with the dismantling of psychic elements linked to experiences of the body, such as perceptions, sensations and movements. This dismantling is such that it makes the subject a prisoner of the world; his or her subjectivity then becomes inaccessible to him or herself. He or she is literally 'out of his or her mind' and, fully identified with dismantled elements of the body, the subject is unable to establish anything but partial relationships with them. The elements that remain unbound will thus appear as persecutors. Melanie Klein's particular insight was to link in a dynamic relationship the old concept of paranoia and the new concept of schizophrenia; the old concept of mania and the new concept of depression. She also advanced the notion of positions and working through as central to the understanding of transformations from one of these states of mind to another. Melanie Klein had no use for the concept or nosological entity known as autism. She was therefore in agreement with Freud when he wrote: 'However, the autistic thinking of Bleuler does not by any means correspond with the extension and the contents of the preconscious, neither can I admit that the name used by Bleuler has been happily chosen' (Freud, 1921).

Kanner's contribution to the concept of autism was to focus on children and to organize his understanding of their symptoms through systematic observation. However, he does not appear to offer new clinical descriptions over and above those of Anna Freud and Melanie Klein. His undeserved celebrity as the creator of the concept of autism (a status attributed to him even by the *Encyclopædia Britannica*) is due mainly to political factors. First, during the Second World War no North American or British psychiatrist would have acknowledged the seminal contributions of German psychiatry. Second, Kanner spearheaded the development of infant psychiatry as some of his early papers show (Kanner, 1943a, b, c). Prior to his papers 'Autistic disturbance of affective contact' (1943c) and 'Early infantile autism' (1944), schizophrenic or psychotic children were considered simply to be 'feeble-minded'. Third, and of paramount importance, at the Richmond Meeting of Psychiatry in America Kanner strongly opposed those who advocated the physical elimination of the mentally ill, including children (1943b). Kanner's 'autistic' children were the original 'feeble-minded' children who, as it turned out, were to be saved from death by extermination in the US. 'Autism' came to mean a way of surviving – and this was a meaning that was to carry great significance. Nonetheless, from a scholarly point of view, it remains the case that many psychiatrists and psychoanalysts have scarcely acknowledged the origins of the concept of autism and its relevance to the views they have developed. Consequently they do not explain their reasons for considering autism to be an altogether different affliction from schizophrenia, rather than, as Bleuler suggests, one of its main symptoms. Psychiatrists and psychoanalysts appear to be at ease with the concepts they use and disregard the lack of congruence between their research and that of their colleagues. Definitions also inevitably play an important role in theories of aetiology, and it is interesting to note that authors such as Kanner, Tustin and Meltzer, and other contemporary researchers in mental health, have not linked the concept of autism primarily to organic malformations or malfunctions. It would appear that clarity of clinical approach requires that autistic children or adults, whose troubles are mostly organic, should not, under these circumstances, be identified as autistic. Even if, late in their studies, authors such as Bleuler or Kanner gave up their research on the psychic origins of autism, thereby yielding to the siren's song of future discoveries in organic research, the task of understanding the changes that take place in these patients remains the paramount one, instead of merely subscribing to the explanations provided by biology, useful though these may be. It is likely that Bleuler and Kanner were discouraged by the failures of their approach to autistic patients and by the fact that they did not have sufficiently substantive conceptual frameworks to permit adequate diagnosis and research. Others have taken up their work. Tustin and Meltzer attempted to pursue research into the psychic origins of autism and the distinctions between autistic and organic troubles that have an impact on the psyche. In contemporary French research, Haag has begun to establish a statistical link between autistic problems and organic malfunction.

Freud and his followers – Abraham and Tausk, Klein and Mead, Searles and Lacan, Aulagnier and Perrier, among others – never thought that organic deficiency could be the main cause of psychosis, or even a primary aspect of psychotic symptoms, even though psychotic symptoms may appear when organic or genetic disorders are present. In other words, psychosis corresponds to intellectual, affective and sensorial functioning that obeys schizophrenic (splitting), paranoid (projection) and exclusion (foreclosure) mechanisms. These are shaped by the trans-generational chain of signifiers, to borrow the Lacanian term, to which the psychotic subject belongs, as well as by his family environment, and give rise to a wide variety of problems. Psychoanalysts influenced by Lacan argue that these problems stem principally from the exclusion or important distortion of major signifiers concerning birth and death, and of the differences between the sexes and generations. These are the symbolic and developmentally crucial 'points of entry' into the psychological system of human relationships that, if jeopardized or effaced, deform and undermine psychic structure. Nowadays, no clinical approach to psychosis would be conceivable without consideration of the psychotic patient's surroundings: and no theory of psychosis is acceptable if it is not congruent with other approaches developed during the century. Conceptual incoherence in a theoretical field implies a breakdown in the relations between theory and reality and this can lead to the rise of ideology. Of course, psychoanalysis is by no means immune from this danger. It is the recollection of psychoanalytical history and the continual return to clinical observations, as Jackson and Williams have demonstrated (Jackson and Williams, 1994), that are of the greatest help in protecting psychoanalysis from the harm that ideology can so readily inflict.

The case history that I shall present is an attempt to clarify some of the links between schizophrenia, paranoia and autism. I have indicated that I personally do not consider autism to be an entity with a necessarily significant organic basis, even if it has organic consequences. Furthermore, it is my view that anthropology or sociology may ultimately prove to be of more value than chemistry and biology in understanding and healing psychosis, in that the most pressing problems of psychosis belong essentially to humanity, rather than to 'nature'. This is not to devalue the contributions of chemistry and biology or their explanatory power, but to stress their strictly limited value in helping us to understand the personal crisis that we term 'psychosis'. As has been well documented, the decision to attribute the care of mental ailments mainly to biology and medicine is, like all decisions, one with a political dimension and this dimension has important and unforeseen consequences for both patients and society. My encounters with little Jeremy focused on an effort to understand the meaning of his troubles for him and those around him.

Meeting Jeremy

I began treating Jeremy at a child guidance clinic located in a rich neighbourhood on the outskirts of Paris. His parents had just moved there. When enrolling their child in the local school, they were advised to consult someone about Jeremy's behaviour. This is a frequent procedure in France when a child presents serious problems. Later, we decided that Jeremy should attend more regular sessions at my private office nearby. How Jeremy should pay for his treatment was, from the very beginning, an important problem. I asked Jeremy to bring me something that he himself had chosen as remuneration. He began by bringing me nuts, shells or small stones that he would pick up in his garden. Now he brings me money that his parents give him before each session. We (including Jeremy) agreed that his parents should not bring their son to my door, but instead leave him at the corner of the block so that he could walk along the street by himself to his session. All of this I considered to be part of the treatment setting.

Jeremy was four years old when I first met him. The colleague who referred him to me wrote that it was not clear whether he was more schizophrenic than autistic or the other way round. Presenting a child in this manner already assumes a theoretical position, in this case separating autism from schizophrenia whilst simultaneously linking them in mutual opposition. Jeremy's drawings, which accompanied my colleague's letter, called to my mind the shapes so often described by Tustin (1986), apart from one of them where it was possible to decipher an attempt at writing his first name. This consisted of intermingled shapeless blots in different colours above which floated scribbles forming vague letters, also in different colours. His first name reminded me of a widely publicized murdered child in France, particularly because my young patient was born at around the same time. As I would later learn, this was just a first, albeit coincidental, indication of the importance of death in this child's life. My experience with autistic children has indicated that death is overwhelmingly present, perhaps even before their conception and birth. It is not simply that their parents may have been severely depressed or in the grip of something deadly, but that they may not have experienced at all the conditions necessary to deal with mourning experiences.

Shortly after receiving the letter from my colleague, I received a letter from Jeremy's mother. In it, she told me that her son's problems were deep rooted and that he refused to eat alone or to dress himself, that he was in no way autonomous and that his fingers lacked tonicity. She recounted that, on his teacher's advice, she was teaching him to help her with cooking, which he did well. He could prepare quiches by himself once she had massaged his fingers. As for everything else, she wrote, he was 'completely mad'. He banged his head on the ground and against the walls, scratched himself and bit his hands until he bled. My response was to consider the likelihood of a severe developmental disorder, but not of real childhood psychosis, because his teacher could at least keep him in class and his mother seemed satisfied with his quiches. As for banging his head, even if it were a psychotic symptom, I wondered what terrifying anxieties could lead a child to such extreme behaviour. When I first met Jeremy in my waiting room, my heart sank. He walked sideways like a crab, as Haag has frequently described (Haag, 1984, 1991; Haag et al., 1995). He also walked on the tips of his toes, as awkwardly as a foal. His hand was limp. He could not meet my gaze nor look at anything else. His head seemed too big in relation to his shoulders or to the rest of his body. His mother hesitated about leaving him with me, but soon gave in and dived back into her book. In the corridor Jeremy took my hand, then let go of it and ran in front of me on tiptoe, waving his arms around as if trying to take off in improbable flight. At four, he still did not speak. He expressed himself by twittering like a bird and occasionally I believed that I could make out the sound of a word. Later on I shall deal with this image of Jeremy as a bird. On entering my office, Jeremy flattened his back against the wall in a corner of the room. The back, and flattening oneself, have a particular meaning. The back is a hard element of the body, as Deleuze pointed out in his comments on Klein (1969). The back stands for a shell and it implies protection, defence or reassurance, much as the walls themselves. As such, the back may signify modalities of parental presence. To flatten oneself seems to be linked to some form of adhesive identification, as indicated by Meltzer (1975). Nevertheless, what I indicate here as an adhesive identification generally corresponds to my experience of children who express the need to get physically in touch with me, by putting their head against mine or their body against mine in some way. Adults also use these kinds of movements: most often they try to hold my hand or, when there is no severe regression, fix their eyes on mine or on my movements. Klein showed how every gesture, posture, movement, look or noise has significance. As Lacan pointed out in his seminar on the logic of fantasy, the body itself is the first signifier. In order for it to acquire meaning for the subject, it must first have had significance for the mother, who receives this meaning from her relationship with the child's father and with their respective families.

I sat down and watched Jeremy's glance slide erratically over the things in the room, the windows, the light emanating from the last rays of winter sun, the mirror in which it was reflected. I felt I didn't exist for this child. He probably glimpsed a shadow, a vague outline, or so I guessed. He, on the other hand, existed for me as a deep sorrow, the sorrow conjured up by wrecks or dead animals. Jeremy spent the time sizing up the place, maybe comparing it with other places he knew, and with his past and current feelings. Meanwhile I wondered about him. My correspondent was evidently right. Here were all the signs of autism as described by the principal authors I had read. I therefore prepared myself for more manifestations of psychotic behaviour from Jeremy, with more obvious schizophrenic elements. Depressed at the thought of having to contradict my theoretical options, I waved toward the jumble of toys in a corner of my office. Jeremy's eyes followed my gesture until he saw the toys. He rushed over to them and knelt clumsily on all fours. He took each toy in turn and lifted it so that it was level with his eyes. The movement of raising the toy was accompanied by a backward jolt of the head, as if he needed to use the ceiling as background in order to examine the toy. He moved quickly and repeatedly from a diving movement into the toys to its counterpart, peculiar to a particular type of transference that I have previously described in relation to Schreber (Prado de Oliveira, 1997). Fantasies of omnipotence tend to correspond with a look that plunges, seeing the world and human beings from above – Godlike – while fantasies of falling, being torn away or abandoned, correspond to a countermovement that sees the other rising into the infinite sky. The *Denkwirdigkeiten eines Nervenkranken (Memoirs of my Nervous Illness)*, the best book ever written on the history of psychiatry, according to Freud, has one single illustration: it depicts the layout of the psychiatric ward where Schreber was admitted, as seen from above. The author meanwhile describes his permanent fear of being forsaken by God and, in order to illustrate this, he describes a picture where women and angels ascend to Heaven high above, as seen from the earth. Jeremy seemed to grasp the toy characters in an omnipotent mode and then to gradually abase himself before them when they seemed ready to forsake him. I watched the little boy, fascinated and sad. The game lasted a long time. Then, to my surprise, Jeremy began to organize the toy figurines into families – the elephant family, the bear family, the lion family, the gorilla family, the human family and so on. I rejoiced and told myself that our game was going in the right direction. Jeremy's behaviour certainly presented many psychotic elements including autism, but there did not appear to be any excessive destructive projective identification, nor was there an overwhelming adhesive identification. Nonetheless, my feelings were largely those of the countertransference he had induced in me and, to that extent, followed his transference, which corresponded to these types of identifications. This session also revealed an oedipal bud that seemed ready to bloom. At the end of the session I said to him: 'Sometimes we think it would be good to be grown up straightaway and yet we feel so very, very small, if we are as little as we imagine ourselves to be.' I now think that this remark implied the designation of a world existing in several dimensions, even if, to my mind, these do not correspond to Meltzer's categories. Meltzer refers to spatial data whereas here I wish to emphasize temporal data, even if they do become intermingled at some levels of mental functioning (Prado de Oliveira, 1996, pp. 287-8). What I said to Jeremy implied distinguishing between what he himself was and what he himself would like to be, as Freud pointed out in his paper on narcissism (1914), and which clearly implies a temporal differentiation. What I said to Jeremy also established the fact that we were able to think and that he and I were together. These are temporal distinctions that make sense in terms of Freudian metapsychology. In a previous paper I have indicated that Klein's theory, as well as her followers' theories, insist overwhelmingly on spatial references, mostly when these acquire bodily expression. These theories, however, tend to neglect temporal references.

At that time I spoke to Jeremy mostly to reassure myself, although I knew this rendered me present to him in some way. It allowed him to at least hear the sound of my voice – an element that is so crucially important in the analysis of very disturbed patients, be they adults or children. When I took Jeremy back to the waiting room, his mother buttonholed me. She wanted to know how the session had gone and my reply that all was going well did not satisfy her. She had lots of things to tell me about her son: she needed to explain details of his education, an accident that happened to him, and so forth. I felt overwhelmed. I can still recall my train of thought. My first response was that Jeremy must suffer a lot with such an intrusive mother. My second, just as banal as the first, was that here was a psychotic's mother, who invades as much as she herself has felt invaded throughout her own life. This was followed by the thought that here was a woman who has passed her schizophrenia on to her son through her invasive hysterical defences. Until finally I thought: this woman suffers so much when separated from her son that he suffers from it as much as she does. I suggested to her that we should all three meet together the next time. This she accepted with relief. I avoided mentioning the father on this occasion. This seemed to be important, because I wished to invite him to join us in the future and wanted to be sure she would not stop him from coming. Experience shows that when a more-or-less permanent couple is set up between mother and child, this corresponds to a difficulty experienced by the father and the mother in creating their own couple at different moments in their history, to a likely attack by mother and child against the father, and even, in extreme cases, to a fading out of the father altogether. On the other hand, to try to separate mother and child under such circumstances not only constitutes a violent step, but, worse, it is a tactic that has often been shown to lead to therapeutic failures in middle term of treatment, if not immediately.

Jeremy, his mother and me

As before, when we had our first interview, Jeremy teetered on tiptoe down the corridor in front of us, waving his arms around. His mother began talking about him using a welter of clichés and denials expressed with anxiety, joy, or scorn. I couldn't get a word in edgeways: she seemed to be speaking to an imaginary interlocutor. On reaching my office, we sat down and Jeremy remained standing with his back glued to the wall. This appeared to plunge his mother into confusion. 'He always does that to me' she repeated, upset and scornful. I reassured her, without being reassured myself: I said, 'It is how Jeremy gets to know the world. He is really very shy. The last time we met, he remained like that for a while, then he played well.' And I was thinking: 'It is not against you he has done it.' I was also thinking that I was wrong and that, in some way, she was right. I was afraid of my thoughts, because they implied that I was becoming aware of the fact that, for each of them, there was barely any difference between them. I was also feeling somewhat split apart. Nevertheless, the difference between them, slight though it might be, also showed me, from my experience with mothers and children, that I was subjected to a dual trans-ference and hence to a dual countertransference, even if I was as yet not properly aware of their nature. I also felt intuitively that my only chance of getting the best out of this situation was to harmonize these transferences in such a way as to create a space where they might link up. The only instrument to achieve this would be if I were to have some success in harmonizing my own countertransferences. The few words I had addressed to the mother seemed to put her at ease. She told me of Jeremy's false timidity, arguing that he was stubborn and knew exactly how to get what he wanted. While deriving comfort from what I had said, she completely invalidated my remark: if what she had said was the truth, her son couldn't possibly be shy and she would not accept what I had just said. She thus confirmed Jeremy's autistic symptoms and disqualified my proposition, placing her son in such a position that being shy and not being shy could be true at one and the same time. Her way of invalidating my statements changed later when she developed what we came to call a 'theoretical-point-of-view-argument', which we gradually understood as her way of seeking a privileged relationship with me, whilst refusing analysis for herself. For instance, when she claimed we were arguing about the need for three sessions per week for her son – although I was not aware that we were having an argument – she would tell me that I was completely right from a theoretical point of view, but that, from a practical point of view, I should do what she suggested and therefore I was wrong. She finally agreed with my proposal once I explained to her that I was not arguing for a particular theory, but for emotional consistency and perman-ence, whereas if she were bringing theory to the fore, we should agree that some degree of coherence between this and our practice is always welcome.

Jeremy generally listened to my words and then went on to play. A temporary mother–child therapeutic relationship was set up between us. For some months, I continued to see Jeremy's mother face to face while her son played with toy characters or with water from the tap, either between us or in a corner of the room. Sometimes he came over to snuggle up to his mother: she was ambivalent about this, both holding and rejecting her son, enjoying and despising him at the same time. At other times, when my questions seemed to disturb his mother, to trouble him or to perturb them both, he threatened me with one of his animals. I then took another animal and the two of us 'fought' for as long as it took his mother and myself to re-establish peace or until Jeremy felt able to return to his own play. Even when he was playing, Jeremy, I suspect, paid very careful attention to what his mother said and how she said it. Once a month, the husband joined us. Even though this rhythm of appointments was not always scrupulously maintained, it is important that it was fixed, and that, whenever an appointment was broken, the absence was queried. (I do not impose too many constraints on the treatment of a child and I always prefer to let the family decide on its rhythm of participation and the extent of its member's individual presence. I think these stand for the family's unconscious movements in relation to me as well as to their own psychic organization.) Much later, I concluded that my conversations with mother and son had given Jeremy the opportunity to work through an adhesive identification and to move more towards projective identification, thus establishing more developed ways of elaborating his identity (as differentiated from identification: cf. Perelberg (1998)). Examples of adhesive identification are Jeremy's previously mentioned practice of gluing his back to the wall, but also his way of clinging to his parents. An example of transformation from adhesive to projective identification would be the boy's practice of bringing his eyes up close to mine when trying to attack me or during our protracted fights. Both of these mechanisms began to fade after a particular session during which Jeremy spent almost the entire time in the toilet. When I asked him what he had been doing in there, he explained that he had had trouble cleaning himself. The risk of his getting dirty during a session was thoroughly worked through during a particular period of his therapy. I need hardly mention that this was linked essentially to the working through of an extreme violence displayed in the families of our toy characters, dirtiness and violence being generally closely related – either imposed or suffered.

Many of the early sessions with Jeremy and his mother were trying. This woman was quite determined to annihilate me, and yet at the same time she idealized me. She talked so much that I could barely say a word. Most of the time she did not look at me while talking and then, suddenly, she would stare at me as if expecting me to work miracles. I often thought that I was going mad or wondered if I ought not to interrupt her and ask her to shut up. At that time, I began to doubt the basis of my approach. Jeremy's play seemed to regress and he became unable to organize the toy characters into families. He started to pile them up, and then blew up the pile or had it blown up by one of his toy animals. This I found discouraging. Sometimes he organized the animals into totem poles, which usually made me feel better. In the meantime, his mother droned on in her nasal way, which had begun to remind me of Jeremy's twittering. Her gaze seemed to shift constantly, like that of her son, but whereas Jeremy's glance usually slid over things, hers met an object or my gaze and then shifted sharply elsewhere. She talked about anything and everything – shopping, neighbours, the car, how she was all alone with Jeremy and how her husband was hardly ever there, how the house was big and difficult to manage, her problems with one of her son's teachers who advised her to consult someone, her sympathy with another teacher who asserted that anything of the kind was useless, and so on. There were times when I got the impression that she wanted to tell me something particularly important, and that she had started to do so, but that in her extreme confusion and desire to confide, something would intervene to prevent her from doing so and she would lose her train of thought. Little by little, however, I got the feeling that she was able to find her way back and recover the thread of what she had begun to tell me. The sessions always ended with a request for reassurance on her part and with guarded encouragement on mine. She made extensive use of me as an idealized and denigrated dustbin breast, all-powerful yet reduced to impotence. Jeremy's totem poles reassured me, as did the fact that once in a while his mother showed herself capable of not losing her train of thought. Tustin once pointed out how shapes could be made out of plasticine. I think that there is something about these shapes that, when they are organized in piles, makes them look like small totems. Freud's studies on the subject made us aware that the construction of totems is related to the working through of destructive drives towards our elders or our beloved ones. Totems are also related to the mourning provoked by their death. Thus, Jeremy's totems seemed to me to be signifiers of the working through of mourning and aggressiveness.

The father and the birth of the son

I was surprised by my first meeting with the father and husband. He introduced himself as a high-ranking businessman, which indeed he is. His wife had always introduced herself more modestly. He made excuses for not having been able to come earlier, but as the director of an important industrial group he was always on the move. When I told him that I couldn't do much without his and his wife's help, he promised to try to do his best. I believe this to be an important psychoanalytical step: to make it clear to patients, discreetly but firmly, that we cannot do much for them if they do not try to help us think about them. What surprised me most about this father was that he seemed to maintain the same confused and split relationship with the mother–son dyad as the mother maintained with the son. His manner of speaking – a mixture of onomatopoeic cartoon sounds, incongruous mimicry and guttural explosions – often made him just as incomprehensible as his wife and son, although somewhat funnier. He waved his arms around a lot in a disorderly fashion when he spoke, which reminded me of Jeremy's attempts to take off in flight. I found myself imagining that Jeremy's was not a case of schizophrenia or autism at all but, given that everyone in this family talked in such a bizarre fashion, it was more a case of a peculiar family subculture.

In time, I also learned that this couple had only just arrived in the Paris region when they came to meet me. The child was born in another big French city. The father's profession had obliged them to move frequently both within France and abroad. They had tried time and again to have a child, but several miscarriages had discouraged them. They had decided that she would take the pill and just as she had started on it she fell pregnant. 'Isn't that funny, doctor?' she asked me. 'The pill stimulated my pregnancy rather than stopping it!' she exclaimed somewhat gleefully. I did not find it funny: on the contrary, I felt it to be catastrophic both for this woman with respect to her relationship with her own mother, but also for the child to whom she had given birth. I perceived a knot of problems presiding over this child's entry into the world and I sensed a shadow of death upon him. If the concept of structure means anything in mental life, this must ultimately lie in its transgenerational historical context and its associations with the compulsion to repeat. Jeremy's birth had taken place in the context of an impossible mourning related to the serious illness and impending death of both grandfathers. The boy was himself the only survivor of multiple miscarriages and was destined to become the redeemer. Thus the shadow of the object fell upon the ego, according to Freud's seminal definition of narcissistic identification (1915). This same metaphor appears earlier in Freud's writings and indicates differentiation between generations, as I have mentioned elsewhere (Prado de Oliveira, 1995). Indeed, Freud writes in relation to mourning and the taboo of the dead: 'If their shadow were to fall on anyone, he would be taken ill at once' (1912). Our experience shows that there is an intimate relationship between children's mental problems and the difficulties experienced by their parents or close relatives in working through mourning, as mentioned earlier. The point that I am stressing is that narcissistic identification is not mainly, or not only, a mirror relationship, but also a trans-generational relationship involving at least three persons, and in which one of them is actively identifying the other with a third dead person whose mourning cannot be accomplished. Indeed, I think that the partition of the mind into unconscious, preconscious and conscious might well acquire an altogether new consistency if transgenerational factors were taken into account.

My intimation of catastrophe when I heard of the failed pregnancies before this first live birth was far from shared by Jeremy's parents. Jeremy's father called him 'ma biche' ('my little doe'), to my intense irritation. According to them, if Jeremy had problems (minor ones, of course) then it was because he had squashed his finger in the door of their previous house, or because they must have looked at more than a hundred houses before deciding which to buy. On top of that, they had not been able to move immediately! 'All that was unlikely to make our son feel secure', they concluded. They were right, from a psychoanalytical point of view. As far as I was concerned, more than a hundred houses, countless moves and several miscarriages are signifiers of a fragmented universe that had dismantled Jeremy's perceptual, sensorial and motor behaviour. And a father who calls his son 'ma biche' is at the very least disturbing the son's possibilities of secure masculine identifications.

Some elements of the parents' history

These splits were far from being the only ones we worked through. In the course of our conversations, I learned that the life of Jeremy's maternal grandparents had been subjected to powerful divisions. His maternal grandparents, who came from a traditional socialist family, and his paternal grandparents who came from a fervent Catholic one, had been forbidden to marry by their respective families. The young couple had disregarded the prohibition and were banned from family life by both families. Not a single member of either family has since contacted them, condemning them to withdrawal into themselves – to a kind of conjugal autism. In my view, it is important that parents arrive at a point where they are able to tell their children their family histories, so that the children can listen to them. It is not only the telling of the history that is important, but also the emotional experience it evokes. Allow me to cite Freud once more: 'Parental love, which is so moving and at bottom so childish, is nothing but the parents' narcissism born again, which, transformed into object love, unmistakably reveals its former nature' (1914). Psychoanalysis has shown us that children do not identify with the conscious system of their elders but, rather, with their unconscious system: most probably, whatever parental narcissism reappears in children has its roots in the reappearance of their own parents' narcissism in themselves when they were children (hence the importance of grandparents to children and the requirement for a transgenerational approach). In the present case, the grandparental families belonged to traditionally opposed groups – socialists and Catholics: these then became signifiers of splitting functions passed on from these groups to the couple and, later, in my view, to Jeremy himself. Whatever the nature of the differences between groups, if these differences are not recognized and worked through, they will support and reinforce the psychic activity of splitting. It is as if, in consti-tuting a couple, those who have set out to meet otherness in a compulsive way are doomed to meet sameness, in an autistic inversion, because of the violence of the splitting they have experienced, almost as if the effort to meet someone from a different background should paradoxically emerge as a way of denying more fundamental differences, such as sexual differences or the difference between generations. It is obviously not the origins of these couples, or the attempt at differentiation, or even the effort to think about the other within the couple, which are at the root of psychosis, but rather the fact that meeting the other is experienced as transgression, as if otherness had become an impossible object of thought. This is counterbalanced by one or several denials or threats of punishment stemming from an archaic unconscious superego, the foundation of which lies within the group, the family or individual masochistic experiences, if not in all of them. Indeed, attacks on linking are always followed by strong masochistic mental functioning. The splitting in the couple, grounded in the splitting in each of its members, keeps them from creating a protective shield for one other and for their children. Jeremy's parents' unconscious mental functioning was unable to keep his projective identifications from splitting.

Jeremy's mother was married once before. Her first husband refused her a child and she expressed her indignation so strongly that, fed up with her, he went off with his best friend's wife. Jeremy's mother and this same best friend consoled one another and ended up getting married. They then left for a distant country where they hoped to live happily ever after. The decision to have a child motivated their return to France but, once the decision was made, the wife developed epilepsy. Miscarriages and epileptic seizures then alternated. Even after Jeremy's birth, and despite the care lavished upon her, she remained panic-stricken at the thought of unexpected crises arising in the large house they had bought. These crises tended to arise in anticipation of visits from friends and relatives – a paradox given that they had bought a large house precisely in order to receive visitors. She never stopped worrying about herself and much else. She worried about the size of her son's head and that maybe his problems were hereditary, a result of family illnesses like those of her father and his relatives. If only Jeremy's father could be with them a bit more, she protested: 'Would you believe that on New Year's Day, Jeremy's father was in Japan and Daddy, Mummy and I were in the living room waiting for his phone call. At midnight, on the dot, Jeremy got up and went over to his grandfather calling him Daddy. Do you think he misses his father too much and that this is the main problem?' I certainly thought he missed his father very much. I also thought that a fantasy of incestuous descent hovered over this family, with poorly resolved oedipal problems. Later, when Jeremy's analysis was well under way, his mother suddenly requested an urgent appointment. Her mother-in-law, Jeremy's paternal grandmother, had made appointments to have her grandson examined by a neurologist, a neuro-psychiatrist and a neuro-biologist, one after the other. 'She has been alone ever since her husband died after a long illness – leukaemia', she explained about her mother-in-law. 'She thought that Jeremy might be seriously ill given that both his grandfathers had been very sick.' And she added: 'If only he had been a girl!' I advised her not to let her mother-in-law trample on her relations with her son like this. 'Wasn't she satisfied with the progress we were making?' I insisted on the 'we'.

I should like to pause here to reflect upon a few points. First, her fantasy of Jeremy being a girl is inscribed in a general reversion of signs, so common in schizo-paranoid formations: proximity and confusion between birth and death, between grandparents and children, between male and female, warmth and coldness, love and hate and so on. The autistic position paralyses or attenuates these reversions and confusions. It may also dislocate them to motor or other body–peripheral experiences. For instance, an autistic child might touch only with fingertips instead of grasping and holding, or walk on tiptoe instead of stamping. Second, 'being a girl' is a particular fantasy described by Fenichel in his seminal paper on the equation between girl and phallus (1949). If we follow a metapsychological approach, Jeremy's dramatic and funny way of walking and waving his arms, which makes me think of a bird, can be understood as obeying a multiple determination. It corresponds to an over-cathexis of experiences of falling apart, in an attempt to hold oneself together, and it is his expression both of the experience of being a phallus to his mother and of the fantasy shared by both parents that he could have been a girl. In his paper on Schreber's 'Memoirs', Freud pointed out this phenomenon of sign reversal and also that 'bird' may stand for 'girl'. I should like to emphasize, from a conceptual point of view, that the subject's 'perceptual background', depicted by Haag and by poets like Henry Michaux as a 'wavy backdrop' (according to our translation) includes a transgenerational dimension, so that any signifier or group of signifiers along the trans-generational chain may be inscribed on the perceptual, sensorial, motor and psychic apparatus of the subject. 'Father', 'mother' or 'grandparents' may be represented by bodily organs, functions or sensations, for instance. This approach to the concept of space implies that space is built on representations of time. Bodies are signifiers of temporal experiences: they are not only organisms but also compounds of identifications. There is no spatial representation in the mind without a simultaneous temporal representation. The first representations of time are representations of rhythm and imply space, just as the first representations of space imply expansion and hence time.

Autism and paranoia

I have tried to indicate how psychoanalytic treatment can be established with a child who, threatened by his own and his family's disturbance, has retreated into autism as a means of self-protection. It would be intriguing to ask Meltzer, Tustin or Haag about the histories of the families whose children they have treated and the work they have undertaken in relation to these families. I do not believe that psychotic children can even begin to solve their problems, whatever the strength of the interpretative devices or talent deployed by their analysts, if concomitant work is not undertaken with their families. Jeremy never failed to participate in the conversations with his parents. When something did not seem clear to me in his mother's account, I asked him if he had understood. At first, he did not seem to hear me; then, after a while, he began to reply, with groans at first, and subsequently with nods. Later on in our analytic work together, he was able to stand up, turn towards us and reply with a firm 'yes', before going back to his toys. As Jeremy matured, his father gradually came to appointments more punctually. I advised them against getting a speech therapist for Jeremy, unless they considered that they all needed one. One day, I asked Jeremy what he felt when his father called him 'ma biche', just when he was getting to be a big, strong boy. Jeremy threw himself on to his father, smothering him with caresses. The father has since thought twice about the way he addresses his son. The conversations we all had together formed an integral part of Jeremy's analysis. Their aim was to let him hear something of the transgenerational background of his history in such a way as to permit him to begin to free himself from its burden. Jeremy's mother and father had always agreed to collaborate with me. They did not avoid my questions and were sincere and dignified, funny and active. This is not usually the case in such difficult analyses.

I should like to point out what I understand to be 'psychotic' in respect of Jeremy and his family. First, undoubtedly Jeremy showed autistic and schizophrenic symptoms when he first came to meet me. These symptoms were enough to make his teacher worry and to make a psychoanalyst confirm this concern. They implied heavy motor problems, an incapacity to speak or to take simple everyday measures, like dressing or cleaning himself. They were counterbalanced by a good quality of play and by the use he made of toys. Nevertheless, schizophrenic adults with mainly autistic symptoms can be very good at repetitive tasks even if they are complex, like solving mathematical equations or other kinds of abstract problems. However, they are unable to learn from experience, as Bion showed. Happily, this was not the case with Jeremy, even though he learned only very slowly at the beginning.

Second, in many ways his mother had and still has an ambivalent way of making contact with him. She holds and repudiates him almost simultaneously. She talks about him as a miracle and as an object of contempt. Nonetheless, she does clearly care for him: she has been and still is ready and eager to take advice and follow it, even when she does not quite agree.

Third, the quality of Jeremy's father's presence has not been entirely reassuring. He does not seem to take things seriously, being ready to make a joke out of everything whilst denying that he is doing so and claiming that he is indeed taking things seriously. Despite this, everyone in this family is striving to help Jeremy, although it is not quite clear what Jeremy signifies to his parents or his relatives. Jeremy himself will have to find his own way through many contradictions. He has been coping quite well and I believe that he will keep on doing so without running into major pitfalls, at least until adolescence, the discovery of erotic sexuality and actual separation from his parents. I must point out that even if the family shows certain signs of psychosis, its members are intelligent and sensitive and Jeremy's parents struggle to be good parents. Quite often we forget that psychotics, just like any of us, are more-or-less intelligent, more-or-less sensitive, that they possess the same human qualities or faults that contribute to forge our particular lives or destinies and that have given us a better or worse chance of dealing with life.

Tustin made a keen clinical remark when she pointed out that whenever she meets an autistic child, a depressed mother is not far away, and that whenever she meets a depressed mother there is almost certainly an absent father (Tustin, 1986). May I add that, quite often, this depression in the mother is not manifest and may be concealed by a playful and well-grounded appearance, just as the father's absence may be not merely a matter of fact but an absent way of being present. On each occasion, we should consider the entire family constellation, including the parents of both father and mother. We need to consider the symbolic, imaginary and realistic inscription of what a father, a mother and a child signify to one another. Experience shows that the development of a child suffering from early psychosis and the consequent diversification of his or her psychic apparatus alters the nature of transference. This induces a change in the countertransference. This development is always accompanied, if not preceded, by transformations of his or her family. A variety of treatments must be placed at the disposal of the families where such psychosis had appeared in order for these processes to take place. In Jeremy's case, it gradually became possible to direct his parents toward a family consultation in such a way as to disentangle the boy's from his parents' complications. Afterwards we offered an individual psychoanalysis for the mother. She strongly resisted this approach and, despite our multiple precautions, ultimately broke off her analysis.

Sessions with Jeremy

Jeremy provided constant reassurance against his dangerous impulses. The quality of his play never stopped evolving, even though my direct interventions during this period were infrequent and largely aimed at bringing conversation into being. His totems were always a great solace to me. Other children build them in plasticene or by drawing circles one on top of the other. As mentioned, Freud in 'Totem and taboo' suggests that totems express the paranoid elements of mourning, which implies at least some attempt at organizing the experience of loss. Our clinical experience shows that schizophrenic patients may go through autistic mourning with fantasies of keeping one or several corpses embalmed in the unconscious. For a long time, Jeremy's play obeyed a strict repetition compulsion: he made a pile of toys then blew them up. The origins of the explosions might vary, but once the pile was scattered all over the room, he would gather them up and rebuild the pile. I would help him collect them, express my sorrow about the explosions and try to link the violence to other violent scenes, words or feelings that his parents had told me about. Sometimes Jeremy took a toy and put it under water. From the way he held it, like bathing a baby, I told him that he was looking after it, trying to heal it. He seemed to accept this. Gradually the explosions became fights between one or more characters.

I took the gorilla family as an example and stated very seriously that gorillas don't fight, but work things out and, in some way, talk to one another. Two scenes at least were created in this way: one where we played, the other where our characters – I should say our objects – met each other. Jeremy's characters met in violent combat, accompanied by all sorts of explosive noises and shouts, whereas mine reflected and commented on these battles. I thus tried to create an additional space within that of the session. Jeremy's destructive projective identifications were then directed into the game. When he decided to attack me, he would attack daddy gorilla, mummy gorilla, gorilla children, or all of them. We then talked about it and he seemed quite interested. Very rarely did he attack me physically and, when he did, I took him in my arms to contain him.

Sessions with Jeremy were often exhausting for me. At the end of one, I heard Jeremy say distinctly that the animals were very tired, and that they were now going to sleep in the warmth until the next session. Not long afterwards, Jeremy came to his session sick and downcast. For some time now, he had made the dinosaur family his favourite toy characters. There was a daddy-saur, a mummy-saur and a little baby-saur who was still half in the egg. The solidity of these toys allowed them to resist Jeremy's numerous attacks, especially upon the baby-saur, which he banged regularly against the wall or on the ground, and then trampled. I intervened to tell Jeremy that perhaps he found this baby who could not manage to get born irritating and he wanted to help him come out of his shell. Another time, I suggested that he felt annoyed by all those babies who had not been born before him and that he wanted them to be dead for good, instead of being kept alive in his mother's heart. On yet another occasion, I suggested that he really wanted to kill all the babies that his mother was not going to have anymore, and that when he banged his head against the wall, he was hurting himself in order to feel alive, because all the babies his mother had lost made him very sad and made him think that he too might have died. After I said this, the daddy-saur was made to leave the scene and the mummy-saur turned toward her baby and said, 'Be careful or I am going to crush the peanuts out of you!' We were both astonished at this expression, which made Jeremy laugh about what he had just made the mommy-saur say. The signifier 'peanuts' implies the notion of 'pee', and, of course, the corresponding organ. We talked about that. But also the gorilla couple wondered what it meant, on the one hand to crush the peanuts out of someone, and on the other, for a mother to threaten her baby like that. The gorilla children asked their parents if a mother could want to kill her child or if a child could get the impression that his mother wants to kill him. The mother gorilla said that if the daddy-saur went away much too often and for too long, the mummy-saur could become so sad that she thought she and her little one were going to die. The daddy gorilla added that children were often sad at being left alone with their mother, and that children often worried about their mummy and daddy. They sometimes even wondered if their father might not be dead when he was away travelling. Jeremy attended to all this with growing curiosity. He then asked me if he could play with the toys I was using and I let him do so. He laid the daddy gorilla on top of the mummy gorilla. I said that all our previous conversation had been very interesting but that I wondered if the main thing he wanted to know was what his parents did together in their bed at night when his father came back from a trip. Jeremy answered me in an uncertain voice, but it was comprehensible all the same: 'Not at all, not in the least. What I want to know is how babies are made.'

An adult patient of mine, a man with an important political career but whose paranoia is unresolved, considers it a psychoanalytical and medical delusion to believe that babies are born from a couple. He thinks that babies are born out of themselves, father and mother serving as very temporary shelters only. I think that at that particular moment in the session, Jeremy emerged from his paranoia just enough to enter into a problematic yet definite oedipal situation. Piera Castoriadis-Aulagnier has shown that the subject in a paranoid position organizes two dyads, but never makes a triangle out of them (1975). The paranoid subject superimposes father–child or mother–child couples, but can only conceive of hate between father and mother, both of whom eventually turn their hatred on to the child in order to acquire an illusion of loving each other. The impossibility of inscribing the name of the father results in soul murder, as described by Schreber during his paranoid episode. My last intervention in the session also showed me how, through my gorillas, I had become for Jeremy a continent for a non-dangerous, father–mother relationship and for a primal scene. Henceforth Jeremy could start to simply be a little boy who was curious about life.

Jeremy later joined a group of children benefiting from group psychoanalytic psychotherapy, whilst continuing his analysis with me. When he arrived for his first group session with my colleague, he glued his back to the wall. I came to the conclusion that he was turning this into a seductive manoeuvre. Anthony Perkins' image suddenly popped into my mind, as did his specific place in the history of cinema, as the actor in Hitchcock's *Psycho*. The murder of the mother or identification with the murdered mother returns incessantly in the analysis of psychotics both adult and child, as I have indicated elsewhere (Prado de Oliveira, 1997).

Five years have now gone by and Jeremy is still pursuing his analytic treatment. Recently, he built a vessel out of plasticene. He called it 'the strange vessel of foreigners who go to discover new worlds'. He says it is 'a very bizarre vessel', but still finds it 'quite beautiful'. All our animals visited this vessel and it seemed a kind of Noah's ark. Jeremy's father recently went on a long professional journey that took him from India to Mexico. He must have told his son stories. Jeremy has also asked me about my country of origin. It is always interesting to work through this material on a transferential and countertransferential level. The scenes of violence have undergone many transformations and these have had the effect of attenuating his own violence, allowing it to be sublimated. For this child, it is no longer a question of violently dismantling his perceptions, feelings or body parts, nor is it a question of enduring the unmanageable violence of projective identification or the violence of his family history. It is, more mundanely speaking, the violence that hunters perpetrate on animals or, as Jeremy puts it, that all hunters on the planet perpetrate on all animals on the planet. In other words, the violence that human beings have always inflicted on nature and nature on them. Jeremy has pointed out to me that human beings may be a threat to the planet and to themselves. He is very funny when, with a scholarly air, he tells me about ecological films he has seen. Man must protect himself from the inhuman within: this is what Jeremy's autism was all about and this is where it relates to our own. Man as a wolf to man is what Jeremy's paranoia was about, and so it merges with our own. Andron paranoia: the condition of human paranoia is common to all of us, as is a corresponding withdrawal into autism, with which we protect ourselves from ourselves. This is where we began.

Acknowledgements

Translated by Lyn Cole. I am grateful to Murray Jackson and Paul Williams for their comments on an early draft of this chapter. Paula Barkay reviewed it afterwards and I thank her for that. Simone Bateman carefully re-read and worked on all subsequent drafts.

References

Bleuler E (1911) Dementia Praecox oder Gruppe der Schizophrenien. Leipzig and Vienna: F Deuticke.

Castoriadis-Aulagnier P (1975) La Violence de l'interprétation: du pictogramme à l'enconcé. Paris: Presses Universitaires de France.

Deleuze G (1969) La Logique du Sens. Paris: Minuit.

Fenichel O (1949) The symbolic equation: girl = phallus. Psychoanalytic Quarterly 18: 303–23.

Freud S (1911) Psycho-analytic notes on an autobiographical account of a case of paranoia (dementia paranoides). Standard Edition. London: Hogarth, pp. 63–6 and 35–6.

Freud S (1912) Totem and taboo. Standard Edition. London: Hogarth, p. 53.

Freud S (1914) On narcissism: an introduction. Standard Edition. London: Hogarth, pp. 90–1.

Freud S (1915) Mourning and melancholia. Standard Edition. London: Hogarth, p. 249.

Freud S (1921) Introduction to J Varendock's 'The Psychology of Dreams'. Standard Edition. London: Hogarth, pp. 271-2.

Haag G (1984) Autisme infantile précoce et phénomènes autistiques. Reflections psychanalytiques. Paris, Psychiatrie de l'Enfant 27(2): 293–354.

Haag G (1991), Nature de quelques identifications dans l'image du corps. Hypotheses. Journal de Psychanalyse de l'Enfant 10: 73–92.

Haag G, Tordjman S, Duprat A, Clément M-C, Cukierman A, Druon C, Jardin F, Maufras du Chatelleir A, Tricaud J, Urwand S (1995) Grille de réperage clinique des étapes évolutives de l'autisme infantile traité Paris. Psychiatrie de l'Enfant 38(2): pp. 495–517.

Jackson M, Williams P (1994) Unimaginable Storms: a Search for Meaning in Psychosis. London: Karnac Books.

Kanner L (1943a) Child psychiatry, mental deficiency. American Journal of Psychiatry 99: 608–10.

Kanner L (1943b) Exoneration and the feebleminded. American Journal of Psychiatry 99: 17–22.

Kanner L (1943c) Autistic disturbance of affective contact. Nervous Child 2: 217–50.

Kanner L (1944) Early Infantile Autism. The Journal of Pediatrics 25.

Meltzer D (1975) Explorations in Autism. A Psychoanalytical Study. Strath Tay: Clunie Press. French translation: Explorations dans le monde de l'autisme. Paris: Payot.

Perelberg RJ (1998) 'The interplay between identification and identity in the analysis of a violent young man: issues of technique', presented at the Société Psychanalytique de Paris, June. Forthcoming International Journal of Psycho-Analysis.

Prado de Oliveira LE (1995) Etre seul avec un mort: solitude et identification narcissique. Dialogue 129: 69–79.

Prado de Oliveira LE (1996) Schreber et la paranoia: le meurtre d'âme. Paris: L'Harmattan.

Prado de Oliveira LE (1997) Freud et Schreber, les sources écrites du délire entre psychose et culture. Toulouse: Eres.

Tustin F (1986) Autistic Barriers in Neurotic Patients. London: Karnac Books.

CHAPTER 9

Psychotic addiction to video games

DAVID ROSENFELD

Introduction

The term 'addiction', from the Latin *addictus,* means 'slave of his debts'. We speak metaphorically of addictive behaviour when referring to a strong dependence on something; for example, a drug. Sometimes, substance addiction is substituted by addiction to an activity. In this chapter, which illustrates the case of Lorenzo who is addicted to video games and computers, I shall present theoretical hypotheses concerning these types of addiction, and their treatment.

First contact

Lorenzo's mother's first contact with me was over the phone: we arranged a meeting and when I asked her if her son would attend she explained that Lorenzo, 17, had been hospitalized in a psychiatric clinic following an episode of violence. 'They have diagnosed schizophrenia', she specified. She wanted to know whether the father should also come, and I said yes, and added that I would prefer to see Lorenzo, too, at the first interview. I met them in my office. They sat facing me: the boy to my left, the father further back, a little distant, to my right and the mother in between them. She began to tell me Lorenzo's history: he had a lot of problems in his relations with people; behavioural problems, he was very violent and, she added, 'We took him out of the hospital a month ago, because we wanted to change the treatment and the doctor.'

Lorenzo was a 17-year-old young man, of medium height and slim but athletic build and with dark brown hair. He walked in a rather strange manner. It was only after beginning treatment that I realized that he sometimes entered my office on tiptoes, which accounted for the strange gait. Lorenzo's eyes were constantly shifting and fluctuating. I think that he was tense and hyperkinetic, perhaps due to the psychiatric medication he was receiving. The mother said: 'Lorenzo has had communication problems since he was 12 or 13 years old. He has almost no friends, but relates quite well with his two sisters who are two and four years younger than him. He had to repeat one year at school because he has problems concentrating on his studies. These problems stem from playing video games day and night for the whole year.' The father, who was not very communicative, said, 'Lorenzo gets so involved in these games it is impossible to get him to stop'. They explained that Lorenzo chose very violent games, with characters that attack and beat each other: the games are full of blows, murders and karate fights. I asked them why he was hospitalized, and the father said, 'Yes, yes, I authorized the hospitalization because one night when I tried to make him stop, he broke all the furniture in the house.' The mother added: 'In the evening we had violent quarrels; he would break the windows, pound on the doors and closets. Once, in a video game arcade, Lorenzo could not beat a video character that was attacking him and there was no way they could drag him from the screen. Finally he broke the machine and the arcade's window, and we had to restrain him with the help of other people. The owners of the shop wanted to call the police.' The father added: 'A boy with so many learning problems and such violence is incurable: it must be genetic.' I think that the father, in front of his son and on the first interview, was conveying a sense of his hopelessness. As we shall see, in the course of the treatment the mother did her best to help her son, to escort him to his sessions, to take him to school and so on.

I tried to talk to the boy, but he could not fix his gaze on anything. He reminded me of a frightened, terrified child – the kind of picture we can sometimes observe in babies during their first year of life. I asked him what goes on in the video games, what he feels and if they arouse him. The patient became enraged, stood up and screamed at me: 'This psycho-analyst is crazy! Look what he's telling me, he's talking about sex, he's mad, mad!' My intervention provoked this reaction: the fact that the patient stood up and reacted so violently against me suggested to me some sort of differential diagnosis. I asked him what he could tell me about his hospitalization, and he answered: 'I'm angry at you, I don't trust you at all! You are mad!' At that point I remembered that it is very common for psychotic patients to undertake powerful projective identification of their madness into the therapist and it drives them crazy to believe that when he speaks, the therapist is returning to them their own madness. It is their own madness, projected on the mind of the therapist, that creates the anxiety. Lorenzo told me one version of his hospitalization: 'I was playing in a video games arcade, and they wanted to make me leave. I screamed because they had no right to make me go. I hadn't finished playing. I hadn't won or lost. And then they took me out of there, they took me to the clinic and they didn't let me play any more.' I asked again if they hadn't let him play again, and Lorenzo answered: 'The psychiatrists confiscated the video game machine I have at home, and they forbade me to go near any video game.' The parents explained that this was a strict order from the psychiatrist. After a few months of treatment, it transpired that the patient remembered that one of the psychiatrists went to his home accompanied by a legal official, and, just so that there would be no doubts about how serious they were about the prohibition, they wrote a notarized document in which it was stated that all video games and video cassettes were to be confiscated.

From then on, I realized that all the characters of Lorenzo's inner world were present on the screen, but they were projected on an outside stage where he could murder them, or they could pursue him. When he heard that I was not going to forbid him to play with his video games and that moreover, I wanted to play with him to understand him better, Lorenzo stopped looking angry, while his parents asked him if he accepted me as his doctor. I told him that I was looking forward to treating him and that I would do my utmost to help him feel better in a relatively short time. I also told him we would be talking together, that I would gradually explain to him what was the matter with him, and that when he got a little better, we would go together to a video games arcade. These were apparently the key words to enter the patient's private world, because he said: 'This doctor is mad, but I accept his treatment because at least he promises to go to the video games with me.' After a week of daily interviews, I considered that he did not need to be hospitalized for a second time, and we started working with my team, where a psychiatrist is in charge of the medication and a psychologist takes care of emergencies when I am temporarily absent. All the team members are also psychoanalysts. Lorenzo's family lives in a town a few hours drive from Buenos Aires, so that we arranged a schedule for sessions, and they decided they would stay at Lorenzo's grandmother's, who lives close to my office, when they had to be in Buenos Aires. Lorenzo stayed at his grandmother's house for the first four months of treatment, and had four sessions each week.

During the first months, he constantly called me on the phone, screaming and wailing. When he returned to school, four months into his treatment, he often called full of anguish, before leaving home to go to the high school. Three years later, the patient still calls now and then to convey his anxieties, but much less often. After four months I decided that Lorenzo was able to go back to school. This was a personal challenge. I acted in an opposite manner to his father. His father told him repeatedly that he would never be cured and that his problem was genetic. As

Lorenzo's treatment proceeded over the years, I gradually discovered how, in his quest for physical feelings and bodily sensations, Lorenzo was ensnared in the lights, the colours and the sounds of video games. I noticed that he performed repetitive movements with his body, could not focus his eyes, gyrated as he walked, ritually tapped his heels when he came into my office on tiptoes or washed his hands at the beginning of sessions. In other words: we discovered in Lorenzo primitive experiences, obsessive mechanisms and movements similar to autistic enclaves or encapsulations from early childhood, which I thought related to his mother's severe depression before his birth.

The importance of teamwork – the multiple support system

The treatment was approached as the work of a team, not only that of a psychoanalyst. As I customarily do, I saw the patient with the psychiatrist and clinical psychologist. The psychiatrist is in charge of medication and family sessions. It is important for me to make my scientific-clinical position explicit – that it is necessary, when treating psychotic or severely regressed patients, to treat the family at the same time. We consider that the patient is a spokesman for the family group and that it is important to detect directly, in family sessions (Correale, 1994; Pichon-Riviere, 1959; Ferro, 1996) and to interpret paradoxical double-bind messages and contradictory orders and their psychogenic effects. The psychiatrist also handles emergencies in case I am out of the city over the weekend. The psychologist intervened when the patient had to be seen at home, and during my summer holiday visited him at home and saw him in his office. This team had regular meetings and frequent communication. When I need to arrange for hospitalization of a patient in a psychiatric clinic I usually include a psychologist or resident in the team, who functions as a qualified assistant or as a representative of the team. He or she spends about two hours with the patient each afternoon and goes out with him when he can for a while. When the patient is better this person accompanies him to my office for sessions.

Our criterion for hospitalization of a patient is the need to contain his psychotic part 24 hours a day. At the same time, we also attempt to recover fragmented aspects of the patient through the reports that we receive from the staff and the medical residents of the clinic or hospital.

Violence and delusions

I shall now relate some instances of violence with delusions and a psychotic transference, during the first year of treatment. Very often Lorenzo began sessions with obsessive rituals like bringing his feet together, tapping his heels and entering the room with his right foot, jumping twice, washing his hands before entering, walking to and fro across my office for a few minutes or pirouetting while he talks. From the first session these movements and gyrations reminded me of what one sees in autistic children, which made me think of encapsulated autistic aspects. Verbal violence was continuous at the beginning of sessions especially because, according to him, the therapist might harm him. He also displayed verbal violence at home and he sometimes said that he did not want to come to his session. His mother often helped to make him change his mind and thought him to the office; she escorted him to every session.

Through Lorenzo I began to get acquainted with the characters and features of the video games that consumed him. In fact, it was clinically vital that I learned what happened to the patient while he played, so I decided to go with him to a video game arcade and get to know the characters he played with, and those he identified with me and with the psychiatrist on my team. The patient projected my attributes on to some of these characters. He wanted to play a game called Street Killer, and another one called Street Fighter, both of which are extremely violent: you have to kill the characters with a sword, cut their throats or hit them very aggressively. When he played with me, Lorenzo won most of the time and he experienced his triumph omnipotently. But after winning at the games he came to his session terrified because he had won, as though he had killed me and cut my throat. The same theme was projected on to many external objects; he was afraid of revenge, of being hounded by a schoolmate or by someone in the street and he was even afraid that I would turn into someone dangerous who would smash his head in and drive him crazy. Sometimes he saw me as dangerous during a session, at other times it was a part of me projected on to the outside world that could hurt him. He confused people on the television screen with real, external people, and this occurred in relation to me. This was a dramatic example of a symbolic equation. The terror he felt about what I could do to him after he beat me at the video games generated in Lorenzo delusional fantasies that were often extremely difficult to manage in transference. In these cases, psychoanalytical technique required relating the transference delusional fears to the fact that he thought he had killed me when I was representing one of the characters in a video game. My countertransference was hard to convey in just a few words, especially in view of the long hours when I was in receipt of his anger and tantrums whenever the game failed to respond to his wishes, aside from the difficulty I had in entering the unknown (to me) world of video games and its characters with mysterious names. It was an enormous exercise in containment and holding. I was also obliged to learn the characteristics and names of all the video characters. The important task was to bring what was formerly projected into the inanimate object, the screen of the video game or the computer, into the transferential relation with the therapist, and to play it out. My most important task was to drive him away from the screen and to connect him with the real, living human being that I am. It was often possible to see Lorenzo's thoughts becoming concrete: there is then no difference between the symbol and the symbolized. The word 'demolish' reflects his fear of what I would do to him during our session *and* exactly what he did to the character in the video game: he demolishes his head with a sword or a karate blow.

A clinical vignette: first year of treatment

One day we played a particularly vicious video game, where the characters fight with laser beams. One week later, the patient began to be afraid of persecution. He thought that his schoolmates would hurt him and he went into frank delusion, afraid that they would attack him with a laser ray. He refused to go out into the street unless he could wear a protective suit against laser beams. His mother tried to calm him down, and made him an outfit of aluminium foil. Lorenzo said he felt protected against the laser beams. This delusion amplified and developed to the point where for a few days Lorenzo did not go to school at all. The psychiatrist increased and modified the antipsychotic medication. We considered hospitalization, but we decided to wait for a week because I was interested in seeing the transferential origin that has triggered the delusion (this is the way I try to reason as a psychoanalyst). He came to sessions every day and he even had two sessions on one day, including at the weekend. Lorenzo came dressed in his protective outfit and he said he wanted to play again the game we played last time. I accepted with reluctance, but also with a good deal of curiosity. After the second session that day, and he had taken off the aluminium suit, we played the laser beam video. Lorenzo won the first time and I won the second game and when we were about to start a third round, he told me: 'Dr Rosenfeld, when you win, you can be transformed and become other characters, so even if I kill you now, you are still alive and have turned into another character.' I am transformed into someone projected in multiple and varied characters, and even if he kills me, I am still dangerous, I go on living through the other characters in the video game. I am a mutating object that becomes other objects and they still pursue him with laser beams. This is a symbolic equation and a disorder of perception and of differentiation of external from internal reality. It is only at that point, after I became aware of this feature of the video game, that I could decipher and work psychoanalytically on the origin of his delusion of being attacked with laser beams. I had metamorphosed and fragmented into his multiple schoolmates and, from there, I was attacking him with laser beams. This description that I was resuscitated and was becoming many other characters was the key, the code-breaker, the rosetta stone, which allowed me access to the delusion in which the different and multiple characters of real life had become fragmented aspects of Rosenfeld, Lorenzo's analyst. We departed from the screen and entered real life. On this basis I interpreted that, when I won at the game, my character became a mutant and he was every other character in the video game. But since the patient confused real life with fantasy, Rosenfeld becomes a character that becomes fragmented and may become any one of his schoolmates who harasses him. The patient thinks that I pursued him not only through the characters on the screen but also through hundreds of people in the real world. His need for the aluminium outfit is a piece of psychotic concretization that, when apparent in the transference, illustrates how the patient displaces on the stage of the real outside world his feelings and his experiences with his psychoanalyst. After interpreting in the transference the origin of the delusion, and after intense work, I was able to resolve what appeared to be a clinical psychosis with delusional episodes. I found the work of Boyer (1983, 1990, 1994, 1999) very useful as a guide for the management of my countertransference. After overcoming this episode, the patient went back to school. One month later, Lorenzo wanted to try a three-dimensional (3D) virtual reality video game. The psychiatrist and I went with him and we decided to play a game that represented an aeroplane battle. While playing, the patient suffered a panic attack when he saw the objects hurling towards him, overwhelmed as he was by the 3D effect. I believe that at that point he felt more acutely than ever before his fear of the vengeful persecution that could attack his mind. In a frenzy of panic, he ran out of the place and refused to play with 3D games again. This event was crucial because with that game, the patient discovered that a two dimensional plane is not the same as a space with depth and a third dimension. This coincided with his discovery that Rosenfeld's live image is not the same as the image of the characters and objects on a flat television screen. I think his encapsulated autistic aspects experienced a kind of evolution from a two-dimensional to a three-dimensional perception of space.

This experience with the third dimension in the new video game indicated a structural change in Lorenzo's mind: it was no longer a flat screen. We were beginning to leave the two-dimensional plane and to get into the real person. I remember that after this game we went to meet with the psychiatrist. We tried to calm Lorenzo's panic in a nearby coffee shop where we had tea, and only after that did we ask him to explain to us in greater detail what he had felt when the aeroplanes were rushing towards him in the third dimension. During one of his subsequent sessions the patient expressed his fear of failing two of the courses at school, and I interpreted that he believed that there was an internal object within his own self that attacked him, abused him or told him that if he failed a course or a test, it was because he was sick. Then, I tried to carry this into the transference and I told him that he often experienced the same with me. I asked him to read to me the essay he had written for his French class: it was the story, which he had created on his own, of a tourist who goes to Paris, and it was very well written. I think he needed me to return to him his valuable, healthy aspects, which he evacuated and deposited in me. I was aware of this mechanism, so I interpreted first the mechanism of projection and only then did I convey to him my astonishment at the essay, which had made me think that he might have copied it.

For a period of time Lorenzo continued to be addicted to video games and to their violence. His involvement with some of the characters in the video-game looked like a 'folie-à-deux', as described by Nicolo (1995). Once, while watching a musical on TV with his parents and siblings, a scene of violence appeared and the patient got up and screamed 'we must stop this fight', bounced on the TV set and broke the screen with his head. This is perhaps the most significant and dramatic example of how he wanted to stop the fights that went on inside his mind among his internal objects, and at the same time, literally stop the part that was projected on the TV screen. I do not think I could have found a better example of a symbolic equation, where the mind is equated to the inanimate object, in this case, the TV set. Segal (1994) has made useful contributions regarding the interplay of fantasy and reality through her distinction between symbol and symbolic equation (in which fantasy and reality are combined). Segal postulates that early processes of symbolic development and their pathological variables are analysable if one understands the patient–analyst relationship, as it offers the chance to explore and analyse the influence of fantasy and reality on the patient's perception of and behaviour toward the analyst. These ideas offered by Segal are extremely important for clinical work and for technique, because sometimes the analyst must decode and descript who he himself is as a psychoanalyst – an individual, a fantasy, or a symbolic equation. Segal's ideas have allowed me to revise my study and understanding of countertransference.

Nintendo versus Sega – collaboration and transition

Nintendos versus Sega

As part of the treatment we used to go to a video games arcade where I could analyse and study the characters in his favourite games. I used the hour of play as if it had been the analysis of a child, but with modern-day toys – the video games. I got to know the characters and I penetrated into his inner world. Lorenzo was given back his small video game, which had been confiscated on his previous therapist's recommendation, and a new issue came up: Sega games and Nintendo games are not compatible. The patient spoke about the problems he had when he tried to connect the games to the device he had at home. I interpreted about the problems he had to 'connect', to connect with me, and the difficulty there was in finding one system through which we could have a dialogue, with two different minds, just like Sega and Nintendo.

Collaboration and transition

During a session, Lorenzo related that he had been playing with a video game, but this was the first time the patient had chosen a game with no beheadings, no karate blows, no sabres and no sword slashes. He said he chose this game 'because there is a monkey who has to jump over a river to save his life, and the monkey finds a giant frog, as large as the desk in this office. The frog tells the monkey to get on her back, and they jump to the other riverbank. Then another animal comes along, who gives the monkey a banana to eat.' The patient said that he had gone to bed early, but had thought about this game for hours. I interpreted that this was the first time that he played a game where there is collaboration and help instead of fights, blows and murders. 'In the game you selected, they get together to help someone', and I added, 'what you saw in the game is like what happens with me in the session. I support you, like the frog; I help you jump and cross the river. I carry you on my back and I give you mental food, which in your game is the banana.' In that session we had good communication, so much so that at one point he lay on the couch as if it were a large frog that supported him. This was the first time he had used the couch. Previously he had stood or walked around the office. During the following sessions, Lorenzo again brought up the frog and comments on my interpretations and on how his therapist and the couch give him support. He seldom showed good humour but one day the patient started joking, laughing and mimicking the monkey, saying 'I am a monkey and you are a frog'.

Periodically, the father and mother would meet with the psychiatrist (Martini, 1995; Cancrini and Pelli, 1995). The patient said that these interviews reminded him of the game with the monkey and the frog. I explained that this was because we are the two people who helped him – the psychiatrist and me. 'You have never seen two people getting together to help you. Mostly, you speak of arguments and quarrels.' At that point the patient remembered: 'On my birthday, my mother cooked Chinese food in a big pan, and just before cutting the cake my mother and father started insulting each other because she said he didn't help her clean up, or pay for my treatment, or make dinner for my birthday. They ended up throwing the pan at each other's heads.' I interpreted: 'You realize that any boy can go crazy with fights like this, especially if it's his birthday.' I think that the real outer world has an impact and intensifies the disorder in Lorenzo's mind. Lorenzo survived his parents' fights by projecting them on to the video games' screen, and thus dislodges from his mind things that happen with real objects: he empties his head of the real events in his house. In my view, the level of violence my patient experienced at home was high and very disturbing for him. Therefore, I indicated to the parents that they needed to have regular interviews with the psychiatrist, which turned out to be useful because the family decided to stay in town for a few days (Izzo, 2000). This was the first time the patient went on an outing with his father, who took him to a movie and for a stroll around the city.

Lorenzo is able to express hatred and anger

Lorenzo began to fear that he would be hospitalized again, and he remembered the first time this happened, at Christmas time. 'Those who sent me to the hospital must have been Jews or atheists, because they didn't care', he said. Around that time, Lorenzo related things that his father had said that bewildered him (I must admit I felt bewildered too): 'My father says that if I ever get married I'll have to go through what he is going through – he is about to separate from my mother.' Lorenzo was jumping and running all over my office as he shoutsed 'Why the heck did he have me, if now he is not interested in this marriage. I could kill him, I could kill him, I could kill him!' I interpreted that he does this in the video games: he projects the hate he feels for his father on to the characters on the screen. I underscored that this is the first time he is capable of shouting his hatred for his father, shouting that he wants to kill him. 'Before, all this was secret, and it was evacuated from your mind into the TV screen. It is very important that you hate and have fantasies about killing, and this doesn't mean that you are really killing him.' Lorenzo continued to scream and run around the office, so I repeated the words, to make sure he heard them.

Collaboration

Several months later, just before I had to go out of town for ten days, Lorenzo appeared to be serene at the beginning of his session, and then said: 'Mother broke a transformer, and I don't know if it can be fixed; I don't know if the technician can make the right connections . . . I don't know if I will be able to catch up on the classes I missed at school, perhaps they will make me pass a test on the environment and health . . . I thought you would be upset because I was a little late today.' I commented that perhaps he is scared of replacements (a psychologist and a psychiatrist) who would be taking my place during my absence. Lorenzo asked himself if human connections can be replaced and be any good, and I interpret: 'You think your communication with me will break, and you don't know if what you called today a "broken transformer" can be fixed.' After remaining silent, he said he had rented some films that he planned to watch with his grandmother. I reminded him that there was a time when he only rented violent video games, full of monsters, in which there were no human beings.

Drawings, letters and dreams – beginning of symbolization

Phase of drawings

During this phase, Lorenzo asked me for a paper pad during our session and began to draw beautiful and willowy women. The men, on the other hand, were sketched in black, very schematically, and this led me to think that he was drawing something about his identity problems and his body image (partly masculine and partly feminine). It was curious to see how, over a few days, his functioning fluctuated between the psychotic and the neurotic parts of his personality. Lorenzo lived far from the city, so we sometimes concentrated four sessions close to the weekend. The week before I was due to go away, Lorenzo fantasized that he had an orifice between his anus and his testicles. A fantasy about the therapist's absence appeared as a hole in his body, or a void in his object relations, and on a different level it could represent an operation he had on his testicles when he was 11, and perhaps also the void left by his grandfather's death. Absence, emptiness, death, loss of masculinity are all mixed together or equated in the fantasy of the hole. Also, it may have represented a confused sexual identity, partly male and partly female (possibly because his mother had so often turned him into a part of her body and her mind). Volkan (1996, 1997) and Quinodoz (1989) state that in transsexual patients who have undergone surgery, it is most often the mother who, via her fantasy, determines the gender identity of her son. Volkan says that the perception the mother inculcates in her son is the core of the 'self infantile core' from which the future development of the self will evolve. 'His future gender identity confusion could be seen in the mother's fantasies about him, which she deposited into the child's evolving self-representation, where it remained partly psychotic.'

Phase of letters

The patient continued with panic and screaming crises, especially before going to school. While in this state he often called me on the phone. His terror and his violence increased towards the end of the school year: he bashed in the doors of his house, afraid he would fail and believed that his teachers and schoolmates were all his enemies. Over these months, the transference was characterized by his violence against me, with claims and accusations: 'Why doesn't he cure me? You want to hypnotize me!' This violence against me provoked intense countertransference feelings in me. But the technical handling of the countertransference was always useful. The violence is now with the human person and not with a non-human screen. Other changes were taking place that also deserved to be taken into account: instead of playing at killing through his video games characters, he began to write long letters that he then brought to the office.

The red ink letter

The patient brought a large, unruled sheet of green board, on which he has written in red ink the following list: 'People I must kill: schoolmates, who think I'm an idiot and make fun of me; Caroline, because of the eternal love disappointment; teachers who want me to fail; the teacher who gave me a low grade; kill the school for everything that's in it and the teachers who think I'm stupid. Kill couples and lovers because they show me what I will never have. Kill Rosenfeld for not being with me when I need him most and for abandoning me at the end of each session, and for setting a time limit to each session instead of being with me when I need him. I also want to kill him for taking money from my mother for each session I come to . . . The Brazilian soccer team for beating Argentina . . . My father, for making me lose all the illusions in my life and for talking to me coldly and sharply and telling me he will have me hospitalized and come and visit me once every six months.' He read to me: 'This Doctor Rosenfeld is a son of a bitch. All he does is debase my father in front of me and debase me in front of my father, he really wants to demolish me, and he pesters me about my masturbating and jerking off while I look at women on TV.' When he finished reading, he tore up the page. The patient was able to convey a message verbally, to read and be heard. This was the beginning of symbolization, and it was a great change from previous years when he spent his nights killing characters through violent video games. We saw the emergence of oedipal levels, mixed with pre-genital levels, but now the patient expressed them during the session in a limited space but no longer within the flat, two-dimensional screen of his video games.

Dreams

During the third year of treatment, Lorenzo began to remember his dreams and to bring them to our sessions. This phase was also characterized by greater eroticization, with sexual fantasies and more masturbation. At the beginning, the images in his dreams or in his imagination resemble those in his comics, where the women are drawn as exuberant, erotic and sensual creatures. I agree with Green (1977, 1992, 1996, 1997) that the sexual instinct is a vital drive for this sexual exacerbation, and it is worth noting that this happens at a time when pre-genital problems and primitive anxieties can be verbalized and interpreted. At times, the tremendous sexual arousal the patient felt was experienced as an instinct that was driving him mad. The inability to contain primitive anxieties and powerful arousal reflects the same problem, perhaps because they are both based in the self's mental space, which is sometimes not appropriate to contain instincts and anxieties (Freud, 1914). Affection and closeness triggered both his fear of not being a male and his fear of homosexuality.

The dream with 'L'

During the next session, he said that once again his father had told him that 'there are things that cannot be changed.' He added that his father and his schoolmates think he is 'weird' and somewhat crazy. I interpreted that perhaps he was confusing real people with the imaginary characters in his head that call him 'weird'. He continued to say that his sister screamed 'crazy' at him, and that he hit her. I decided to give him a second session on that day because I was afraid he might turn violent against his sisters. This is when we discovered that violence was his defence against sexual arousal. Lorenzo felt contained by me on this day and at the next session he related a dream: 'I see myself as a woman and I look for a name like mine, with an "L", like Lorenzo, and it is "Lenora". I don't know if I have a penis or not', he adds. I interpreted his fear of losing his sexual identity as a male; he feared that if he received affection or was taken care of by his therapist (who is a man) he will be homosexual, or become a woman. I added that he thinks that this is the only way he can be accepted, loved by me. Lorenzo believed that to be loved by his father, he has to be a woman, like his sisters, because they were his father's favourites. Lorenzo responded to the interpretation with a sexual comment: 'My schoolmate Carol arouses me.' And he went on to tell me that he was also aroused when he saw a couple who were students in his school kissing and necking on a motorcycle (cf. Resnik, 1994). At the end of the session he said that at his grandmother's there isn't the fighting that goes on at his parents' house; he would like to go to his grandmother's more frequently, so he could come more often to the sessions. I think we can see here how he was afraid that he will not be accepted as a male by a male therapist. Moreover, primitive lack of differentiation with his mother's female body emerged. He was scared of being close to his doctor, of discovering that he could feel affection for him, and this leads to dreams such as the above. This is a transferential recurrence of his history with his father.

Negative therapeutic reactions and insights

Negative therapeutic reactions

Negative therapeutic reactions (NTRs), as Freud (1923) describes them, appear after progress has been made during treatment, especially in neurotic patients. In Rosenfeld (1992), I describe certain varieties of NTRs, amongst them a silent variety in severely disturbed or psychotic patients. In my experience with psychotic patients, I have noted that with the onset of perception of insight – simply with its onset – psychotic patients often violently attack the therapist, and I have developed a hypothesis that may explain this mechanism. The patient's perceptual apparatus, capable of insight, is emptied, evacuated, projected outside the patient, into the therapist. When the patient begins to have a first outline of an insight, an outline of a perception of who he is, he wants to attack his perception of himself. The next step consists in attacking his own perceptual apparatus, which has been evacuated and projected into the therapist, and he therefore attacks the body and mind of the therapist. When I say 'attacks' I am referring to real experiences in treatments of psychotic patients. This theory differs from Searles' theory on violence in schizophrenic patients (Searles, 1986). Lorenzo, our patient, after his moments of insight, of getting closer to the depressive position, begins to perceive who he was when he was psychotic, and who he is now. The so-called NTRs cannot always be explained by a theory of envy, which is extremely useful in other pathologies, as Klein has taught us (1975).

Some dreams related to insight

When the patient came to the next session he was in a hurry, but he was not scared. He remembered once again that his parents had had a fight at the dinner table, and ended up throwing pots at each other. Then he said he had a dream: 'I was with an adult, I must have been around 12 years old. The adult could have been an uncle or a grandfather. It was night, and we were going through a place with all kinds of gangs and criminals. A train arrived, which came from where my grandfather lives. My uncle and I had to fight against all of them.' (When he said 'them' he used the feminine pronoun, 'ellas', in Spanish.) In my countertransference, I thought that Them (ellas) could be the gangs as a feminine slip of the tongue, but it could also be a change of sex as in the video games' characters. At that time I thought that Lorenzo tried to survive his parents' real fights and screams by trying to project them and empty his mind of them, either in a video game or in a dream. The patient continued his narrative: 'Then I was with my uncle and I killed the woman, the big one, and I threw her on the railtrack: the blow as she landed on the rails killed her. Then I suggested killing the young one. Later an ugly woman came along, like a witch or a thin, bony, ugly nursemaid. She was with a young girl of my age who was just as evil as she was.' I asked him to explain why there were so many women, and exactly who was with whom, and he explained: 'By the look on their faces, I think they all wanted me to lose, they wanted to beat me, they defended themselves well, but there was a stalemate. I could do nothing to them, and they could do nothing to me. Then I realized I liked the young one.' A little overwhelmed by the confusion of characters, I asked him which young one he is talking about, and he answered: 'I see her with long blonde hair, partly straight but with some curls, white skinned; and then I thought that this girl was not worthwhile, but I still forced her to be with me that night. I wrapped my arm around her waist, and we went walking like we were a couple. Then, the adult in the dream changed into my grandfather and told me "now, we are all doing all right." My grandfather followed us and took care of us.'

Dr R: Was he protecting you from some danger?

Patient: I was just a 12-year-old kid, I wasn't ashamed if my grandpa took care of me.

Dr R: Perhaps I was the grandfather?

Patient: No, no. The grandfather was my grandfather. I miss him since he died. It would be wonderful to have a girlfriend like that and a grandfather. (His voice has changed dramatically as he says these words; he had never shown such emotion during his years of treatment.)

Dr R: Tell me about your grandfather.

Patient: I think I was 11. Oh yes, he loved me very much and I loved him too.

He then said that in his dream there was a restaurant where he went with his girlfriend, it was quite a simple and plain place, but they served good food. In the countertransference, I felt moved and remembered vividly an important scene from my childhood with my own dear grandfather. In my countertransference I was able to deduce that Lorenzo had felt moved when he talked about his grandfather whom he loved so dearly, and now he had found in his treatment a place where he felt good, a simple place, but with good and abundant food. 'In the end, we didn't go into the restaurant, grandfather took us someplace else because he had work to do', he says.

Dr R: This is the first dream where you recover your grandfather, who loved you so much. In your dream, he protects you from your fears, and you recover him, this character who was so important when you were a child, at a time when you feel protected by me from your nightmares and your inner monsters that pursue you within yourself.

The session ended in silence, which was unlike him, but I did feel that he was in the process of recovering his internal objects.

Phase of insight and infantile dependence

In another session, Lorenzo brought a letter, and read it to me:

> OK, doctor, I understand that during sessions I must answer for myself, and not through somebody else's mind . . . a) I feel many kinds of hatreds, but I wonder why all my hatreds must be directed towards you; b) Video games represent my mind; c) The rituals I perform are aimed at cleansing my hatreds; d) I am afraid that you will do something to me in retaliation for my hatred of you.

The next point in his letter is extremely important, and I quote it verbatim: 'The development of my mind depends on the video game, but only in part. I have the absolute right to attack you if you behave like an ass-hole.' We must remember that once he tried to illustrate how he wanted to attack me, which he called defending himself, and while he was pacing in my office he gripped my head and my neck from behind to show me what he would do to me. I admit I was scared. At that moment, I remembered a schizophrenic patient who once punched me in the face because, as he said, I looked like his father because of my glasses and moustache. But once I took hold of myself, it allowed me to decode his act and to under- stand that he does to me what he is continually afraid I will do to his mind. 'There is a video game I can never beat; when will I stop being driven to play it, unable to quit once I've started it? Will the video game in my brain never be erased?' These words that the patient had thought, spoken and written, are a sign that he has understood the interpretations that indicate that the characters fighting and killing each other in the video games, that fascinated him so much, were already within his mind since he was a little boy, his parents fought, slaughtering each other in a sadistic coitus, with him in between, in a terrifying mental video game. In the same letter, some fragments reflect his infantile aspects, in need of help, more clearly than ever before, when he wrote: 'I know a boy that, if you are any good, really needs you, because he leads a miserable life, he can't find peace within himself.' He went on to list other items, related to his masculine identity, which he brought to his sessions under different guises: 'I think I will remain short . . . I don't ejaculate any more . . . Is the physical male in me dead?' I admit that after the session, I felt surprised and moved when I reflected that this had been written by the same young boy who had been hospitalized in a psychiatric institution when I was first asked to treat him.

Theoretical conclusions

In my opinion an accurate perception of countertransference is primarily the result of a good psychoanalytic treatment of the therapist himself and is associated with responsible supervision of his work. If we take black-and-white photographs we shall end up with black-and-white pictures, and we might even say that colour does not exist. The same happens if we work without the full richness provided by the proper use of countertransference.

The setting or frame

The setting is a dialectic creation that takes place over a period of time. It is created by patient and therapist together. The setting consists in what is fixed or formal – the hours, the place or space, the fees – and in what is mobile, which is the dynamic aspect, the process that occurs within the setting. This is essentially a human relationship. We can say that this interpersonal or intrapersonal relationship is empathic and is an attempt to get to know about the unconscious, the inner world, its internal objects and the primitive transference that unfolds. In particular, it takes into account the countertransference in order to decode primitive levels of communication, which, in infancy, had no words available for their expression. Countertransference will be the most important tool for research in psychosis. The order, time of day and place is important as are messages that convey stability and order in the object relationship, rather than the chaos and disorder that are experienced as mental disorganization in the therapist's mind. In my regular work with patients hospitalized in hospitals or private psychiatric clinics, I always saw the patient at the same fixed hours. But at other moments in the process, especially in acute psychoses, the dynamic part of the process is more important, and in this case, the frame or setting is the creation of holding and of mental space in the psychoanalytic field (Anzieu, 1986; Boniamino, 1998; Painceira, 1997). Then, it is the analyst's interpretation and attitude as a person that is fundamental for creating the holding. Within the mental space of holding we include the team, which always shares the work. Here I refer to the psychiatrist and the psychologist on the team and I also include the hospital residents and assistants who have contact with the patient while he or she is hospitalized. In the case of Lorenzo I went to great lengths to protect the setting, despite the patient's difficulties and the daunting task facing the team. The team must be a unit that the patient experiences as adequate and holding. What is important is to be able to think psychoanalytically about the transference and the patient's inner world, as well as about the countertransference. No one can prevent me from thinking like a psychoanalyst, even when I am walking through the hospital with a patient, or going to a shopping mall and playing video games. Here, what is important is to create a mental space in common that is appropriate for holding and for psychoanalytic work. Even in a classical setting, which includes a couch, the psychoanalyst's existence can sometimes be denied. In my patient, Lorenzo, we see that not everything could be based on verbal or symbolic elements. It is the psychoanalyst who must decode and differentiate these distortions or different systems of communication.

The setting or frame is more than something passive, as Goldberg (1990) points out.

> The environmental provision of holding revealed to us by Winnicott involves much more than a passive state of empathy: indeed, the holding environment must sometimes be actively sought and created within the therapist, a process that may involve the therapist in a great deal of internal activity and struggle . . . [and] . . . not necessarily any external activity at all, but rather a certain internal activity or experimentation with internal mental states.

Lorenzo had several simultaneous defence systems that were used interchangeably and that were modified throughout the course of the treatment. Some of these are:

- powerful projective identification;
- symbolic equations;
- confusion, especially between the human and the inanimate;
- behaviour based on autistic manoeuvres or mechanisms.

Projective identification

The video-addicted patient emptied his mind in the imaginary space represented by the screen, and projected on to it the characters of his inner world; he was like a glove, which was turned inside out and emptied its content on to the screen. The characters in the video games – imaginary on the screen, but with some correspondence with persons from the patient's childhood – became real for him and pursued him with unforgiving vengefulness. The patient wielded an omnipotent power over these characters, through powerful obsessive mechanisms, but he feared they would treat him as he treated the characters in the games.

Symbolic equation

The real outer world is also projected on the video game's screen. To explain this type of functioning I use the theoretical model described by Segal (1994), which I find useful to explain the differences between a symbol and a symbolic equation. Segal insists on what I believe is crucial for our work with severely disturbed patients: the first symbolization processes, as well as the alterations or pathological distortions to which the symbol is submitted, can be analysed and understood because they surface in the patient–analyst relationship. This is where we analysts have the unique opportunity to analyse the influence of fantasy on reality, and how it supports the patient's perceptions. Our most important task is to understand how the patient distorts his perception of the analyst. 'In a concrete symbolism, the symbol is equated with what is symbolized. Concrete symbolism leads to misperception and false beliefs' (Segal, 1994).

Transference and interpretations

By emptying his mind through projective identification this patient elicits states of confusion. I postulate that Lorenzo could not relinquish his video games because he needed to evacuate into the outer world – a non-human world – the violence, hatred, murder and brutal sex that occupy his fantasies. Thus, until he does not succeed in killing the characters that pursue him and that he hates, he cannot abandon the video game or the screen. With regard to transference and technique, we use the concept of psychotic transference, also called delusion or regressive or primitive transference, to describe a type of transference that has extremely intense, primitive and undifferentiated emotional characteristics, based on part objects (Rosenfeld, 1980).

Autistic sensations

Quite often, patients induce autistic sensations in their own body, in order to create protective manoeuvres. Through bodily sensations or feelings they create what Tustin has called 'a world of sensations that envelops them and in which they live' (Tustin, 1990). This is a primitive survival system and a way of achieving an equally primitive concept of identity – a way to avoid disappearing. Autistic children usually touch objects in the office, or rub up against them. They may, for example, lick the windows or the furniture, or rub the curtains or the analyst's clothes with their arms and hands. They search for bodily sensations in order to create a protective shield. I found some drug-addicted patients who, as children, had some autistic features and who survived by creating their own world of sensations through drugs. In adolescents and adults the search for this type of feelings is pursued through increasingly stronger drugs in order to try to obtain powerful bodily sensations, which reflects how autistic children obtain these sensorial experiences through the body using bodily movements (Rosenfeld, 1994 and 2000). Autistic children use autistic manoeuvres in order to surround themselves with a world of sensory stimuli in order to protect themselves from all that is terrifying on the outside. This is a world of sensations created by their own body and these are experienced in a concrete way. The main purpose in using parts of the body in this way is to shut out threats of bodily attacks and, ultimately, annihilation. For them, any separation or absence is a tearing apart, and any absence is experienced as a hole. For example, with this patient, when I interrupted the treatment because of a trip, only then was he able to symbolize it in a fantasy. He expressed it by dreaming that he had a hole, a hollow, between his anus and his testicles. He expressed this separation and loss as a loss of a part of his body. Tustin (1990) says: 'Autistic patients are fearful, despite having this protective shell.'

We have described some behaviour of our patient, Lorenzo, which we also observe in the treatment of autistic children. One example is his coming into my office on tiptoe; to be precise, on the tips of his big toes. Another activity was his whirling around and around, which is typical of the repetitive movement of autistic children (Reid, 1997). Another was his repeated seeking of sensory stimuli by twisting his fingers and hands and rubbing his hands together vigorously. I think that the autistic manoeuvre most closely linked to his addiction to the video games and the computer was his autistic-like attempt to procure sensory stimuli through the bright lights and colours on the video screens, the loud noises of his games and the vibrations he felt in his body. This is another way to procure, as Tustin defines them, 'bodily sensations'. Autistic children, absorbed by and closed in by this sensory world, cannot use projection and therefore are unable to make contact with the outside by means of projective identification (Bion, 1984). Learning is held up and, of course, symbolization is arrested. The contribution of Ogden

(1994a, b) on the autistic-contiguous position is particularly important, theoretically and clinically. In this position, primitive sensory experiences provide the self with a sense of cohesion, an envelope for the skin. For Ogden, this is the starting point for the formation of a rudimentary structure of subjectivity and an incipient experience of an integrated self. This is still a non-symbolic area, a non-separation of self and object. Regarding the effects of television, video games and computers on the child's mind during the first stage of childhood, I should like to comment on some interesting issues described by Amati-Mehler (1987, 1992, 1998), regarding the influence of television and video games on children's mental processes. Amati Mehler begins by saying that 'parents and teachers have become increasingly interested as well as alarmed vis-à-vis the invasion of games such a video games'. Certainly, the unsettling issue of the 'technological child', symbolized at a symposium by a cartoon representing a child with a cap (computer) on his head, proposes an area of study that has been largely unexplored. A more recent symposium about the same subject was entitled 'The "On-off" Child', in reference to the uninhibited use of all types of buttons and keys. We know that the development and functioning of the psyche result from the variable and unique interaction between the exquisitely individual innate intellectual equipment that every child is born with, and the world surrounding him or her. The mind is constructed by virtue of experiences and perceptions that we have within the scope of human relationships and the surrounding environment. Therefore, we cannot avoid thinking that changes in the psychic organization of children do occur. The lack of boundaries or differentiation between true horror and fiction are introjected with natural and increasing nonchalance. This leads to a massive invasion of the perceptive field and influences the time and mode of reaction to events which, in order to be mentalized and elaborated, would require adequate internal space and time. Subsequently Amati Mehler says: 'We are particularly interested in establishing the boundaries within which certain objects, such as TVs or computers – when used at a very early age or inappropriately – may interfere with the mode in which the inner self establishes the subjective capability of valuing and generally understanding the events and information coming either from the inner or the outer worlds.' Amati Mehler adds (assigning value to the introjective aspects of outward invasion): 'I will particularly dwell on the interaction with the computer and television. This doesn't mean that video games or other electronic games, to which I will refer later, are not important, but I believe that the TV and computers are the instruments that have most influence on the adjustment of mental mechanisms and mainly on the development of the symbolic function.'

This is one of the main reasons for the alarm expressed years ago when the computer was triumphally promoted – the earlier the better – with the rationale that it stimulated the development of logical processes in children. But, how can we use logic when an adequate sense of reality has not yet developed? Or when fiction cannot be distinguished from reality? A sequence of facts may be very logical and true, but its adequacy to a certain situation requires more complex judgement and the appreciation of other contextual circumstances.

And the author continues: 'Play is one of the more important elements in children's lives, because it is the natural arena for experimenting the difference between reality and fiction, between animated and inanimate objects, construction and destruction, finding and losing, pleasure and displeasure, interest and boredom, between the interaction with oneself and that with others.' And about the influence of television on children younger than age 6 she says:

The excessive leniency of television decreases children's ability to properly focus on a problem during sufficient time. This is a very relevant point, since attention, a fundamental requisite for learning, may already be compromised before entering school. The capability of forming mental representations is also affected, and these are the building bricks for later categorisations and more complex mental operations. Television, in contrast with reading or play, precludes experimentation, exploring and a whole series of other mechanisms.

'But while our fantasies spring spontaneously from within, the images that dwell in our head while we (passively) watch TV, come from outside.'

Final comments and summary

In this chapter we have presented the clinical material of a youngster addicted to video games and computer games. We presented clinical material, including dreams. We offered hypotheses about the mechanisms employed by this patient and believe that such hypotheses may be useful for understanding other patients with similar psychopathology. We described the mechanisms of projective identification, symbolic equation, confusional defences or mechanisms and autistic mechanisms. In these final conclusions and summary I should like to expand on the concept of autistic mechanisms and especially on the encapsulation of autistic aspects, which may occur in a patient who at the same time functions in a reasonably adapted way to reality with the other part of his neurotic self (Klein, 1980; Tustin, 1986). Carrying out an in-depth study of the mechanisms used by this patient we should find different mechanisms, as I mentioned earlier. But I should like to emphasize the autistic encapsulated areas because part of the material seems to point to the mechanisms of autistic encapsulation. In the encapsulation model, there is a shielding or early identifications that are later found to be fairly well preserved in this patient. As an explanatory model I would suggest that there is a dialectic interplay between all the systems: one aimed at encapsulating (which does not mean integration but preservation) and thus shielding identifications, and another that, despite everything, loses valuable identifications as a consequence of powerful projective identification. The inner drama develops between these mechanisms. Technically it is advisable to bear all these mechanisms in mind. We need to pay attention to projective identification mechanisms in order to avoid a mental emptying due to massive projection. This may lead to either mental emptying or severe confusional states, or even to the loss or dismembering of early identifications. It also plays an important role in disorders employing symbolic equations. Encapsulation is a way of shutting out and protecting oneself from the external world, against the unknown – the non-ego. These are children whose internal wounds are always open and painful. One of the aims is to preserve the precocious integration of personality, which has occurred far too hastily.

Conclusion

On the basis of experience it may be concluded that in many neurotic children the processes of secondary encapsulated autism have become isolated in a 'pocket' of functioning, so that the developmental process seems to continue normally. This is my hypothesis transferred to adult patients. This hypothesis (Rosenfeld, 1986) in which autistic encapsulation is also useful to preserve early identifications, was originally described by the author in the paper presented at the International Psychoanalytical Congress, Hamburg, 1985, on 'Identification and the Nazi phenomenon'. Two years after discontinuing treatment with me, Lorenzo came to see me, following the advice of his current psychoanalyst who was going on vacation and suggested the need for containment. Lorenzo came to the office, and I saw a slimmer young man, dressed quite elegantly and with properly combed hair (which was never the case in the past). He said that he was currently sharing an apartment with his sister in downtown Buenos Aires, and that both of them were studying. This would not have been possible had they stayed at their parents' house, which is very distant from the large schools, colleges and universities. Lorenzo later related that he sat for the English course's exam and passed the 'FIRST CERTIFICATE'. Now he was about to sit another English test, for a higher level. But he had been very violent and anxious due to this and has had quarrels with his older sister. Later, when he remembered the discussions at his parents' house, he denied the occurrence of arguments where they yelled and even threw pans of food over their heads during his birthday party. I believe that forgetfulness or denial sometimes occurs in severely disturbed patients, when they deposit in their therapist extremely sick or crazy periods of their lives and then refuse to tolerate remembering and resuffering these periods. We were also able to talk and remember good moments whilst he was in treatment with me, especially when he finished high school and had won three awards: for best qualifications in economics-mathematics, best in French and a prize for best overall results in his class.

References

Amati-Mehler J (1987) Il Bambino e la Tecnologia. ULISSE Enciclopedia della Ricerca della Scoperta. Vol. 13. Milano: Editori Riuniti, p. 273.

Amati-Mehler J (1992). Reflessione sul 'Bambino Tecnologico'. Revista di Picoanalisi. Rome: Editore Il Pensiero Scientifico.

Amati-Mehler J (1998) Informazione e Formazione della Mente. Lima: Peruvian Psychoanalitical Society.

Anzieu, Annie (1986) Cadrages. Construction du cadre, construction du Moi. Journal de la psychanalyse de l'enfant 2: 64–77.

Bion W (1953). Notes on the theory of schizophrenia. International Journal of Psycho-Analysis 35: 113–8.

Bion W (1984) Diferentiation of the psychotic from the non-psychotic personalities. In Bion W (1984) Second Thoughts. London: Karnac.

Boniamino V (1998) Personal communication.

Boyer B (1983). The Regressed Patient. New York/London: Jason Aronson.

Boyer B (1990). Countertransference and technique. In Master Clinicians. Northvale, NJ/London: Jason Aronson.

Boyer B (1994). Introduction: Countertransference: Brief History and Clinical Issues with Regressed Patients. In Master Clinicians on Treating the Regressed Patient. Northvale NJ/London: Jason Aronson.

Boyer B (1999) Countertransference and Regression. Northvale NJ/London: Jason Aronson.

Cancrini G, Pelli M (1995) Lavorare 'con' le famiglie e lavorare 'sulle' famiglie: alcune reflessioni tra approccio sistemico e intervento psicoeducazionale. Rivista Interazioni 1: 151–8.

Correale A (1994). Famiglia e psicosi. Rivista Interazioni 1: 136–9.

Ferro A (1996) Nella Stanza D'analisi. Milan: Raffaello Cortina Editore, p. 115.

Freud S (1914a). On narcissism: an introduction. Standard Edition. London: Hogarth.

Freud S (1914b) Remembering, repeating and working-through. Standard Edition. London: Hogarth.

Freud S (1915). The unconscious. Standard Edition. London: Hogarth.

Freud S (1923a) The ego and the id. Standard Edition. London: Hogarth, pp. 49–50.

Freud S (1923b) Lectures on psychoanalysis. Standard Edition. London: Hogarth, pp. 109–10.

Goldberg P (1990) The holding environment: conscious and unconscious elements in the building of a therapeutic framework. In Boyer L, Giovacchini PL (eds) Master Clinicians On Treating The Regressed Patient. Northvale NJ/ London: Jason Aronson.

Green A (1977) Le Discours Vivant. La Conception Psychanalytique De L'affect. Paris: Presses Universitaires de France.

Green A (1992) La Folie Privée. Gallimard: Paris

Green A (1996) La sexualité a-t-elle un quelconque rapport avec la psychanalyse? Revue Francaise De Psychanalyse 60: 829–48.

Green A (1997) Les Chaines D'Eros. Paris: Odile Jacob.

Izzo E (2000) Más Allá De La Interpretación. Interpreting In The Treatment With Severally Disturbed Patient. Buenos Aires Symposium held at the Argentinian Psychoanalytical Association, April.

Klein Melanie (1975a) The Writings of Melanie Klein. Vol. 1. Love, Guilt and Reparation And Other Works. London: Hogarth Press.

Klein Melanie (1975b) The Writings of Melanie Klein. Vol. 3. Envy and Gratitude and other Works. London: Hogarth Press.

Klein, Sidney (1980) Autistic phenomena in neurotic patients. International Journal of Psycho-Analysis 61: 395–402.

Martini G (1995) Dinamiche tra gli operatori dei servizi di salute mentale e i genitori dei pazienti psicotici: un terreno che scotta. Rivista Interazioni 1: 81–94.

Nicolo Corigliano A, Borgia F (1995) Tra l'intrapsichico e l'interpersonale. La folie à deux: come ipotesi-modello di un funzionamiento interpersonale. Rivista Interazioni 1: 40–51.

Ogden T (1994a) Subjects of Analysis. Northvale NJ/London: Jason Aronson.

Ogden T (1994b) Analyzing the matrix of transference. In Master Clinicians on Treating the Regressed Patient. Volume 2. Northvale NJ/London: Jason Aronson.

Painceira A (1997) Clínica Psicoanalítica a Partir de la Obra de Winnicott. Buenos Aires: Lumen.

Pichon-Riviere E (1959/ 1970). Del Psicoanálisis a la Psicología Social. Buenos Aires: Galerna.

Quinodoz JM (1989) Female homosexual patients in analysis. International Journal of Psychoanalysis 70: 55–63.

Reid S (1997) Developments in Infant Observation – The Tavistock Model. London/New York: Routledge.

Resnik S (1994) Erotizzazione e Psicosi nella Famiglia. Rivista Interazioni 1: 73–81.

Rosenfeld, David (1986) Identification and the Nazi phenomenon. Internat Journal Psych 67: 53–64.

Rosenfeld, David (1994) Primitive object relations in drug addict patients. In Boyer B, Giovacchini P (eds) Master Clinicians on Treating Regressed Patients. North Vale NJ/London: Jason Aronson.

Rosenfeld, David (1992) The Psychotic: Aspects of the Personality. London: Karnac.

Rosenfeld, David (2000). Dictionaire De La Psychanalyse. Toxicomanie, addiction, et transfert psychotique. Paris: Calmann-Levy.

Rosenfeld, Herbert (1987) Impasse and Interpretation. London: Tavistock.

Searles H (1986) Transference Psychosis in the Psychotherapy of Schizophrenia. In Collected Papers on Schizophrenia and Related Subjects. London: Hogarth/Karnac.

Segal H (1994) Fantasy and reality. International Journal of Psycho-Analysis 75(2): 395–401.
Tustin F (1986) Autistic Barriers in Neurotic Patients. London: Karnac.
Tustin F (1990) The Protective Shell in Children and Adults. London: Karnac.
Volkan V (1996) The Infantile Psychotic Self and its Fates: understanding schizophrenics and other difficult patients. Northvale NJ/London: Jason Aronson, p. 106.
Volkan V (1997) The Seed of Madness. Madison CT: International University Press.

CHAPTER 10

Psychotic developments in a sexually abused borderline patient[1]

PAUL WILLIAMS

Prior to referral for analysis Miss A, 40, was assessed by an experienced analyst in whom she confided her crippling, lifelong feelings of depression and loneliness. During a painful assessment the analyst made a simple statement which has stayed with the patient: 'You seem to have no people in your mind.' By this I believe the analyst meant that no whole object of either gender had been internalized. Miss A's subsequent analysis has shown this to be the case. This paper seeks to show how Miss A's capacity for mature object relationships has been severely compromised by unresolved immature identifications, the origin of which lies in her early relation with her mother. It also shows how a profoundly damaging, apparently incestuous relationship with her father was constructed on this basis. I shall describe Miss A's borderline pathology and the significance of anorexia nervosa in it. Miss A has been diagnosed as suffering from a paranoid psychosis, to which she remains vulnerable. A pathological narcissistic organization (cf. Rosenfeld, 1964, 1971) to which the patient has given the name 'The Director', and through which her psychosis found expression, has controlled her mental life leading her to try to take her life. The difficulties involved in analysing the transference in such a disturbed patient led to certain modifications in technique, which I shall describe. Finally, I consider whether the patient's shifting identifications and difficulties in distinguishing between fact, memory and fantasy constitute a discernible pattern or syndrome.

In trying to orientate myself in a mass of complex material, I was influenced by the work of Henri Rey on double identification in anorexia nervosa and claustro-agoraphobia. This work, a development of Klein's observations on projective identification, refers to a type of fixation in the mother–infant dyad that leaves the adult prone to regress in relationships in such a way as to experience himself or herself as both a baby relating

175

voraciously to a mother, and at the same or other times as the mother exposed to the baby's attacks. A turning in fear and frustration from the mother to the father occurs in early life as a consequence of this fixation, and this is expressed symbolically as a failure to differentiate breast or nipple from penis, leading to associated disturbances of function (cf. Rey, 1994). Prior to her analysis Miss A had exploited her psychotic pathology in her unusual work. She was an operational member of a branch of military security. She was frequently required to pursue and confront dangerous males. In carrying out this work she has had little hesitation in placing herself at risk of injury or even death. Her senior officers held her abilities in high regard.

History

Miss A is the middle child of a working-class couple from the north of England. Her parents are, at the time of writing, alive and in their 70s. She has an older and younger brother by eighteen months and five years respectively – Ian and Anthony. She described her childhood as bleak and affectionless. She feels she had no relationship to speak of with her mother, who was so enamoured of her first child that she rejected Miss A, pushing her on to the father. He appears to have resented the attention paid by his wife to Ian, whom he treated badly. The boy suffered a depressive breakdown in his teens. Miss A's impression of her mother is of a fragile, narcissistic woman, and of her father as an alternately paranoid and ill-tempered loner capable of exuding great charm. Miss A's hatred of her seemingly unavailable mother has had the quality of an *idée fixe* – a consuming, unremitting grievance. The atmosphere at home seems to have been one of contrived normality and falseness. The children were told that they were loved and that theirs was a happy family. Miss A appears to have had some happy moments with her father. She has several memories of walks in the countryside with him as a little girl. No criticisms were permitted at home, especially of mother, and any fuss was, according to Miss A, punished by the father, who beat the children. During Miss A's first three years of life her father, a builder, spent time working away from home. This left Miss A, her mother and her brother Ian alone together. Miss A feels that she was excluded by her mother and Ian from the start, and took to playing on her own whilst surreptitiously studying them. At some point she began to experience them, and others, staring and laughing at her. At such times she wished she could turn to her father. Her mother then became pregnant with Anthony and Miss A took to hiding in the under-stairs cupboard space ('to get away from their stares', she said) where she developed an elaborate fantasy life. She has disclosed that since making the cupboard her 'home' as a child, she has experienced uncertainty as to whether people she speaks to are real or are part of her fantasy world. In her isolation she constructed a grandiose fantasy; a family romance in which she lived on a country estate adjoined by another. Her parents had been killed in a car crash. Her upper-class neighbours had two sons, Peter and David, who were her friends. They shared adventures such as horse riding, rambling and 'special assignments' in which she accompanied Peter on missions to free hostages or capture bad people. These forays could make David jealous. On her missions, Miss A could be male or female or neither. Two further fantasies arose as she became, I think, more isolated and disturbed. She developed friendly relations with creatures from outer space who promised her they would come and take her away. This gave her hope, but she could not allow herself to go with them as she didn't know where they would take her. At this time (she was aged five) she complained to her father of a high-pitched ringing in her ears. After several weeks of this she was taken to the doctor who found nothing amiss. The patient wanted to tell the doctor, but was unable to, that the noise was the creatures making contact with her. A final, pervasive fantasy has been that she is a famous actress managed by an ominous, protective, pimp-like figure who was to feature prominently in her analysis as a pseudo-hallucination – 'The Director'.

On the basis of Miss A's account and my transference and countertransference experiences, which I shall describe, I came to a tentative view that Miss A may have been sexually abused from about the age of five, at or around the time of the birth of the third child. Miss A said that the father, feeling excluded by his wife caring for a newborn baby, took Miss A into his bed and persuaded her to masturbate him. This occurred perhaps weekly, and was interrupted by father's trips away. These absences left Miss A feeling abandoned. By the time Miss A was seven she was, she said, masturbating and fellating her father in his living room armchair, while her mother was out with baby Anthony. If Miss A did not feel like obliging her father, it appears that he persuaded her with flattery or if this failed became angry and occasionally hit her. The father appears to have attempted vaginal and anal intercourse without success, but from what I have learned full intercourse apparently occurred at around 10 and continued until the age of 14, at which time Miss A, fearing pregnancy, insisted that sexual relations stop. When left unsatisfied by her father, or when lonely while he was away, Miss A has indicated that she would masturbate to a fantasy of her father, or of a queue of men, waiting to have sex with her. As an adult, intense affects have continued to be eroticized and infused with violence, and until recently she has been compelled to find men to masturbate or to mistreat her sexually. At school, Miss A was aggressively passive and withdrawn, teased and occasionally bullied. She has said she was overweight and by puberty seems to have developed a pronounced anorexic tendency, dieting, wearing a large coat and refusing to shower naked with the other girls: she insisted on wearing a towel in the shower. She was confused and ashamed by the changes taking place in her body. By 16 she was masturbating schoolboys, an activity which made her feel wanted, and by 18 a pronounced anorexic-bulimic cycle had set in. Academically, her achievements at school were negligible in relation to her intelligence, which is high.

Relations between Miss A and her parents deteriorated steadily in her teens. Having apparently broken off sexual relations with her father she felt he became extremely strict, opposed to her seeing boyfriends and controlling her life because he could not tolerate the thought of another man having a relationship with her. Relations with her mother were so estranged that when Miss A thought of her it brought to mind images of her mother with her older brother and these ignited unmanageable jealousy and hatred. For many years she was excessively protective of her younger brother, maintaining a fantasy that he was her baby by her father. Occasionally she lost her temper and beat him. Miss A left home at 18 and went to France where she worked in cafés and restaurants. She made sado-masochistic relationships with uncommitted or aggressive men until she fell for Antoine, a car mechanic, who seems to have cared for her. Her schizoid functioning made Antoine's demands for emotional intimacy intolerable, and after a few months he announced that he was to be engaged to a girl from his village. Miss A, distraught but relieved, returned to England where she took a job as a security guard, work that bore a striking resemblance to her childhood daydreams. She applied for a position with the armed forces, was accepted, and was eventually placed in intelligence fieldwork. She was effective in tracking down political and civil lawbreakers, commanding a certain awe, if not respect, from her colleagues for her fearlessness. It was common for her to be confronted by guns or explosives, or to witness woundings and deaths. During her work Miss A became friendly with a minor criminal whom she married. The relationship deteriorated into sadomasochistic brutality, with Miss A being assaulted and beaten. She has told me that she required her husband to hit her in the stomach, 'to kill the crying baby in there', as she put it. They had no children, although she arranged for the abortion of two pregnancies early in the marriage. They divorced shortly after she entered analysis.

Accounts of objective history such as this one, provided by extremely disturbed patients suffering florid fantasies, often of a hysterical type, are extremely difficult for the analyst to verify, to say the least. Can one believe anything such a person says, and if so, in what sense? Only over an extended period can the consistency and detail of the accounts be assessed and, even then, distinguishing between fact and fantasy remains, in my view, an ongoing, ultimately unresolvable problem. In Miss A's case I was eventually left in little doubt as to the essential truth of some of the facts reported here, but the overriding 'truth' of her statements lay, for me, more in the transference and countertransference experiences of the sessions.[2]

Analysis

My initial meeting with Miss A was unsettling, as she was anxious to the point of incoherence. She wore dark, masculine clothes (the same as, I was to discover later, those worn by 'The Director') and large sunglasses. She stood before me shaking visibly, clipped a bleeper to her belt and said: 'Where do you want me?' I replied that she was free to talk from wherever she liked. She could stand, or use the couch or the chair, but as she seemed to be feeling anxious perhaps the chair would feel most comfortable. She responded compliantly and told me about herself, as though reading from a newspaper article. Her isolation, unhappy marriage and feelings of helplessness were recounted mindlessly, with no trace of emotion. A moment of apparent distress overtook her when she interjected: 'My father kissed me once.' She dismissed the incident, saying it was a harmless lapse. Towards the end of the meeting she again appeared to drop her falseness, becoming angrily seductive: 'They are all men in my unit' she remarked scornfully 'I am the only woman. I can handle men. Women are scared of me.' Transferentially, I thought that this display of tough independence might have something to do with her being about to leave; otherwise, our first meeting was intense and enigmatic. So split and massively projecting did I experience Miss A to be that I felt that interpretations that went beyond acknowledging her initial, extreme anxieties might be felt as an assault likely to persecute or excite her. In the early stages of the analysis I proceeded by trying to establish an atmosphere in which a space might be created for tolerance of the fear and latent violence that beset her, and which might facilitate her telling me something about herself.

I think it is important to stress at this point that Miss A did not behave at any time in the way one might have expected an analytic patient to behave, until perhaps comparatively recently. The ideal working model of 'interpretation–response', if such a thing exists, cannot be achieved with such a patient (perhaps not with any patient) for a long time, if ever. My comments went ignored, at least outwardly, for years. Most of her dreams remained unexamined, comprising, as they did, unmediated expressions of primary process about which she could not think. And acting out dominated the treatment. The sessional material from which I shall quote represents certain moments of candid engagement. More often I was reduced to confusion and silence by her dismissal of me, and to querying in vain her transferential state from seemingly incomprehensible utterances and my own chaotic experience of sitting with her. Any *post hoc* coherence that this chapter might convey should not minimize the perplexities and confusions that suffused the analysis, now in its seventh year. One might ask: why consider such a patient for analysis in the first place? Despite my many misgivings, both the assessor and I felt that her request for help was serious, and more importantly that her distress was accessible. However, I had little confidence in our prospects, but as things have turned out the patient has done better than one could have expected. How and why this has happened was important for me to understand.

During the first three months of analysis Miss A talked in her newspaper-reporting style, and I learned a good deal of what was conveyed as fact. This was interrupted by what I took to be a number of references to possible sexual abuse, although it would be three years before I would succeed in any serious exploration of these with her. For example, her analysis was to be kept a secret from work. Her superior officer must not find out as she would be sure to be discharged (even though her employers in real life accepted that she was in analysis). She felt nervous about having analysis with a man. It made her want to cry. On hearing that she had entered analysis, her father had taken her aside and said: 'Your illness might have something to do with what happened between you and me when your brother was born.' There were further statements on the theme of concealing secrets. Alongside these fears arose, immediately, severe difficulties with weekend and holiday breaks. Miss A's initial solution was to write me innumerable letters assuring me of the value of analysis. Attempts to explore this behaviour proved futile. They abated only when more serious acting out supervened. She experienced my statements about her separation problems as either narcissistic demands or as rebukes. She was unable to regard me as capable of empathic understanding. Unconsciously, her dependence on the analysis and outrage at its frustrations had drawn her into acting out, and this became increasingly masochistic (for example, missing sessions, excitedly placing herself in danger at work, and so forth). After eight months or so she reported the following dream: *'I am being fed. A hand then slaps me across the face hard. Then I am on a terrorist exercise, rolling down a hill clutching a male officer. We fall off a cliff or shelf.'*

It was possible to discuss briefly this dream with her, which was unusual as she was unable to think about her dreams despite dreaming prolifically. Her associations were to feelings that something catastrophic was going to happen, and to the excitement she felt when on dangerous military exercises. I felt that she was communicating, in the transference, a sense of loss of the breast, followed by an incestuous solution. I said to her I thought that for her to take something from me in her analysis gave rise to feelings of disaster that had to be stopped. Although I thought she needed help, and that was what analysis was for, she had little or no hope that her needs could be met. For several minutes her anxieties seemed to abate and she appeared to think about what I'd said. She told me calmly that she had never relied on anybody and that to do so was bad. Her anxieties then returned and she appeared to no longer be able to think. Two further themes became prominent at this time. One was a complaint that her mother had given her elder brother Ian more food when they were children. Her tone was one of unspeakable injustice. The other was an expression of triumph as, for example, when she told me of an army psychiatrist with a Welsh name who had been drafted in during an assignment and with whom she had worked well, once she had shown him the ropes. I felt that her principal injury – deprivation in her primary relationship – and its incestuous, sado-masochistic resolution had, transferentially, surfaced in earnest. From this point on she no longer missed sessions. I became an object of curiosity and idealization, whilst her violent, perverse pathology was acted out. She instituted a divorce against her husband, apparently seduced men and took such operational risks as to provoke reprimand by her superior officers. She had once told me how, in her childhood fantasies, she, Peter and David had used special codewords to organize their adventures. Now, on a recent real-life assignment, she had become confused between her private fantasy codes and the real-life military operational codes, creating near-disaster for herself and her colleagues.

By the middle of the second year she had become convinced, on the advice of The Director, that she was being trailed by assassins and that the woman who lived next door to her hated her, 'because I [Miss A] am an individual' (meaning a person with her own opinions which could not be tolerated). For several days she brought to her sessions – in reality – a disabled friend whom she insisted was in a suicidal state and installed her in the waiting room, whilst Miss A, in tears, angrily assured me of her own sanity and goodwill, and that she desperately needed her analysis to succeed. This is an extract from a session at the time:

The patient arrived about five minutes late in a distressed and dishevelled state. She hid in the corner of the waiting room, trembling. She seemed agitated, as though possibly hallucinating, and on entering the consulting room walked around unsteadily, sat on a chair and then sat on the edge of the couch. She cried intermittently, staring ahead.

When Miss A spoke she said

P: 'You don't understand. My mother never understood me. When my grandmother was dying, she was very old, I tried to give her the kiss of life. I was breathing into her. I was trying to get her heart going. My mother thought I was hurting her. I wasn't. I wanted to keep her alive, not die. She didn't understand, she just didn't understand. You don't understand' [she cried, paused, and then resumed her complaint that I didn't understand her for several more minutes, before suddenly stopping and shouting out, in alarm].

'You're trying to kill me.' [Pause]

A: 'I think you are afraid of what you could do to me if you make demands on me. When you complain about me, as you are doing now, a voice in your head warns you that I will retaliate, even want to kill you. I think that the voice is trying to stop you from letting me know what you're really feeling.'

P: [Pause, calmer] 'It is true, isn't it? People don't like people, they don't, do they? Nobody wants an individual. They can't cope with an individual. That is what happened to me. I wasn't an individual. It's the only thing I know [long pause]. My mother didn't understand me [pause and again shouts angrily]. You're going to stop my analysis. I know it.'

P: 'It sounds like you're being told again that I can't stand you, and that I will reject you. You are upset, you're trying to tell me about it, and something is interfering to try to stop you. I think this must feel confusing.'

P: 'I do feel confused [pause, cries]. I don't feel well. The Director tells me I'm fine. I don't feel fine. I want to be in hospital. Everything's going wrong and I don't know why. What's wrong with me? I don't know what to do. Please help me'.

A: 'I do understand that you need my help but we need to understand that when you try to get it the Director voice shouts that your needs don't matter, and that we will both be destroyed if we talk. This makes you want to push me away, even though you need to talk to me.'

P: 'I think I know what you mean. He says that I don't need help, I'm fine. I feel sick . . . I want to vomit [pause] there's no other way [pause] when people get too near I want to vomit. People take you over, you see. I don't want you to misunderstand me. I know you understand me. You do understand me.'

There was a pause. I felt she might be feeling overwhelmed by the contact taking place between us. Eventually I said:

A: 'I wonder, when you feel that I do understand something about you, it can feel as though something bad is happening inside you, which you must stop.'

The patient became alarmed by what I said.

P: 'That's sexual. It's wrong. I'm sorry. I don't want you to misunderstand me [cries]. I worry all the time that you might misunderstand me. Nothing must go wrong this time'.

One way of understanding these anxieties is as an expression of depressive guilt leading her to self-destructively act out in order to protect me from her overwhelming impulses. She feared that emotional closeness would destroy me, and thus her. Yet what interested me particularly about this and other similar sessions was the discovery that when the psychotic voice that influenced her was interpreted as an autonomous, frantic outbreak of concern (no matter how overtly destructive) that erupted in the trans-ference without warning at times of acute paranoia, seemingly to protect her from the consequences of having her needs met, Miss A felt relieved and momentarily coherent, prior to being readvised by her psychotic personality of my unreliability and malevolence. This way of understanding and interpreting her transference anxieties had certain implications for technique, which I discuss below, the principal of which was the need to understand that the thoughts of the psychotic personality present when Miss A was in my room were distinct from those of my patient. Her under-standing of my final comment as being sexual seemed to relate to her experiencing making emotional contact as the same as engaging in sexual activity. At other times contact could be equated with a threat of death or as the death of me or of someone else. Shortly after the above session Miss A began to cut herself lightly on her arms. She took a non-fatal overdose and a month later jumped from a moving train as it entered a station, injuring her leg. This behaviour was a prelude to a period of highly destructive acting out as her paranoid psychosis asserted itself, and which could not be contained by interpretation. Certain dreams drew attention to the crisis:

There was a baby bird in a nest with its beak open. It was starving. Nobody came to feed it. I watch it die. I am crying.

*

A minibus crashes through the front of a food store. There is a huge explosion. My older brother helpfully leads people away. There are many dead pregnant women. I touch the stomach of one but there is no life. Tins of food are embedded in people's faces. They are missing arms and legs. The manager says 'We carry on, we stay open.' I desperately try to stop him but can't.

*

I am lying on a bed surrounded by cut-up foetuses. I can't look at them because they are parts of the devil.

*

I am waiting in a doctor's waiting room. There are other patients waiting. You come out, look around smiling and call me into your consulting room. You take your trousers down and tell me to suck your penis. There is shit on the end, but I have to do it.

Miss A was unable to associate to these dreams. It is probable that what is being depicted in them concerns an extremely deprived child, perhaps with a mother who was unable to contain her child's murderous aggression (lacking in Bion's alpha-function) and there is portrayed a perverse experience with a man. Yet their meaning is far from transparent. The dream data are close to primary process. The condensation of imagery (for example, conflation of penis-breast-anus) and absence of symbolic elaboration, together with little or no secondary process, confirm that they are psychotic experiences. In the first dream, how identified has Miss A become with the person who does not intervene, as well as with the starving, dying bird? In the food store dream, is she communicating confusion between reality and fantasy, as well as murderous wishes against siblings? She believes her projections destroy people, yet a store manager is saying 'We carry on, we stay open.' Does she think he is undamaged by her attacks, or is he denying terrible suffering? What kind of person does she think her analyst is? Affective contact seemed to be felt to annihilate a vulnerable and rejecting mother analyst – a situation felt by the patient to have been created by herself. At the same time murderous, perverse and suicidal fantasies consumed and persecuted her. This impossible conflict gave rise to manic states in which she attended religious or other public meetings and denounced them in favour of psychoanalysis, until she was thrown out. She apparently tried to give away her life savings, and to buy her local village hall to turn it into an orphanage. She attempted to visit orphans in Romania. She bought baby clothes, took to waiting outside nursery schools and on one occasion was overwhelmed by an impulse to abduct a child and was deterred only by the arrival of the child's mother. The weekend breaks were experienced as too long, leading to instructions by The Director to kill herself. In view of the increasing self-harm, I encouraged her to see her GP and area hospital psychiatrist with a view to receiving appropriate medication so that her analysis could continue. A hospital bed was to be available should it prove necessary in the future.[3]

Her basic functioning improved with the containment provided by medication, in this case lithium. Whereas Miss A had for 18 months sat in the chair, she now expressed a wish to use the couch. She experienced panic that 'a man will see through me' or that she would be attacked with a knife. She covered the lower half of her body with a rug and held her head, as though anticipating blows. Intermittently she brought into sessions a pillow, towels, toys, a kitchen knife and razor blades. The references she made to these indicated that they served as either comforters or protectors. This was not simple to understand, as the knife could be experienced as a comforter due to the promise of relief offered by suicide. Notwithstanding these fears, she was able to tell me of past times with a schoolteacher who had been kind to her, and of some happy moments with her grandmother, in addition to her customary, harrowing accounts. Her benign memories generated anguish and she found it more difficult to finish her sessions. She complained: 'my bleep goes off outside' and 'men touch me up when I'm not here'. A dream seemed to depict the dangers of dependency:

I am walking along a country lane. A mangled baby, half-human, half-animal, is lying dying in the lane. I see a beautiful woman in a garden and go and ask her for help. She can't hear me. I go back to get the baby but suddenly a huge, black lorry comes towards me, filling the lane. I don't make it to the baby.

Her associations to the dream indicated a yearning for a good mother, which she believed could never be fulfilled. In addition, she thought that the baby she could not reach might have been herself or one of her brothers. She felt that she had died as a child. I said that I thought she felt she had never been allowed to have a mother. She now felt the same with me, that she could never have me, and this made her feel frustrated, angry and desperate.

'The Director'

Overt communication by The Director – the executive aspect of her paranoid psychosis – emerged as problems of separation became intolerable. Initially I was told of his influence outside the sessions. For example, he told her that she must sit immobile on the floor of her bathroom at weekends and neither eat nor go to the lavatory. By assuming a catatonic posture, the woman who lived next door would be stopped from coming through the walls and killing her. She hallucinated bulgings in the walls. The Director said they were the neighbour trying to get in. She associated the bulges to the shape of a pregnant belly. The Director, located in the same room as the patient and experienced as some feet away from her, eventually appeared in the consulting room as a pseudo-hallucinated figure standing by the door or sitting in the chair at my desk, issuing compelling instructions. These were, for example:

- 'He [your analyst] is rubbish. Chat him up and have sex.'
- 'You [Miss A] are a famous actress. Everything is wonderful.'
- 'They want to take you over and kill you. Swallow all your tablets now.'

Depending upon her anxiety levels, Miss A could feel subsumed by The Director, forced to obey him like a compliant child or respond as would a lover. She could not resist his communications. In one sense I had no patient to talk to, but rather a set of shifting identifications over which she had little control. This posed technical problems that space does not permit me to develop fully here, but to which I alluded earlier. Briefly, I came to realize that if Miss A was to be able to understand my interpretations of her psychotic pathology, it was necessary for me to understand that the Director figure appeared to function independently of my patient's thoughts or wishes. His paranoid-schizoid responses controlled her thoughts and behaviour according to specific, concrete wishes. His statements were automatic, immediate, totalizing, omniscient and required no thinking on my patient's part. They were symbolic equations of pure economy. This psychotic organizer provided instantaneous, unfailing responses whenever Miss A engaged in human relating, an activity that 'he' knew with certainty was ludicrous and irrelevant. 'He' ensured that she adopted his views by insisting that she would be destroyed by other people if she did not. Compelling psychic scripts were repeated, which immobilized her thinking and evoked ritualized behaviour leading to isolation and, ultimately, to despair. These scripts were, of course, transference communications: the patient's difficulties in using transference interpretations necessitated the communication of *both* her psychotic and non-psychotic transference states to her in any transference interpretation.

As a result of this work with Miss A, and with certain other severely disturbed patients, I have come to appreciate the significance of separating analytically these two phenomena – the psychotic personality, which acts asymbolically, and the personality capable of symbolization and thinking. Often, the psychotic personality is so influential as to be assumed to *be* the patient's personality, a confusion that can reduce the patient to despair. In Miss A's case, analysis of these distinct personalities in the transference led to her gradually becoming able to think about and express verbally the meaning of her psychosis and its impact on her sanity. For example, on the occasions when she was able to tolerate and observe a violent upsurge of psychotic disparagement of me, a space was created to then explore its meaning, aims and methods. This was for a long time the means by which it was possible to interpret psychotic paranoid anxieties in the transference. Later, as splitting and projective activity decreased, so more conventional transference interpretations became possible. The Director's outbursts became recognizable as ruthless interventions purporting to guarantee Miss A safety in the face of perceived threats to her life, even if saving her necessitated suicide. Closer scrutiny revealed that what was in fact taking place was the repeated expression of outrage by a psychotic mind violently opposed to any activity different from its own. Miss A's psychotic personality intervened in anything *not already reduced to a symbolic equation,* the aim being to reassert a psychotically rigid status quo in which an illusion of self-sufficiency was maintained through the use of fantasy objects. For me to have made transference interpret-ations that required Miss A to subsume her psychotic trans-ference anxieties via a superordinate ego or rational self, would have been to make unrealistic psychological demands leading to compliance. This would also have rendered transference interpretations meaningless.

The co-existence of psychotic and non-psychotic personalities has been described by a number of analysts, Bion in particular. In my opinion, these co-existing personalities in the psychotic person need to be analysed as distinct phenomena if impasse is to be avoided. To try by interpretation to reduce one to the other or to pursue premature attempts at integration can give rise to annihilation anxiety, unconscious guilt and severe negative therapeutic reaction, not to mention a conviction that the analyst is insane and in need of the patient's help. I believe that the psychotic organization itself is not modifiable, regardless of how much analysis is received. What seems to alter over time is its relationship to the patient's non-psychotic personality, as a result of change and development in the latter. When the gulf between the two systems has been reduced and the patient's capacity for thinking can be re-established, a non-paranoid interest in the status of the psychosis and of the patient's affective states may prevail. Miss A seemed, in her own way, to be aware of these problems. She talked, brought dreams and gave rudimentary associations in an effort to provide what she believed the analysis required, but was under continuous pressure from the Director to remain oblivious to their significance. This meant that she felt she had no alternative but to resort to attending to my apparent narcissistic needs, which seemed to mirror the loss of her relationship with her mother and her turning to satisfy her father's sexual and emotional demands. She would recount in a detached manner dreams that were vivid and often difficult to listen to. Occasionally their impact would reach her and she would clutch her body in pain, but generally she remained unable to think about them. The following dreams indicate some of her preoccupations after starting to use the couch:

A small male faun is lying on a bed, tied down. A telephone wire runs from its mouth through its body and out of its anus and limbs. Blood is spattered on the bed. I (Miss A) am in the clouds, an angel looking down. The faun cannot be touched because it would cause too much pain.

*

My genitals are covered in maggots. Only my legs and the bottom half of my torso exist. The rest of me is missing.

*

A man comes up to me in a gym and talks sexily. Suddenly he becomes violent and sticks his fingers up my anus, threatening to kill me.

Miss A found these dreams, which refer amongst other things to fears of sexual abuse, especially difficult to think about or talk about due to the degree of violence they evoked in her. A further obstacle was a fusional identification with an idealized mother-analyst. Acknowledgement of difference or separation generated unmanageable pain and hatred, which The Director advised could be resolved only by committing suicide. This was suggested when she thought reflectively or made emotional contact with me. His most frequent suggestion was that she cut her throat, in order to stop speaking. Any notion of progress in the analysis seemed to me to occur at moments when she was able to grasp, in the transference, that I was alive and remained interested. Depression and confusion followed these experiences. Unpredictable acts of sanity also occurred from time to time, including admitting in full her psychiatric condition to her employers, ceasing to drive her car for fear of killing herself or someone else, requesting a review of her medication as she felt increasingly ill and confiding in me aspects of the sexual abuse. At the same time, alterations in her defences could also be included in a broader, omnipotent fantasy of control over the analysis. After deciding to use the couch Miss A explained, in stages, The Director's function, which was to protect her from being taken over and destroyed. She feared merging above all, a state of mind in which she was overwhelmed by the near-delusional experience that the other person would get into her food, face, legs and stomach and want to eat or murder her. The Director would signal when he perceived these dangers: when the coast was clear he would invite her to enjoy manic and perverse gratifications as alternatives to object relationships. His scripts, reminiscent of her childhood fantasies but reworked for contemporary use, often included a dangerous person who would be vilified or destroyed in fantasy. The 'famous actress' would be evoked and told to give a performance culminating with an imagined or enacted seduction or exhibitionistic act. Such theatrical confusion reflects how Miss A evolved from a lonely, imaginative child into a woman with a hysterical psychosis in which fantasy could take over reality. The scripts ended according to the law of talion, with Miss A retreating into a persecuted, claustrophilic state in a corner of her house contemplating suicide at the invitation of a solicitous Director. The Director's exhortations reached a peak two years or so into the analysis when, for about 12 months, Miss A became increasingly psychotic. At weekends and during breaks she took airline flights to different parts of the world seeking out men for sex and female prostitutes whom she paid to cuddle her overnight. After these trips she would arrive at the consulting room confused and paranoid. On one occasion she recounted how she had spent the weekend consorting with the criminals she was employed to apprehend, although how true this was I do not know. After a trip during which she had 'sought out a lady in Brussels who gave me an ice-cream when I was little, but I couldn't find her', she returned home so depressed that her internal voice told her to kill herself. She obeyed, taking a near-lethal dose of lithium. She had sufficient sanity before passing out to phone for an ambulance, was taken to hospital and thanks to the prompt action of the staff her life was saved. It was during this period that I was made to experience something of the violation of boundaries that I suspect Miss A suffered as a child. So overwhelming was The Director's influence that I despaired of any alteration to her pathology. I felt I had no option but to continue to interpret that I thought she was trying desperately to preserve our relationship whilst being instructed to destroy it, in order to prevent a worse catastrophe, and that we were being prevented from talking about any of this. There were times when I felt convinced that I could no longer help her. I had no reason to believe that anything of value could proceed from this crisis, and I often feared for her life. I did not realize at that time that by continuing to interpret, I was responding to an unconscious need in her to make me bear certain primitive, infantile projections, particularly her partly denied feelings of despair, in order that she could begin to work her way towards the construction of a mental space in which she might internalize the rudiments of dependency on an object. The genuineness of this nascent internalization was of ongoing concern to me. Her psychotic personality dealt with feelings of abandonment and loss by slick adaptation. However, following this period there occurred only one further, mild overdose, which caused her to panic and rush to hospital. Also, The Director's influence gradually seemed to alter, taking more the form of a war of attrition with Miss A's infantile needs and depressive anxieties. With hindsight, I had the impression that the influence of her psychotic personality had not decreased so much as had become proportionally less effectual as her identification with me and the analysis had begun to develop.

In the ensuing and rather confusing fourth year of the analysis she seemed to become more able to think about and work with interpretations, whilst being assaulted by frequent attacks of psychotic anxiety. I attributed this development to her having experienced a certain amount of containment of her basic separation anxieties. The malignancy of her paranoia and its relationship to envy and jealousy began to be seen by her. Families, including fantasies of my own family, women with babies and images of her mother with her older or younger brother, evoked massive envy and murderous jealousy, which she began to talk about. The birth of her younger brother, which had apparently precipitated her sleeping with her father at the age of 5, was at one point refracted through a memory of having been given a scarf by her father, which she wore continuously as a child. She recalled how she used to tighten it round her neck to induce a sense of being strangled. In her later sexual life strangulation had become a motif. As these paranoid and depressive anxieties became more conscious, so impulses to steal, fears of being intruded upon and other manifest-ations of her own invasive wishes emerged. She became preoccupied with break-ins – to houses, cars and my consulting room, and to her mind and body. There occurred an increase in her sense of guilt and shame, particularly in relation to her envious, murderous, need-filled fantasies. An odd period of lying occurred when she attempted brazenly to manipulate her sessions. She declared that she had only ever said that she loved her brothers, denied saying things she had said minutes before, and stopped bringing dreams, insisting she was cured. Interpretation of her fear of exposure to her need for love, her greed and the humiliation these could create gradually led to disclosure of a longstanding fantasy in which The Director assured her he could satisfy all her needs without exposing her sad or, above all, her loving feelings to anyone. Miss A did not object to me knowing about this fantasy. In fact, she seemed to feel relieved whenever I interpreted the spurious aspects of her contact with me, even though to do so gave rise to further depressive anxieties. It was as though a desperate, sane part of her had remained alive and was saying: 'This is all I can do. Please understand that and continue to try to help me.'

The Director's overt involvement may have abated somewhat, but verbal outbursts of sexualized violence continued to be bellowed when he decided that merging threatened. Between these, low-level mutterings were designed to maintain an atmosphere of chronic suspicion. Miss A began to make a number of more direct, heartfelt rejections of object relatedness, and these revealed unalloyed envy, fear, resentment and anger, including towards me. The hatred she harboured against her mother became more conscious. For a time she became extremely upset that her former husband did not want her, even though they had been apart for years. It seemed that a weakening in her identification with her abusing father had begun to threaten her with isolation and despair, as the catastrophe of her primary attachment came to the fore. She suffered a recrudescence of anorectic symptoms and extensive bouts of eczema, in particular during breaks. Her ambivalence toward me increased markedly. As I became increasingly identified with her 'bad' mother, so she instituted a mental search for her father. A dream illustrated this conflict: 'I was walking through thick mud with my mother. I left her to go to my father who was looking for his lost child. I get to a house, but the mud on my shoes is too heavy, and I can't walk up the stairs to my father.'

We were able to begin discussing the hatred she bore against her mother and her turning to her father, and in so doing the horror of the psychological murder of her mother and of her siblings, and its paranoid consequences, virtually overwhelmed her. Nightmares portrayed her and others as dead or paralysed in wheelchairs. She dreamed of being murdered by gangs in retaliation for her badness; or of being turned into a skeleton or a rotting corpse. One day, in the midst of this torment, she expressed a tentative wish to talk to her mother, whom she had avoided for years. Over a period of several months she took to spending an hour or so with her at weekends, and her mother prepared meals for her. A dream followed: 'I am in a house like my own house with another woman. I think we like each other. I suggest that we go for a walk in the middle of the road, which is empty of traffic, each of us wearing our separate space suits.'

She associated to a need for, fear of and feelings of contempt for her mother and how confused these made her feel. Depressive feelings followed and gave rise to a series of nightmares in which her ex-husband stabbed her in her stomach. Although this violence terrified her, containing, as it did, her own projected rage, it did not prevent her from producing further dreams in which talks, walks and arguments with her mother (or another woman) took place, often culminating in Miss A trying to climb inside womb-like spaces. A further occurrence was awareness of her isolation, and of her inability to do anything about it. It seemed that the bare beginnings of a perception of separation anxiety on a whole object basis had brought about an awareness of intense loneliness and need. The need for dependence on her mother and a reduction in the necessity for absolute compliance with The Director, brought about a further period of extreme despair. This she endured without serious acting out. Her sessions seemed to comprise repeated attempts to articulate her infantile needs only for these to be dissipated by destruction of her thinking, leaving her exhausted, depressed and often driven compulsively in search of sex. I thought that the effects of The Director, although less violent, seemed to be more pervasive in that he now advised at every turn against having feelings or needs met, and I interpreted this as her transference response to needing me.

It had become fairly clear that she would be unable to continue with her military security work, as part of an overall regressive collapse – or perhaps, a progressive collapse of her falsity. Her employers agreed to her taking a desk job. Her demeanour became more timid and depressed and she experienced regular suicidal impulses, although these remained at the level of ideation only. Her transference behaviour exposed more detailed splitting of her objects. A yearning for an ideal mother offering the physical and emotional contact she needed was contrasted by a dread of 'lesbianism', which she felt would be the outcome of contact with another female. This was interwoven with familiar fantasies of usurping, abusing and murdering her mother, her brother and anyone who stood in her way of the mother. She could no longer find significant relief in perverse fantasies. She began dreaming of exposing an adult male psychopath to the authorities, who would be shocked by his misdeeds and ensure that justice was done. This enabled me to interpret her growing recognition of her hatred for her father and her psychopathic tendencies projected into him (an ideal container for them) and into me. A confusional state regarding her parental objects prevailed, and as her depression deepened so conscious fear of loss of her objects grew. Past infantile defensive behaviour re-emerged: for a time she hid in corners and in cupboards. She tried to make contact with creatures from outer space by staring out of windows. She bought a quantity of second-hand shoes to comfort herself (the cupboard she hid in as a child contained the family's shoes). Nonetheless, her outward appearance had improved. She looked more ordinary and relaxed, although very distressed, compared with the gaunt, sinister figure I had first encountered. She was sleeping better and had begun to read, something she had avoided for years for fear of being taken over by the story (a concrete, almost literal fear of being consumed or eaten by a person, place or thing illustrates the psychotic, as opposed to borderline, quality of her thinking). She had resumed contact with her brothers, and had become better able to deal with her new work colleagues. She also viewed the patients who came and went from my consulting room in a somewhat less paranoid way. Clearly she was beginning to project less of her internal world on to the external world and to acknowledge her miserable, hate-filled childhood, including her confusion, envy, rage and guilt towards her mother, in increasing amounts towards her father and towards me. Until recently, the sadism of her father was mitigated by the narcissistic gratifications of the incestuous relationship. Her hatred had been reserved for her abandoning mother. I came to think that Miss A displaced her rage towards her abusing father on to her mother for having failed to protect her, in order to avoid a state of objectlessness (the experience of believing that neither parent could love her). There is at least hope in attacking a recalcitrant mother who might change, whereas to confront the known but repressed knowledge that the father is the conscious agent of so serious a violation, *in addition to* a sense of loss of the mother, might be considered equivalent to psychological death. Latterly, her outrage towards her father has at times seemed to equal or exceed any of her murderous fantasies against her mother and siblings.

The mood of the analysis gradually seemed to take on a depressed, grief-stricken quality compared with its previous, often histrionic disturbances and distortions. Although functioning better in certain respects, Miss A had become consciously far more unhappy and confused. Her anorexia, a symptom since the age of 17, took on an increasingly emotional rather than physical form in that she became preoccupied with calculating the degree to which she was permitted contact with others. She was eating better and maintaining a normal weight. In the past she had often confined her eating to occasional potatoes and milk, whereas she now ate a range of foods, all vegetarian. She remained anxious about desserts, which, she said, over-stimulated her appetite. Her sessions became characterized by expressions of bitterness, regret and despair as she faced the many losses in her life. Hatred of her father and of me was accompanied by sexualization of needs and affects, sometimes to the point of demanding that I molest her when she was extremely angry with me. The overall direction of the analysis seemed to move into a long, painful struggle in which her mutilated, infantile, female self attempted to resume her arrested development. She committed herself to this task and has begun to acquire a certain capacity to think and to reflect. Although attacks of paranoia are less frequent, she remains vulnerable to them and to states of depressive collapse, particularly around holidays. An extract from a Thursday session a few months ago illustrates an improved capacity to tolerate her affects and something of a shift from paranoid to more symbolic thinking and depressive concern:

The patient began the session in a tearful and quietly distressed way.

P: 'I did something stupid yesterday. I went to the hospital where Dr X (her psychiatrist) works and parked my car next to her. I kept thinking of just sitting next to her. We wouldn't be saying anything special, just chatting. I wanted to go in but I was afraid she wouldn't have the time to see me. I know she's busy. I went home' [cries quietly for some time].

A: 'Perhaps knowing that she would find it difficult to see you without an appointment spared you from feeling that you were being too demanding.'

P: 'I knew I probably couldn't see her. You see, as a child I was always told to be good, to never ask for anything, never cry. I wanted to sit with her, that's all. I like her. She's been good to me. I can't make demands on anybody. The only thing that ever counted at home was being well behaved and being good.'

A: 'I think you feel that to be demanding here will disturb me greatly, but I think the truth is that you do feel demanding and angry when you feel I don't meet your needs.'

P: 'Yes I do [there is a pause]. You are a rotten analyst, you know. Sometimes I don't think you care about me at all. You don't give me enough time. I want more time, I want to read your books, ask you things, but you don't let me . . . I'm sorry [cries, pause] . . . I remember there was a boy in primary school who complained and he got to play in the sand pit. I never said anything, I was good and got nothing [angry]. My mother was always smiling. Even at the doctor's once when he found something wrong with her, she just kept on smiling. It's quite ridiculous. I do nothing and all I have for it is the empty. I can't stand the empty. I miss you so much sometimes. I feel so lonely. [Shouts] Oh, fuck off!'

A: 'Fuck off?'

P: 'The Director's telling me to fuck off. He wants me to be quiet, stop complaining. You know that I'm not supposed to speak to you. It's difficult for me, you know. Don't take me literally . . . I don't mean it, what I say. I do mean it but it's just . . .' [pause].

A: 'I think you do mean what you say. You are upset and angry with me because you feel I neglect you. The Director warns you against complaining. But I think you want me to listen to you when you feel like getting rid of me or simply telling me to fuck off.'

P: 'I'm always afraid you'll throw me out. I want to be demanding . . . do what other people do. I see them outside you know, they just do simple things like talk to each other or have a cup of coffee. I want to know how to do that, I want to have a life instead of always having to be good and be on my own.'

[There is quite a long pause of about five minutes. It seems fairly calm and I do not feel it appropriate to interrupt the silence].

'I want to know what a psychotic is. There's a book on your shelf which says 'psychotic'. What does it mean? Is it a psychopath?' [Pause.]

A: 'You're not sure?'

P: [Pause] 'No . . . no, I'm not sure, really' [she cries].

A: Perhaps you can see how much you need to find out why things have gone wrong, and why you have been unwell for so long.
[The patient cries quietly]

Discussion

Miss A's early identification with her mother clearly miscarried, leading to vulnerability to psychosis. She experienced her mother as incapable of loving her, and this gave rise to extreme feelings of exclusion, hatred, envy and jealousy. Her stated grievance consistently centred around food. A fixation in her development occurred based on a double identification. After the birth of Anthony when she was 5, Miss A seems to have felt rejected for ever by her mother and turned in desperation to her father. She appears to have been encouraged in this by her mother, a frequent precursor to incest noted in a number of studies (Eisnitz, 1984; Herman and Schatzow, 1987; Price, 1993). Up until this point we can understand how, under normal circumstances, the father might have helped Miss A with the difficult task of separating from her mother. Yet it is here that Miss A's development underwent lasting further trauma. Her attempt to establish an alternative object relationship was vitiated by the sexual abuse, leaving her with no viable object relationship of either gender. The father came to represent, in Miss A's mind, a breast in the form of a penis, which was to be masturbated and fellated. Father was a 'penis-breast mother' ejaculating 'semen-milk'. This combined 'penis-breast-mother-father' figure made actual relationships with father and mother, and the construction of good inner objects, impossible. Another way of describing the father is as a perverse transitional object, perceived as comforting but also exciting in a terrifying way. The relationship created absolute confusion of objects. Miss A actively built up a daydream life around her confused identifications, involving contact with sexually exciting, occasionally dangerous males. Her later work in military security was based on her unsuccessful attempt to identify with her father. She became a 'heroic man' fighting for and protecting the motherland. Ultimately, her identifications were neither male nor female, but rather a part object confusion of both.

The clinical material reported earlier lends support to the view that Miss A established a double identification early in her development, with fateful consequences. A manifestation of this is that in a dependent situation she feels herself to be a dangerous baby who endangers her mother, and who is in turn endangered by the mother. Her anorexia denotes a wish to regress to a pre-oral state in order to avoid destroying the mother by eating. Dreams and sessions consistently referred to food. One dream showed a baby bird starving in a nest and nobody came. Another had her being forced to suck her analyst's penis, which had shit on it that she must eat. In the violent food store dream tins of food were embedded in people's faces. Could an image like this be an unconscious reference to what it might feel like for a child to feed from an ejaculating penis? The search for food via the penis makes her later compulsion to masturbate schoolboys seem not unlike the hand-milking of cows. Miss A's deepest anxieties, however, concerned her mother's body and the siblings that emerged from it. Her anorexic-cannibalistic crisis arose from terrifying feelings of starvation, rage and envy towards her mother's body and towards her siblings. The dream of the baby in the country lane, whom

Miss A cannot save from the truck, is likely to be an expression of thoughts about a newborn sibling she wished to murder in order to gain access to her mother, aside from other meanings it may have. She dreamed of being surrounded by cut-up foetuses. Fantasies of invasion of the mother lay behind her fears of burglary, stealing and occupation of 'maternal spaces' such as rooms, cupboards, houses and bodies. When Anthony was born, Miss A retreated into a cupboard under the stairs. Perhaps this makes most sense as regression into the mother's womb, taking the place of Anthony. It was at this point that her anorexic-bulimic pathology came into being: with no object in sight to provide reliable nourishment, her never-to-be-satisfied hunger was joined by a deep fear of destructiveness if she ate. Feeling herself to be a biting baby who endangers her mother and her siblings placed her, by projection, on the receiving end of this violence. She could destroy by eating or be destroyed by being eaten. The anorexic's fear of taking in the analyst's food for thought is similar: either the analyst will be devoured by the patient's greed, engendering guilt, or the patient will be consumed and destroyed. In later life, after menstruation and when pregnancy is possible, the sexual act may become confused with oral wishes so that the anorexic fears that the inside of her body will be taken over and destroyed by a penis containing her own projected, avaricious desires. Rey (1994) has noted such confusions in anorexia, especially the unconscious conviction that mothers have babies by eating them, and that birth takes place via a bowel movement.

The Director, the patient's psychotic adviser usually seen as a caretaker, appropriated the task of protecting her from these terrible fears. His comments led to her becoming catatonic or not eating or going to the lavatory – paranoid-schizoid solutions to the projective problem of 'the woman next door' seeing or hearing her. Eating and shitting were felt to be highly dangerous to her mother, analyst and neighbour. The hallucin-ation of bulging walls, which a woman with a pregnant belly is trying to break through, is a graphic example of claustrophilia in which Miss A located envious, murderous little-girl wishes about her mother and siblings in the mother neighbour. These wishes threatened to return and break through her defences ('She is coming through the wall to kill you', The Director would advise), which would then lead to a state of psychotic claustrophobia. It has been by persistent interpretation of her severe paranoia *in the transference* that Miss A has been able to begin to withdraw some of her projections towards her mother, her mother's body, her siblings and me. To achieve this I needed to understand that her psychotic and non-psychotic personalities were distinct, functionally and organizationally, and for some considerable time transference interpretations took this into account. This led to more conscious depression and grief in Miss A. Her grief has been of a magnitude as to be tolerable only fleetingly. Nevertheless, after years of upheaval, she has become able to take an interest in and responsibility for her attitudes, including her anxiety and guilt at wishes to consume and destroy her objects.

It has become clear to me that, in view of her damaged identifications, Miss A's search for an identification with a mother amounted to a descent into unbearable confusions and losses. She has been required to address her psychotic anxieties knowing she did not possess the psychological equipment to think or imagine them, only to enact them (cf. Jackson and Williams, 1994). Survival of the failure of her relationship with her mother was sustained through the use of borderline defences. The incest, however, consolidated her confusion between fantasy, memory and fact, leaving her gravely vulnerable to a psychotic process that very nearly destroyed her.

Obviously, not all patients who form a double identification or who are sexually abused suffer the type or degree of psychopathology shown by Miss A. However, these two developmental crises – serious failure in early identification with the mother and a turning to the father, often with incestuous consequences – are reported by clinicians with increasing regularity, usually in the context of accompanying anorexic pathology. It is my view that, taken together, these obstacles may usefully be thought of as a single syndrome, and that the psychotic anxieties that accompany them affect the entire lives of afflicted individuals as a result of their being prevented from forming object relationships with members of either sex.

Notes

[1] This chapter was awarded the Rosenfeld Clinical Essay Prize by the British Psychoanalytical Society.

[2] In attempting the extremely difficult task of distinguishing between fact and phantasy, I think it is important when dealing with schizophrenic or borderline patients to study the precise, even uncanny ways in which they select the objects or part objects into which they proceed to projectively identify. To separate the behaviour of the object who is doing certain acts or responding in specific ways, from the alike projections into that person becomes a highly complex problem. It is analogous to dreaming, only when we wake up the reality situation is restored, or at least we hope so. In psychosis it becomes difficult, if not impossible, to separate delusions and hallucinations from reality. Addressing this confusion in Miss A has been a central problem in her analysis.

[3] I was fortunate in receiving the support of Miss A's GP and her psychodynamically oriented hospital psychiatrist who provided inpatient treatment when needed and outpatient care. Without their involvement the analysis could not have continued. This kind of support is, I believe, a prerequisite for the psychoanalysis or psychotherapy of a

severe borderline or psychotic patient. However, even though I felt that no alternative to medication presented itself in the case of Miss A, I am unsure in retrospect if the decision to propose it to her was a wise one. Medication given to help the analysis can have complex consequences over and above any pharmacological benefit. The patient may become convinced that the analyst cannot stand his or her pathology, and therefore has to resort to medicines. The pills are then taken ultimately for the analyst's benefit. More seriously, pills given to help can be turned into weapons of death. Such abuse can constitute a devastatingly destructive attack on the analyst and the analysis. Soon after commencing her medication, which helped her, Miss A embarked upon a series of very serious self-destructive acts using her pills. I am unsure as to whether the suggestion of medication acted as a provocation to a part of Miss A's mind, which then seized upon the opportunity to attack the analysis, or whether the ensuing acting-out would have occurred anyway.

References

Bion WR (1967) Differentiation of the psychotic and non-psychotic personalities. In Bion WR (1967) Second Thoughts. London: Maresfield, pp. 43–64.

Eisnitz AJ (1984) Father-daughter incest. Internat. J. Psychoanal. Psychother 10: 495-503.

Grand S, Alpert JL (1993) The core trauma of incest: an object relations view. Professional Psychology: Research and Practice 24(3): 330–4.

Herman JL, Schatzow E (1987) Recovery and verification of memories of childhood sexual trauma. Psychoanal. Psychol. 14(1): 1–14.

Jackson M, Williams P (1994) Unimaginable Storms: a Search for Meaning in Psychosis. London: Karnac.

Price M (1993) The impact of incest on identity formation in women. J. Amer. Acad. Psychoan 21(2): 213-28.

Rey H (1994) Universals of Psychoanalysis. London: Free Association Books.

Rosenfeld H (1964) On the psychopathology of narcissism. In Psychotic States. London: Hogarth Press, pp. 169–79.

Rosenfeld H (1971) A clinical approach to the psychoanalytic theory of the life and death instincts: an investigation into the destructive aspects of narcissism. Internat. J. Psycho-Anal 52: 169–78.

Rosenfeld H (1987) Projective identification in clinical practice. In Rosenfeld H (1987) Impasse and Interpretation. The New Library of Psychoanalysis. London/New York: Tavistock/Routledge.

Winnicott DWW (1960) Ego Distortion in terms of True and False Self. In Winnicott DWW (1960) The Maturational Processes and the Facilitating Environment. London: Karnac, pp. 140–52.

Index

addictions, 11
   psychotic (case study), 149–65
adhesive identification, 132, 133, 136
affect, 62, 72
   affective outburst, 118
   affective contact, 185
   affective state, 43, 60
   attunement, 19
   deregulation, 18
aggression, aggressiveness, 60, 62, 137
Alanen, Yrjo, 4, 119;
   see also need-adapted care
ambitendency, 62
amnesia, 76; *see also* memory retrieval
anger, 110, 158
anorexia nervosa, 45, 175, 178, 196–7
anxiety, 45, 76, 105, 110, 118, 121, 190
archaic structure, 103
archaic universe, 101, 112
assimilation, 59
asylums, 32
attention deficit, 61–2
attachment, 54–5, 107, 108–9
auditory hallucination, 49
autism, 15, 126ff, 127–9, 168
   autistic projection, 168
   autistic sensation, 167
   case study, 130–47
   chronic autistic development, 56
   and maternal depression, 131, 143
   encapsulated, 171
   and motility, 131
   and paranoia, 142–4
   secondary, 171

auto-eroticism, 69, 127
axis I and II disorders, 10, 15, 16, 19

Balint, Michael, 52
behaviour
   bizarre, 41, 42–3
   modification therapy, 15
   need satisfying, 61
behaviourism, 75
Benedetti, G., 56
Bion, Wilfred, 9, 11, 16, 43, 47, 56, 71,
   74–5, 79–80, 81, 184, 187
bipolar disorders, 11, 14
Bleuler, E., 127, 128, 129
body
   bodily sensation, 168
   image, 61
   as signifier, 132, 141
borderlines, 16, 17, 95n
   case study, 175ff
Boyer, L. Bryce, 9

Cameron, J.L., 56–7
catalepsy, 62
catastrophe, 105, 110
   psychic, 99–100
cathexis, 60, 102
   libidinal, 104
chemotherapy *see* pharmacotherapy
claustro-agoraphobia, 45, 175
cognitive disorganization, 57
cognitive function, 60, 61
cognitive therapy, 15
cognitive unconscious, 75, 94 n

201